THE POLITICS OF
EDUCATION IN
THE NEW SOUTH

THE POLITICS OF
EDUCATION IN
THE NEW SOUTH

Women and Reform
in Georgia, 1890–1930

REBECCA S. MONTGOMERY

LOUISIANA STATE UNIVERSITY PRESS ✺ BATON ROUGE

DESIGNER: *Amanda McDonald Scallan*
TYPEFACE: *Galliard*
TYPESETTER: *G&S Typesetters, Inc.*
PRINTER AND BINDER: *Edwards Brothers, Inc.*

Library of Congress Cataloging-in-Publication Data

Montgomery, Rebecca S.
   Politics of education in the new South : women and
reform in Georgia, 1890–1930 / Rebecca S. Montgomery.
— 1st printing.
      p. cm.
   Includes bibliographical references and index.
   ISBN 0-8071-3108-3 (cloth : alk. paper)
   1. Politics and education—Georgia—History—19th
century.   2. Politics and education—Georgia—History—
20th century.   3. Middle class women—Georgia—Political
activity.   4. Georgia—Social conditions—19th century.
5. Georgia—Social conditions—20th century.   I. Title.
LC72.3.G46M66 2005
379.758′09′034—dc22

                                        2005004465

CONTENTS

ACKNOWLEDGMENTS

Since the origins of this study lie in my doctoral dissertation, many debts of gratitude are owed those who pored over early drafts. LeeAnn Whites at the University of Missouri—Columbia worked tirelessly in applying her exceptional analytical skills to incisive critiques that helped me to see the larger potential of the project. Her colleague at Missouri, Mary Neth, and Victoria Bynum at Texas State University also gave generously of their time and provided insightful comments and suggestions. I am grateful as well for the comments of the reader for Louisiana State University Press, which were of immeasurable benefit. LeeAnn Whites, Vikki Bynum, and Gregg Andrews deserve special thanks for their continued mentoring as the project evolved into a book, and for their steadfast friendship throughout the ups and downs of academic life. Little did I know at the onset of my academic career that the school of hard knocks would not be confined to my working-class past, but that I would find the class and gender hierarchies just as entrenched in academia. I truly am fortunate to have had the support of such talented and generous scholars. Their commitment to social justice is exemplary. The Southern Association of Women Historians and the Rural Women's Studies Association also merit acknowledgment for providing a nurturing environment for young historians despite the competitive individualism that all too often characterizes the profession.

Finally, I must thank my family for giving me the fortitude to pursue my passion whatever the obstacles. My partner, Gary Gerbstadt, has endured more moves and more disruptions of our household than he probably cares to remember. Despite the drawbacks of having an academic in the family, both he and my sisters, Beth LaRose and Sheryl Micyk, have shown a gracious willingness to understand and respect exactly what my work means to me. Their love, courage, and integrity will forever be my inspiration.

INTRODUCTION

In Georgia as throughout the postbellum South, middle-class women emerged in the late nineteenth and early twentieth centuries as some of the region's most visible supporters of a more socially activist state. Their leadership role in the multitude of reform campaigns aimed at building upon the Reconstruction foundations of socially responsible government warrants a closer look at the motivations that drove them to seek greater public authority. How could southern white women, many of whom paid homage to the Lost Cause and states' rights principles, have come to support state intervention in and interference with the most intimate rights of male citizenship, the authority of fathers over dependents? What caused them ultimately to reject southern laissez-faire political doctrine and to advocate greater government protections for the welfare of women and children? What were the origins of the distinctive political culture that distinguished their activism from that of Progressive men, and why was education the centerpiece of their plans for creating a more democratic and prosperous South? It is only in answering these questions, in understanding the complex nature of women's political activism, that historians can develop a truly thorough picture of the character of southern progressivism and regional exceptionalism, and of the role of education in the construction and reconstruction of the postbellum social order.

To begin the task of answering the above questions, this study takes as its starting point works that portray the social relations of the southern antebellum household as the model for, and indeed as the material basis of, power relations in the larger society. The dynamics of household domination and subordination constructed not only "manliness," the essence of gender identity for antebellum white men, but also the legal parameters of acceptable behavior that defined the public and political authority of white men even as it circumscribed the personal liberty of dependents. White male independence was defined in opposition to female and black dependence, and the formal and informal distinctions contained therein supported a social hierarchy in which the fruits of all labor accrued to white male heads of household. In examining the implications of this hierarchy for post-Reconstruction reform, it becomes clear that education was central to the struggle of southern white women to gain personal freedom and the full rights of citizenship through a reconstruction of household relations and a widening of economic opportunity. Historians have readily recognized the role of education in this struggle for African Americans but rarely have looked at its significance for the postbellum white women who also were emerging from the plantation household. Perhaps because white women still shared their households with white men, at least with what was left of them, their struggle was less visible to the historical eye. They shared race and class privileges with their men, so their gender struggles appeared as a personal matter unrelated to the larger political battles over control of state resources.[1]

Because household social relations were so central to the construction of the social hierarchy, the meaning and significance of postbellum female activism can be understood only within the context of the rapid transformation of the southern economy and household after the Civil War. In the antebellum era, slavery stunted industrialization and the development of a mature market economy. In the slave economy banking and commerce were tied to slaveholding interests and generally did not invest in industrial expansion and long-term economic development. Antebellum Georgia was fairly typical in that slave ownership absorbed most of the capital, and the state ran slightly behind the rest of the South in the development of manufacturing industry. These characteristics of the slave economy had multiple implications for white women, and not the least was the continued integration of home and work in the plantation and yeoman household. A more fully developed market economy with burgeoning industrial capitalism would have resulted in a devaluing of women's domestic labor, because economies of scale eventually make it easier to buy rather than to produce items, and because men's in-

1. See in particular Peter Bardaglio, *Reconstructing the Household: Families, Sex, and the Law in the Nineteenth-Century South* (Chapel Hill: University of North Carolina Press, 1995); Victoria Bynum, *Unruly Women: The Politics of Social and Sexual Control in the Old South* (Chapel Hill: University of North Carolina Press, 1992); Stephanie McCurry, *Masters of Small Worlds: Yeoman Households, Gender Relations, and the Political Culture of the Antebellum South Carolina Low Country* (New York: Oxford University Press, 1995); and LeeAnn Whites, *The Civil War as a Crisis in Gender: Augusta, Georgia, 1860–1890* (Athens: University of Georgia Press, 1995).

creasing association with formal economic structures outside the household renders the value of their work more visible. In the Old South, where the profitability of plantation agriculture kept commercial and industrial activity at a minimum, women's labor continued to be an integral part of the household economy.[2]

There were certain aspects of the slave economy that made women's productive work within the household particularly important. One of these was a perpetual shortage of wage labor. An abundance of free land meant that virtually any white man could acquire property, and Georgia's lottery system for confiscated American Indian lands resulted in a more democratic distribution than occurred in most Deep South states. Hired help was therefore in short supply: few white men would choose to work for others when they had the option to work for themselves. Slavery allowed wealthy planters to circumvent the problem through the purchase of their workers, but farmers who could not afford that option had to depend upon family labor. Consequently, the amount of land that a farm owner could till was directly tied to the size of his family. This was true of frontier areas more generally, but in the South farmers' options were limited in comparison to other regions. Mechanization—and more specifically the manufacture of agricultural implements—was one type of internal development suppressed by the system of slavery. Slaveholders found it most beneficial to expand production through acquiring more slaves and planting more cotton rather than by mechanizing, a strategy that discouraged entrepreneurial activity in implements manufacturing. In the 1850s, when cotton prices were high, the value of agricultural implements in the Deep South actually declined.[3]

The isolation and relative self-sufficiency of households in the slave South made white women's labor equally important in the planter and the yeoman classes. The plantation was "a community and a business rolled into one," and its mistress was the household administrator. Planter-class wives presided

2. Eugene Genovese, *The Political Economy of Slavery: Studies in the Economy and Society of the Slave South* (Middletown, CT: Wesleyan University Press, 1965; repr., 1989), 19–26 (citations are to the 1989 edition); Numan V. Bartley, *The Creation of Modern Georgia* (Athens: University of Georgia Press, 1983), 23–25.

3. Bartley, *Modern Georgia,* 17; Gavin Wright, *The Political Economy of the Cotton South: Households, Markets, and Wealth in the Nineteenth Century* (New York: W. W. Norton, 1978), 45–55.

over virtually all domestic affairs and acted as "delegates of the master" in their husbands' absence. They kept account of domestic production and expenditures, and they directed and participated in the feeding, clothing, and nursing of all household members, including house and field slaves. They also had primary responsibility for the daily duties of child-rearing. Women's work was central to the reproduction of family and labor (which also was human capital) and, by extension, of class status. Similarly, among the successful yeomanry, women's labor was critical to self-sufficiency and thus to the maintenance of economic independence. Women performed much of the work necessary to meet basic subsistence needs, and surplus goods such as eggs and cloth could be bartered for other items with neighbors or local merchants. Unlike planter-class women, they also went into the fields when necessary, sometimes laboring beside slaves and free blacks. The white community overlooked this evidence of class difference so long as yeomen women could conform to other status markers of race privilege, such as meeting local standards for appropriate behavior and personal appearance.[4]

The irony of white women's status in the Old South was that even though industrialization was too limited to obscure the value of their labor by relegating it to a separate, private sphere, slavery achieved much the same end through different means. Certainly, slavery bolstered white women's status in many ways. The inferior position allotted slave and free black women relieved many white women of the most menial tasks in the same way that white men's status rose on the backs of black male laborers. Furthermore, in denying African Americans the gender roles that white people had—assigning them the hypersexual stereotypes of Buck and Jezebel or the asexual ones of Uncle

4. First quote from Katharine Du Pre Lumpkin, *The Making of a Southerner* (New York: Alfred A. Knopf, 1946; repr., Athens: University of Georgia Press, 1991), 22 (citations are to the 1991 edition); second quote from Elizabeth Fox-Genovese, *Within the Plantation Household: Black and White Women of the Old South* (Chapel Hill: University of North Carolina Press, 1988), 110; see also 111–132; Catherine Clinton, *The Plantation Mistress: Woman's World in the Old South* (New York: Pantheon Books, 1982), 18–29, 38–40; McCurry, *Masters of Small Worlds*, 72–85. Daniel Blake Smith found that in eighteenth-century Chesapeake society, planter-class fathers took an active interest in child-rearing, but it is likely that most of the responsibility for physical care (especially of infants and small children) fell to mothers and female relatives and slaves. *Inside the Great House: Planter Family Life in Eighteenth-Century Chesapeake Society* (Ithaca, NY: Cornell University Press, 1980).

Tom and Mammy—white southerners could "naturalize" racial discrimination and create for their women a special, privileged category of womanhood. Conversely, in other ways white women realized the benefits of the slave economy only indirectly, filtered through their men, since their reputation as pure and productive was contained within the politics of dependency that constructed white manhood. Planter-class and yeoman men were tied together across class lines by a concept of a natural social order in which all relationships were based on the "domestic relations of domination and subordination." Even though white women were located above African Americans in the social hierarchy, their subordination was constructed similarly, justified by supposedly innate characteristics that made them naturally dependent. White men's private and public authority, their very economic and political identities, depended upon this interpretation of household social relations.[5]

The structural basis for white women's peculiar position in the Old South can be found in the way the institution of slavery obscured and privatized their material contributions to the household economy. This aspect of the southern rural household represented an anomaly compared to social and economic developments occurring elsewhere in North America. Historians and social theorists have described the rural household operating within the early market economy as an integrated and complementary unit in which domestic production and commodity production were two sides of the same coin. Women's work, both their physical labor and their "organizational and managerial role," was an obvious part of this integrated enterprise, and its material value was plainly visible. In this household structure, female productive contributions could confer status and perhaps even become the basis for civil and political rights. It was only when the emphasis shifted overwhelmingly to commodity production (with the corporate form of property-based capital eventually replacing the household enterprise) that women's household labor began to appear as a private contribution to individual men, its material value obscured and no longer serving as a positive basis for the private and public status of women.[6]

5. Deborah Gray White, *Ar'n't I a Woman? Female Slaves in the Plantation South* (New York: W. W. Norton, 1985), 27–61; McCurry, *Masters of Small Worlds*, 215–220, quote 213.

6. Dorothy E. Smith, "Women's Inequality and the Family," in *Inequality: Essays on the Political Economy of Social Welfare*, ed. Allan Moscovitch and Glenn Drover (Toronto: University

While it might seem that the antebellum women in plantation and yeoman households were an obvious part of the household enterprise, public acknowledgment of their role was limited by the social relations stemming from the slave economy. In the Black Belt cotton-growing region of the Deep South, an emphasis on large-scale, slave-labor commodity production hindered recognition of planter-class women's productive role from the beginning of settlement. This was not necessarily true of the yeomanry, who often combined subsistence production with cash crops in a classic version of the integrated household. However, slaveholders' need to protect their capital investment in black labor required that they withhold acknowledgment of women's productive activities. For all practical purposes, physical labor was designated black, and in the context of growing national demands for the abolition of slavery, strictly maintaining this definition as natural and beneficial to both races became even more critical. Perhaps more importantly, the concept of a natural order that justified denying blacks ownership of their labor necessitated divorcing productive contributions from civil and political rights; there could be no connection between productive value and access to power for subordinate members of the household.[7]

Despite the disadvantages of the slave economy for women, it subdued gender conflict among white men and women just as it ameliorated class differences among white men. By restricting capitalist industrial development, slavery minimized economic competition and exploitation for all whites. This claim of the proslavery argument was sound. Even though the institution of slavery confined women within the household and denied them public authority in their own right, it offered some compensation. Most white women were saved from the hardest toil, and even those who labored in the fields usually did so for the benefit of their own households and worked under men

---

of Toronto Press, 1981), 156–195, quote 162; for a broad overview, see Julie A. Matthaei, *An Economic History of Women in America: Women's Work, the Sexual Division of Labor, and the Development of Capitalism* (New York: Schocken Books, 1982).

7. The cotton boom of the 1830s induced many planters to migrate westward in search of large tracts of land. Joan Cashin has found that the increased exploitation of slaves was central to the development of the southern states west of Georgia (she considers Georgia a border state between seaboard and frontier, with characteristics of both) and that as paternal race relations broke down, sexual inequalities increased *A Family Venture: Men and Women on the Southern Frontier* (New York: Oxford University Press, 1991).

who had a personal investment in their well-being. The slave economy may have continued to subsume women's public identity under that of their men, but it also created a protective mantle for women who maintained respectability by upholding the race and gender order. So long as white women could realize the benefits of the artificial hothouse of the slave economy, even if indirectly through men, most could at least tolerate that their public economic and political representation would also occur indirectly through their men. The marked reluctance of more conservative postbellum southern women to endorse female suffrage represented, in part, the cultural fragments of this trade-off between dependence and support embodied in antebellum gender relations. Antisuffragists such as Georgia's Mildred Lewis Rutherford intended female abnegation of the right to direct political representation to serve as a sharp reminder to white men of *their* corresponding duty to protect and provide for their women.[8]

This is not to say that white women did not chafe at the limitations imposed by slavery. Indeed the seeds of postbellum female activism can be found in the antebellum plantation household as well as in the disintegration of male protection during and after the Civil War. No doubt women's hurt and anger at the double standard that allowed white men to sexually exploit female slaves while it required strict chastity of their wives gave added meaning to organized women's later crusades for social purity. It was easier for the wronged plantation mistress to blame miscegenation on black female sexual precocity than to hold her husband responsible, but some were able to step over the line and make the analogy between their own subordination and that of slaves. Their willingness to overlook the uneven power relations that char-

8. Elna Green, "'Ideals of Government, Home, and of Women': The Ideology of Southern White Antisuffragism," in *Hidden Histories of Women in the New South,* ed. Virginia Bernhard, Betty Brandon, Elizabeth Fox-Genovese, Theda Purdue, and Elizabeth Hays Turner (Columbia: University of Missouri Press, 1994), 96–113. Even some suffragists could not make a clean break with proslavery ideology and stubbornly adhered to a "states' rights" approach to the female franchise. Marjorie Spruill Wheeler, *New Women of the New South: The Leaders of the Woman Suffrage Movement in the Southern States* (New York: Oxford University Press, 1993), 133–171. The most remarkable evidence of the gender politics underlying Mildred Lewis Rutherford's antisuffragism can be found in the handwritten notes for her speech delivered to the Georgia House of Representatives Committee on Constitutional Amendments. Mildred Rutherford Scrapbooks, Hargrett Rare Book and Manuscript Collection, box 1, folder 8, Special Collections, University of Georgia Libraries, Athens.

acterized the social order under slavery diminished further during the Civil War, as the reality of who had to pay the costs of maintaining the system hit them full in the face. As they managed plantations on their own, wrangled with hired hands and slaves without the master's ultimate authority to back them up, and buried entirely too many fathers, husbands, and sons, many came to realize that the protected household was no longer a viable option. In the war's aftermath, even as they honored the dead and living with Confederate memorials and services for veterans, white women increasingly found the former construction of gender relations inadequate to meet their new needs.[9]

Some of the core problems facing Georgia women after the Civil War were shared by their sisters across the nation, even if southern needs were more acute and public resistance more daunting. Throughout antebellum America, marriage constructed the independence of men in opposition to the dependence of women and children, serving as a basis for male civil and political rights. Under the system of coverture, women's legal identity was similar to that of slaves: husbands owned their wives' labor, wages, and even their actual bodies and volition. Moreover, since women relinquished their property to their husbands upon marriage, they lacked any basis for the integrity of thought and action deemed necessary for the franchise. Women's status as citizens who lacked political rights appeared so axiomatic and unquestionable to most men that it often surfaced as justification for denying the vote to other groups, such as working-class men and free blacks. If women's citizenship rights were not violated by representation through men, then the rights

9. On elite women and the sexual exploitation of slaves, see Catherine Clinton, "Caught in the Web of the Big House: Women and Slavery," in *The Web of Southern Social Relations: Women, Family, and Education,* ed. Walter J. Fraser Jr., R. Frank Saunders Jr., and Jon L. Wakelyn (Athens: University of Georgia Press, 1985), 19–34, and " 'Southern Dishonor': Flesh, Blood, Race, and Bondage," in *In Joy and in Sorrow: Women, Family, and Marriage in the Victorian South, 1830–1900,* ed. Carol Bleser (New York: Oxford University Press, 1991), 52–68. On the effects of the Civil War on white gender relations, see Drew Gilpin Faust, *Southern Stories: Slaveholders in Peace and War* (Columbia: University of Missouri Press, 1992), 113–140, 174–192; Ann Firor Scott, *The Southern Lady: From Pedestal to Politics, 1830–1930* (Chicago: University of Chicago Press, 1970), 81–102; Whites, *The Civil War as a Crisis in Gender;* and Jane Turner Censer, "A Changing World of Work: North Carolina Elite Women, 1865–1895," *North Carolina Historical Review* 73 (January 1996): 28–55.

of laborers and blacks were not violated by representation through white elites. This argument was particularly effective because it was difficult to make the reverse point, that disfranchisement violated the rights of women. It simply was unthinkable that women would not fully identify their own interests with those of their husbands—that they would break the "sexual contract," in which they surrendered independent agency in exchange for male support and protection, to embrace the rights and obligations inherent in the social contract.[10]

Following the Civil War, women were able to take advantage of new state interests and authority to improve their status inside and outside the home. The electorate was expanding, with universal white male suffrage within sight and the Fourteenth and Fifteenth Amendments seeming to promise political equality for black men. These developments undercut the concept of natural categories of subordination and diminished the importance of property ownership as a necessary condition for independent agency, thus strengthening arguments for female civil and political equality. At the same time, the growth of industrial capitalism gave the state an increased interest in the productive and reproductive functions of the family. New legislation and court rulings established direct contractual relations between household dependents and the government (primarily at the state level), gradually eroding the old practice of recognizing male heads of household as the sole interested parties in matters concerning dependents' property, wages, and physical well-being. The political activism of middle-class women played an important role in helping to push forward these changes, revealing their high regard for the state's potential as mediator. They agitated for and got married women's property rights and divorce-law reforms, and they attempted to ride the tide of franchise expansion by organizing for woman suffrage. They also lobbied

10. Carole Pateman, *The Sexual Contract* (Stanford, CA: Stanford University Press, 1988); Nancy F. Cott, "Marriage and Women's Citizenship in the United States, 1830–1934," *American Historical Review* 103 (December 1998): 1440–1474; Lori Ginzberg, "Pernicious Heresies: Female Citizenship and Sexual Respectability in the Nineteenth Century," in *Women and the Unstable State in Nineteenth-Century America*, ed. Alison M. Parker and Stephanie Cole (College Station: Texas A&M University Press, 2000), 139–161; Linda K. Kerber, "A Constitutional Right to Be Treated like American Ladies: Women and the Obligations of Citizenship," in *U.S. History as Women's History: New Feminist Essays*, ed. Linda K. Kerber, Alice Kessler-Harris, and Kathryn Kish Sklar (Chapel Hill: University of North Carolina Press, 1995), 17–35.

for greater state protection of abused and exploited children, frequently arguing that the state's economic and humanitarian interests in the welfare of children justified government intervention in their behalf.[11]

Southerners felt the influence of these national trends, but they faced conditions more unique to their region that limited the impact on women. In the postbellum South, the subordination of women and blacks remained linked in the politics of private and public life. The untimely end of Radical Reconstruction allowed the basic structure of the old social order to survive, while the need to divorce productive value from civil and political rights was particularly acute for those holding the reins of power in the New South. The dilemma of the freedmen had induced national political leaders to move toward defining ownership of one's own labor as the basis of political rights (rather than ownership of property), and southern white elites countered with persistent attempts to deny blacks and women control of their productive capacities. Redemption allowed them to tighten control of black labor and eventually to disfranchise black voters, using old arguments of a natural order that now were bolstered by scientific racism. The maintenance of patriarchy was arguably more important than ever before; just as it had diminished differences among white men in the slave economy, there was a need for its preservation in the competitive industrial economy in which class relations were laid bare. All white men could continue to stand on common ground as rulers of household and dependents, facing together the problem of how best to protect their families from other dependents run amok. For many assumed

11. Norma Basch, "The Emerging Legal History of Women in the United States: Property, Divorce, and the Constitution," *Signs* 12 (Autumn 1986): 97–117; Ginzberg, "Pernicious Heresies," 152–155. For an overview, see Morton Keller, *Regulating a New Society: Public Policy and Social Change in America, 1900–1933* (Cambridge, MA: Harvard University Press, 1994). Most scholarship on the changes in both women's legal status and the relationship between family and state emphasizes the ways in which reforms perpetuated the gender hierarchy, for example, Peter Bardaglio and Eileen Boris, "The Transformation of Patriarchy: The Historic Role of the State," in *Families, Politics, and Public Policy: A Feminist Dialogue on Women and the State,* ed. Irene Diamond (New York: Longman Press, 1983), 70–93; Cott, "Marriage and Women's Citizenship"; Sonya Michel, "The Limits of Maternalism: Policies toward American Wage-Earning Mothers during the Progressive Era," in *Mothers of a New World: Maternalist Politics and the Origins of Welfare States,* ed. Seth Koven and Sonya Michel (New York: Routledge and Kegan Paul, 1993), 277–320; and Amy Dru Stanley, "Conjugal Bonds and Wage Labor: Rights of Contract in the Age of Emancipation," *Journal of American History* 75 (September 1988): 471–500.

that blacks, once released from the "beneficial" restraints of slavery and able to pursue their own interests, could only represent a serious threat to social order.[12]

There were a number of ways in which the connections between patriarchy and white supremacy negatively impacted the postbellum status of southern women. Whites who wanted to strictly limit black independence had a stake in continuing to define manual labor, and especially *female* manual labor, as black. In the minds of many southerners, the naturalness of white female dependency counterpoised the unnaturalness of black freedom as evidence of the superiority of the old order. The separation of white women from the formal labor market and their isolation in the home continued to stand as rhetorical and symbolic evidence of the superiority of southern culture and society, even though real conditions had changed dramatically. In the aftermath of war, large numbers of widows and orphans no longer had the choice of realizing their economic and political identities through men and had to find new sources of security and protection. Moreover, those with surviving male relatives might not have the option of complete dependency, since many white men had lost their livelihood. But despite abundant evidence of need and growing numbers of female workers, women who sought unprecedented access to higher education and upward mobility in employment often found their efforts thwarted by men who accused them of betraying the South and degrading its culture. They continued to suffer severe civil disabilities as well; in Georgia married women did not gain clear ownership of their wages until 1943, and as late as the 1920s they endured one of the most restrictive divorce laws in the nation.[13]

12. Bardaglio, *Reconstructing the Household,* 27; Joel Williamson, *The Crucible of Race: Black-White Relations in the American South since Emancipation* (New York: Oxford University Press, 1984), 111–119.

13. Between 1860 and 1870 the wealth of the average white man in Georgia fell from about $4,000 to little more than $1,400. Bartley, *Modern Georgia,* 30; Scott, *The Southern Lady,* 106–133; Suzanne D. Lebsock, "Radical Reconstruction and the Property Rights of Southern Women," *Journal of Southern History* 43 (May 1977): 195–216. The connection between the race and gender hierarchies is most often discussed in terms of the dual purposes of lynching in reinforcing the subordination of both women and blacks. Jacquelyn Dowd Hall, *Revolt against Chivalry: Jessie Daniel Ames and the Women's Campaign against Lynching* (New York: Columbia University Press, 1974), 149–156; and Nancy MacLean, *Behind the Mask of Chivalry: The Making of the Second Ku Klux Klan* (New York: Oxford University Press, 1994), 142–148.

Important changes did occur in the South as a consequence of the Civil War, but white male political culture militated against assigning significant powers to the state as mediator between household members. Although the Confederate defense of slavery was rooted in the right to local rule and community control, during the war it became necessary for the state to take on an expanded role in social and economic matters. Afterward, when Reconstruction governments met to create new constitutions, most took up the issues of married women's right to own property and wages and to have reasonable access to legal separation and divorce. Reforms usually were minimal and were uneven from state to state, most likely because politicians were motivated more by the desire to protect inheritance and shield part of household income from debt than by genuine support for female civil equality. Redemption governments tried to reverse much of the liberal legislation of Reconstruction, although the use of state power to regulate gender relations was in itself evidence of the diminished authority of men as individual heads of households. As Redemption brought an infusion of northern capital, economic growth (and an emancipated labor force) produced the same state interests in the South as it had in the North, so that contractual relations eventually linked women and children directly to the state rather than indirectly through men. However, race and gender politics and the connections between the two systems of power—as well as a fierce regional loyalty to the republican ideals of limited government and localism—continued to limit change and to hinder the creation of a socially activist state throughout the nineteenth century and into the twentieth.[14]

In Georgia, there were further structural impediments to Progressive reform that frustrated female activists and contributed to the development of their political culture. The electoral process was designed to ensure disproportionate representation among rural elites, the large-scale landholders who controlled state politics through their power and influence at the local level. After a brief moment of Reconstruction, these elites quickly moved to stifle government expenditures on anything that did not directly benefit themselves

---

14. Bardaglio, *Reconstructing the Household*, 124–137, 150–156; Victoria Bynum, "Reshaping the Bonds of Womanhood: Divorce in Reconstruction North Carolina," in *Divided Houses: Gender and the Civil War*, ed. Catherine Clinton and Nina Silber (New York: Oxford University Press, 1992), 320–333; Lebsock, "Radical Reconstruction and the Property Rights of Southern Women."

and the cotton economy. They fought the establishment of a public school system and the most basic social services, and they fiercely opposed any measures that might have limited access to cheap labor or distributed more equitably the expense of maintaining a government bureaucracy. The new urban elite, New South boosters who wanted to remove all impediments to economic growth, provided some challenge to their political power.[15] However, in the eyes of women reformers, neither of these political factions acted quickly enough or went far enough in addressing the rural and urban poverty that took such a heavy toll on families and communities. White male leadership was engaged in a battle over the economic future of the South, and financial concerns were primary. Humanitarian issues such as illiteracy and rural poverty, for example, surfaced in male political debate as part of the larger struggle over industrialization and control of workers, as New South men sought to transform cheap agricultural labor into an efficient manufacturing workforce that would attract capital investment.

Women's perspective on reform also was shaped by the sexual division of labor that situated women in a particular location in relation to family and society. The material basis of women's existence and the very structure of their everyday lives were organized by a division of labor in which they assumed responsibility for the emotional nurture and physical care of family members. Even women who could afford domestic help had primary responsibility for making sure that the fundamental needs of household members were met. Whether comforting, counseling, educating, or peacekeeping, their activities tended to be other-oriented, necessitating a cooperative approach and a spirit of mutuality (enhanced by their subordinate status) that sharply contrasted with the competitive individualism of men's work. Whether or not women used separate spheres ideology with its assumption of female moral superiority to justify their activism, their strategies and goals were shaped by its material reality. Viewing female political culture from this perspective acknowledges the role of personal experience in shaping public activism while avoiding the pitfalls of both the "essentialist" and the "socially constructed"

15. Georgia's county unit system gave rural counties disproportionate power in the electoral process because it was an indirect system of nomination that utilized unit votes, with the ratio of unit votes to population dramatically favoring less populated counties. V. O. Key, *Southern Politics in State and Nation* (New York: Vintage Books, 1949), 119–125; Alton DuMar Jones, "Progressivism in Georgia, 1898–1918" (Ph.D. diss., Emory University, 1963).

concepts of the female politics of reform. It can explain women's needs-based arguments for collective social responsibility as well as their considerable skill at cooperative grassroots organizing, which male reformers acknowledged and appreciated.[16]

When female voices began to emerge in public debate in the 1880s and 1890s, the issues of social justice and political reform they took up on the part of children, workers, and rural Georgians spoke to their own struggles for equality. Historians have noted how middle-class women's need to establish their social usefulness within the context of separate spheres propelled them into lives of public service. While this perspective provides important insights, it tends to limit women's motivations for activism to their emotional needs as individuals. Although Georgia's organized women had a self-conscious awareness of their privilege as persons who did not carry heavy burdens of labor inside or outside the home, their activism was grounded in a conception of social inequality that both encompassed and transcended personal need for self-fulfillment. Their sex represented a civil, political, and economic liability. Shut out of the formal political process and denied the full benefits of state institutions and services, many middle-class women identified with other groups neglected or ignored by governmental representatives. Although women's need for state mediation could blind them to the undemocratic impact of reform on other groups, from their perspective the political system already was undemocratic. Female citizens dedicated to public service were denied the franchise and other basic political rights while corrupt "courthouse rings" enabled rural elites to ignore the needs of the poor and the interests of the wider community. Many southern Progressive reformers—male and female—came to believe that the ends (the public good) justified the means (limiting local control).[17]

16. Maureen A. Flanagan, "Gender and Urban Political Reform: The City Club and the Woman's City Club of Chicago in the Progressive Era," *American Historical Review* 95 (October 1990): 1032–1050; Paula Baker, "The Domestication of Politics: Women and American Political Society, 1780–1920," *American Historical Review* 89 (June 1984): 620–647; Nancy C. M. Hartsock, "The Feminist Standpoint: Developing the Ground for a Specifically Feminist Historical Materialism," in *Feminism and Methodology,* ed. Sandra Harding (Bloomington: Indiana University Press, 1987), 157–180.

17. On women's activism as a product of middle-class angst, see James L. Leloudis II, "School Reform in the New South: The Woman's Association for the Betterment of Public School Houses in North Carolina, 1902–1919," *Journal of American History* 69 (March 1983):

The limitations of white male political culture eventually led middle-class women to openly draw parallels between their own struggle for the full rights of citizenship and the need of other groups for greater access to state resources. In 1890 the average Atlanta club woman was educated, socially prominent, and about forty years old; thus, much of Georgia's female leadership had witnessed the tremendous changes wrought by the Civil War and Reconstruction. The women who began a flurry of organizational activity in the mid-1890s frequently expressed the belief that southern women were being left behind in the march of social progress, that they were losing out on opportunities gained by women in other parts of the nation. Rebecca Douglas Lowe, founding member of the Atlanta Woman's Club and the Georgia Federation of Women's Clubs, often connected the inferior status of southern women with the lack of social progress experienced by other disadvantaged groups in the region. At the state Federation's first annual meeting in 1897, she expressed exasperation with persistent opposition to gender equality in higher education, claiming that she was "almost convinced that Rousseau lives again" and that the South had returned "to the days of old, when education was denied women as a means of keeping them in better subjection." In this case as in others, Lowe argued that the benefits of education rightfully belonged to all, rich and poor, male and female alike. Perhaps it was because they saw their fate as tied to that of other groups that Georgia's female political leaders rarely based their demands for change on what historians have labeled domestic feminism. They were more likely to argue from a position of economic justice and its benefits to the state, and they usually portrayed equal educational opportunity as an inherent right of citizenship.[18]

Public education was central to women's reform campaigns because the

---

886–909; and William A. Link, *A Hard Country and a Lonely Place: Schooling, Society, and Reform in Rural Virginia, 1870–1920* (Chapel Hill: University of North Carolina Press, 1986), 77, 80–81. Jane Addams spoke to this very motivation for reform in her memoirs, *Twenty Years at Hull House* (New York: Macmillan, 1910; repr., New York: Penguin, 1981). On Progressives' opposition to localism and tendency to accept undemocratic means, see William A. Link, *The Paradox of Southern Progressivism, 1880–1930* (Chapel Hill: University of North Carolina Press, 1992), and *A Hard Country and a Lonely Place,* 92–94.

18. Darlene Rebecca Roth, *Matronage: Patterns in Women's Organizations, Atlanta, Georgia, 1890–1940* (New York: Carlson Publishing, 1994), 84–90; Lowe quote from "Clubwomen at Rome," Scrapbook 1, Atlanta Woman's Club Collection, Atlanta History Center Archives, clipping.

restrictions and limitations associated with it (discussed further in chapters 1 and 2) provided such clear evidence of the undemocratic structure of state services, and the reform of education had the potential to effect change on multiple levels. The establishment of a fair and just system of education could distribute public resources in a more equitable manner, providing economic opportunity for women and the rural and urban poor. Furthermore, reform could make the value of female domestic labor more visible by highlighting women's interests in the welfare and training of children, thereby justifying their presence as educational professionals and public policy experts in the field. At the most intimate level, enhancing their own possibilities for intellectual development and professional training gave female activists a tool for renegotiating household relations. The New South and its women needed new men whose honor and integrity was constructed on the basis of the obligation and duty to serve family and society rather than on individual liberty rooted in the domination of subordinates. What white women needed was a realignment of gender relations, a form of white male citizenship that acknowledged the new conditions and defined economic and political agency in more egalitarian terms.[19]

African Americans would have been logical allies of female activists, since the common roots of their subordination in the antebellum household put the two groups on parallel paths. In the case of both women and blacks, restrictive notions of their innate capabilities continued to be used as justification for segregation, discrimination, and denial of civil and political rights. Both groups were struggling for the basic human right to self-realization, and both stood to benefit tremendously from fairer access to state resources. Despite such common ground, however, the repressive conditions that pushed Atlanta's white female leadership in the direction of democratic reforms simultaneously worked to limit their willingness and ability to identify with black Georgians. The intense sense of competitiveness for access to scarce re-

19. Bertram Wyatt-Brown has discussed the ways in which antebellum southern white men's honor was constructed on a more localist and individualist basis than that of antebellum northern white men, in *Yankee Saints and Southern Sinners* (Baton Rouge: Louisiana State University Press, 1985), 183–213. On white women's efforts to reconstruct concepts of male citizenship, see Rebecca Montgomery, "Lost Cause Mythology in New South Reform: Gender, Class, Race, and the Politics of Patriotic Citizenship in Georgia, 1890–1925," in *Negotiating the Boundaries of Southern Womanhood: Dealing with the Powers That Be,* ed. Janet Coryell, Thomas H. Appleton Jr., Anastatia Sims, and Sandra Gioia Treadway (Columbia: University of Missouri Press, 2000), 174–198.

sources that underlay the discriminatory policies of white men affected white women as well. In their eyes, private philanthropic aid to black education justified women's claims to a greater share of public funds. Furthermore, defining physical labor as black benefited female educational reformers by supporting their argument that working-class white women deserved better. Household relations also discouraged recognition of black women as equal sisters in need, because the use of black domestic labor continued to underpin the race and class privilege of white women. Equally importantly, the sexual politics of white supremacy and the rise of reactionary racism sharply limited interracial cooperation prior to World War I; the risks and costs associated with crossing the color line appeared too high a price to pay for most reformers. This complex set of factors made white women reluctant to fully include blacks in their campaigns for social and economic justice.

Perhaps not surprisingly, the process through which organized women pursued their goals began with reform of their own education. Chapter 1 examines how white women's new economic vulnerability led to their efforts to improve female educational opportunity. In addition to petitioning male politicians and university trustees for full access to the state's colleges and universities, club women assisted female colleges and teachers in promoting more rigorous and consistent academic standards in the education of women. Persistent male opposition to the campaigns for coeducation and curricular reform profoundly impacted female political culture by enhancing women's understanding of how education underpinned and reproduced the social order. In relation to their own status, this knowledge forced women to look at how the gender relations of the household worked to constrict their opportunities for personal and professional growth. It also influenced them to express solidarity with working-class women, as they recognized that women of all classes were being denied opportunities for upward mobility simply on the basis of their sex. Gender-based double standards in education were a problem that connected the interests of women who chose to work (or to not work) with those who had to work. As middle-class women developed a broader analysis of social inequality, they came to see the ways in which class-based double standards similarly limited the options of rural and mill children.[20]

20. For a critique of the opposing social-control interpretation of reform that does speak well to this context, though it does not refer to the South or to female reform specifically, see

Organized women's reform interests branched outward in the early 1900s, when they tackled the problems of the rural community. Their ambitious efforts included multiple campaigns designed to improve living standards, increase individual opportunity for women and children, and promote new definitions of gender and citizenship. Developing a strategy that would become common to virtually all facets of reform, women used educational institutions to make the value of domesticity more visible so that they could leverage that visibility into a fairer division of household and public resources. Chapter 2 looks at how women's rural school improvement work was an attempt to open up households and link them together in a community of interests. Creating a network of teachers, parents, and students, club women used the rural school as a medium through which to create a more female- and family-centered localism to replace the male-centered localism that primarily served the interests of propertied white men. They counteracted male politicians' reluctance to enact effective legislative reforms by building support at the grassroots level. The movement was successful at improving the quality of rural education and increasing community interest in rural schools, in large part owing to female reformers' cooperative approach and their ability to stand outside the corruption and violence of formal politics as representatives of the public good.

The campaign for the establishment and expansion of home extension services sought to build upon the foundations of the school improvement movement by more directly targeting the structural causes of rural poverty. Chapter 3 examines how female reformers attempted to use extension work to divert public resources away from male heads of households and toward the households themselves, thereby lessening the subordination of family needs to the demands of cotton production. Reformers also hoped that increasing cash-earning possibilities for rural women and girls would both improve their status within the household and widen their options outside of it. This cam-

---

Linda Gordon, "Family Violence, Feminism, and Social Control," in *Women, the State, and Welfare,* ed. Linda Gordon (Madison: University of Wisconsin Press, 1990), 178–198. On racial differences in female class politics, see, for example, Paula Giddings, *When and Where I Enter: The Impact of Black Women on Race and Sex in America* (New York: Bantam, 1984); and Mary Martha Thomas, *The New Woman in Alabama: Social Reforms and Suffrage, 1890–1920* (Tuscaloosa: University of Alabama Press, 1992), 88–90.

paign played a critical role in opening the University of Georgia to women and resulted in female educational and occupational opportunities in domestic science, but it was less successful than the rural school movement at wresting control of funds away from men. The complicity of the U.S. Department of Agriculture in institutionalizing gender and race discrimination in extension services, as well as the use of racial rhetoric to obfuscate the class politics of agricultural woes, hindered women's efforts to influence policy at the state level. Georgia officials' ability to ignore the needs of black families enabled them to deprive all women and children of the full benefits of state resources. Consequently, the extension division never achieved its potential to become an agency that recognized the equal value of male and female productive labor.

Chapter 4 wraps up the discussion of rural reform by looking at women's campaign to help the most rural of all Georgians, the mountaineers. In this effort, female reformers had to combat cultural and political prejudice against highlanders while also finding avenues of influence into isolated mountain communities. Women were able to at least partially overcome the former obstacle by drawing upon regional and national concerns regarding racial purity and race suicide. They attempted to gain support for highland educational reform by focusing on the racial purity of "Anglo-Saxon" mountain families, and especially mountain girls, as justification for assisting them. Turning the gender conservatism of eugenics on its head, club women also used the reproductive role of highland white women to justify providing them with alternatives to early marriage and motherhood. Although funding remained a problem, female activists and educators were able to promote greater gender equality through the establishment of boarding schools run and taught by women. The schools were too few in number to close the gap of educational opportunity between highland and lowland communities, but they acted as avenues of reciprocal influence nonetheless. As mountaineers shaped the schools into true community institutions, resident teachers and administrators went about reconstructing manhood by teaching mountain boys to respect and value domesticity.

The final chapter turns to the urban campaigns for public kindergartens and child welfare reform. Inspired by new insights into the importance of early childhood development and by their own struggle for equality of opportunity, women in educational reform used the kindergarten movement to promote public recognition of the welfare of all children as a common interest. Like the rural schoolhouse and the mountain boarding school, the kindergarten overlapped private and public, creating a new space for female activism that broke down the barriers of the old construction of gender relations. The teachers who dominated this space, the "kindergartners," acted as conduits through which national reform movements could influence southern attitudes toward the relationship between parent and child and between family and state. A growing familiarity with the field of child study influenced club women to directly challenge white male individualism, as the issue of child labor convinced them that the problems with the construction of the state and the construction of white manhood were linked. Their efforts to implement legal reforms met with stubborn resistance from state legislators who refused to recognize public kindergartens as a social obligation. Even that, however, could not fully defeat women's efforts to reform child labor practices and to transform early childhood education into a democratic promise of self-realization and upward mobility for the state's working poor.

Much as club women and kindergartners saw themselves as agents of reconciliation between private family needs and the greater public good, female reformers more generally regarded the state as a mediator between competing interests. Their reform campaigns sought not to transfer patriarchal power to the state, but rather to create an altogether different model of power relations grounded in reciprocal obligation as well as individual rights. To that end, they sought to make the state an arbiter of relations between men and women, between heads of household and dependents, and between the market and the family. In pursuing this goal, female reformers faced a problem inherent in centralized social services: enhancing the powers of the state increases the potential for infringement of personal prerogative and individual liberty. Southern middle-class women, operating within a region pervaded by laissez-faire doctrine, patriarchal plantation culture, and Lost Cause mythology, were aware of the tension and the controversy surrounding the issue. But they believed that that the costs of white male individualism were too high a price for women and children to pay. They argued that the individualism of capitalists and fathers should not interfere with social progress for the good of all, that it should not restrict the basic human right to a fair chance and a healthy start in life. In their eyes state regulation and educational services were a means to these ends, a tenuous democratic thread that connected all those who paid the costs of the Civil War and postbellum industrialization.[21]

21. David J. Vold, "Democratic Tension and the Future of the Public School," in *School Reform in the Deep South: A Critical Appraisal,* ed. David J. Vold and Joseph L. DeVitis (Tuscaloosa: University of Alabama Press, 1991), 155–167, argues that the bureaucratization and consolidation of public schools reveals the inherent tension between the need of society for unity and the requirement of democracy for expression of diversity. Studies that focus on women reformers' assertion of authority over poor and working-class women include Molly Ladd-Taylor, *Mother-Work: Women, Child Welfare, and the State, 1890–1930* (Urbana: University of Illinois Press, 1994); Gwendolyn Mink, *The Wages of Motherhood: Inequality in the Welfare State, 1917–1942* (Ithaca, NY: Cornell University Press, 1995); and Robyn Muncy, *Creating a Female Dominion in American Reform, 1890–1935* (New York: Oxford University Press, 1991).

1

REFORMING WOMEN'S EDUCATION
Changing "the Equation between Being and Living"

The campaign by Georgia women to improve female education played an essential role in the evolution of their political culture, and in this sense it was a precondition for their activities in behalf of other groups. From the very inception of the state's most powerful women's organizations, female activists were vitally interested in equality of educational opportunity. They were most concerned about the plight of women who needed means of support, but they also understood, like black Georgians, that access to education was an important deciding factor in their own struggle for political agency and self-determination. They quickly found themselves faced with the private origins of public policy, as men who opposed their goals often praised the supposed cultural value of women's containment and subordination within the household. The economy that had maintained that dependency no longer existed, and it seemed to women that men wanted to have their cake and eat it too—to maintain the false image of female dependency in the household while exploiting women's labor in stores, factories, and mills. National trends in women's education gave female reformers a rationale for acting upon their heightened sense of injustice by offering alternative, activist concepts of domesticity. Believing that "it is education which changes the equation between being and living," Georgia women demanded the right to configure that equation for themselves.[1]

1. Mrs. Charles A. Perkins, "Open Doors in Woman's Education," in *Southern Educational Association* [hereafter SEA] *Journal of Proceedings and Addresses of the Tenth Annual Meeting, Held at Richmond, Virginia, December 27–29, 1900* (Richmond, VA: SEA, 1901), 81–91, quote 81. Southern blacks' recognition of the importance of education in shaping the New South social order, and their further recognition of the significance of controlling their education for themselves, provided white women with both a blueprint and a call for action in the transformation of female education. James D. Anderson, *The Education of Blacks in the South, 1860–1935* (Chapel Hill: University of North Carolina Press, 1988), 4–32; and Jacqueline Jones, *Soldiers of Light and Love: Northern Teachers and Georgia Blacks, 1865–1873* (Chapel Hill: University of North Carolina Press, 1980; repr. Athens: University of Georgia Press/Brown Thrasher Books, 1992), 61–74 (citations are to the 1992 edition).

Southern women needed only to look to the recent past for evidence that their educational opportunities had deteriorated. Before the Civil War, female education in the South mirrored that in the North, and many southerners proudly proclaimed their region a national leader in women's higher education. Georgia Female College (later Wesleyan College) opened in Macon in 1839 as the first women's college in the nation with a curriculum and degree program similar to that of men's colleges. Roughly a decade later, thirty-two of the thirty-nine chartered women's colleges in the nation were in the South. Antebellum southern women's colleges were more likely to offer courses in the fine arts, but their curricula changed along the same lines as those of northeastern colleges, gradually including more of the classical studies that characterized male education. It was only after the Civil War that northern improvements in women's education began to surpass those in the South. Many southern public colleges were damaged or destroyed during the war, and state governments had limited funds for repair of old campuses and construction of new ones. The situation was worsened by the absence of public school systems, which forced private institutions to focus on secondary instruction. Most postbellum southern women's "colleges" offered a combination of high school and junior college studies, and before 1890 none were ranked by the U.S. Bureau of Education as meeting the "Division A" standards of a four-year liberal arts college.[2]

In trying to remedy this situation, postbellum female activists had to face other problems related to the Civil War. Restricting female intellectuality had become linked to the preservation of slavery during the intensification of the sectional conflict, serving as an integral part of the fiction of a "natural order" that justified unequal and undemocratic power relations. Antebellum southern men were far from being in agreement on women's intellectual capacities, but they generally accepted female education because it served useful purposes. Southern states' lack of public schools meant that formal education of any kind indicated class privilege, and higher education for both men and

2. Clipping on Wesleyan College, Clara Nelms Scrapbook, Georgia Department of Archives and History (hereafter GAH); Christie Anne Farnham, *The Education of the Southern Belle: Higher Education and Student Socialization in the Antebellum South* (New York: New York University Press, 1994), 12–13, 25–28; Shirley Ann Hickson, "The Development of Higher Education for Women in the Antebellum South" (Ph.D. diss., University of South Carolina, 1985), 136–145, 203–204; Joseph M. Stetar, "In Search of a Direction: Southern Higher Education after the Civil War," *History of Education Quarterly* 25 (Fall 1985): 341–367.

women was restricted to elites. Daughters who could pursue advanced studies, thereby providing public proof that white female productive labor was not needed in their households—and that slavery enhanced white cultural achievement—bolstered men's status. The educational "finishing" of girls also could result in lucrative marital partnerships that primarily benefited the property-owning heads of households joined together by matrimony. However, as the abolitionist movement began to loom more menacingly in the North, southern men increasingly expressed concern about the nature of female education. They sought to distinguish its purposes from the northern model linked with abolitionism and women's rights, arguing that female education more narrowly defined by its social and cultural value was a necessary genteel counterbalance to the harshly pragmatic intellectuality of men. Support for gender equality in higher education declined, women found their ability to travel north for advanced study curtailed, and male speakers admonished female academy students to embrace confinement within the home as evidence of the privileged status accorded southern women.[3]

These attitudes regarding the purposes of female education persisted into the twentieth century, indicating that institutional discrimination became more critical to maintaining the social hierarchy when the parameters of power relations no longer were defined by slavery. Recent studies have shown how the power struggle taking place in the postwar South involved attempts by women, African Americans, and common whites to establish individual autonomy and household integrity. In their search for positions of respect and authority, subordinate groups drew upon concepts of womanhood and manhood that assumed inherent differences. However, elites sometimes utilized these same concepts in manipulating political and legal institutions for the preservation of their own dominance. This process can be seen at work in the tremendous opposition to opening southern state universities to women. The segregation of higher education by gender as well as by race contained

3. Eleanor Miot Boatwright, *Status of Women in Georgia, 1783–1860* (New York: Carlson Publishing, 1994), 5–24; Farnham, *Education of the Southern Belle,* 12–13, 25–28; Mary V. Woodward, "Women's Education in the South," *Educational Review* 7 (May 1894): 466–478. The classic works that first attempted to address regional differences in female education are Eleanor Flexner, *Century of Struggle: The Women's Rights Movement in the United States* (Cambridge, MA: Harvard University Press, 1959; repr. New York: Athenaeum, 1972); and Thomas Woody, *A History of Women's Education in the United States* (New York: Science Press, 1929), vol. 1.

and controlled the social and economic mobility of subordinates. State policy-makers pointed to the inherent differences that separated men from women and whites from blacks—the same differences that justified female and black dependency under slavery—as justification for separate classroom environments and curricula. The end result was a dilution of state resources through duplication of services and a constriction of options for female and black students, because their institutions rarely matched the quality and occupational diversity of colleges historically white and male.[4]

In Georgia, women of all classes faced a set of structural obstacles that exacerbated the negative impact of institutional discrimination. One way in which Redemption legislatures attempted to reverse the liberal reforms of Reconstruction was through placing severe restrictions on the use of government funds for public schools. As a result, women seeking an education beyond the elementary level faced numerous barriers. The state's constitution restricted use of common school funds to elementary education, which meant that public high schools (normally the level at which industrial and vocational training was instituted) could be established only in districts with private patronage or in those with a sufficient local tax base and a willing citizenry. Few districts had such resources, and most women simply could not afford a private education. The problem of affordability was just as acute at the college level, since women's colleges in Georgia were so poorly endowed that financial aid was virtually nonexistent. Women who had the money to pay for their education faced difficulties as well. Teachers in private secondary schools were inadequately prepared themselves, so graduates were ill prepared to undertake college-level studies. Even women with good academic skills had no guarantee of receiving an education that met any established regional or national standards. Educational institutions could call themselves acade-

4. Laura F. Edwards, *Gendered Strife and Confusion: The Political Culture of Reconstruction* (Urbana: University of Illinois Press, 1997); Glenda Elizabeth Gilmore, *Gender and Jim Crow: Women and the Politics of White Supremacy in North Carolina, 1896–1920* (Chapel Hill: University of North Carolina Press, 1996). C. Vann Woodward, in *The Strange Career of Jim Crow* (New York: Oxford University Press, 1955; repr., 1974), describes the power struggle between blacks and whites as a state of flux, the outcome of which was not certain until southern states mandated segregation in the late nineteenth century. As late as 1910, the state universities were closed to women in Louisiana, Florida, Georgia, South Carolina, and Virginia. Woody, *Women's Education in the U.S.*, 253–254.

mies, colleges, universities, or whatever they wished, and the Georgia legislature, not a professional accrediting organization, granted them the right to confer degrees. The exclusion of women from the University of Georgia further cemented the likelihood that they would enter and remain in the lower levels of their employment fields.[5]

By 1890 the impact of these developments on female education was evident. The census data of that year showed that the greatest regional discrepancy in educational opportunity as measured by illiteracy rates was between northern and southern white women. The illiteracy rate among native white females ten years and older was seven times as high in the South Atlantic Division (which included the Carolinas, Georgia, and Florida) as in the northeastern states that comprised the North Atlantic Division. Black females were worse off than white females in both regions, but their incidence of illiteracy in the South Atlantic was only three times as high as in the Northeast. The ratio of female to male college students among whites in the two regions provides further evidence that inadequate funding and single-sex institutions limited southern women's access to schooling. In the South, there was one female student for every three male students enrolled in a public college or university, while in the North Atlantic, where coeducational schools were more prevalent, there were two female students for every man enrolled. Clearly, women benefited disproportionately from state-supported coeducational institutions. The female-to-male ratio in private colleges was much more favorable to women in the South in comparison to the Northeast, but the uneven and substandard quality of most southern private institutions made the value of their diplomas questionable. In addition, southern women were extremely underrepresented in commercial and professional schools, especially in comparison with their northern and northeastern counterparts.[6]

White female activists began publicly protesting the inadequacies of female education in the 1880s, as teaching became an increasingly important

5. Dorothy Orr, *A History of Education in Georgia* (Chapel Hill: University of North Carolina Press, 1950), 263–264; Celeste Parrish, "Some Defects in the Education of Women in the South," in *Proceedings of the Second Capon Springs Conference for Education in the South* [hereafter CES], *1899* (Raleigh, NC: Edwards and Broughton, 1899), 61–76; Celeste Parrish, "The Education of Women in the South," in *SEA Proceedings, 1900*, 45–62.

6. U.S. Census Office, *Compendium of the Eleventh U.S. Census, 1890* (Washington, DC: Government Printing Office, 1894–97), part 2, 225–227, 230, 246–252; part 3, 305–306, 314–316.

source of financial support for women. The death and destruction of the Civil War left many women in need of additional household income but with few ways in which to earn it. Teaching was an occupation that enabled middle-class women to earn money without losing respectability and status, and for several decades after the war it was common for "better educated ladies of good families" to open private schools in their homes and communities. Establishing schools allowed them to alleviate their pressing need for income while also performing a public service through the reduction of illiteracy among postwar youth. Many of these new educators found that their own formal education fell short of the demands of teaching, leading them to publicly criticize the quality and availability of teacher training. The fledgling public school system established during Reconstruction only magnified the need for female normal schools by highlighting the serious shortage of teachers and, at the same time, attracting women as the majority of applicants. Prior to the Civil War, women held less than one-quarter of the teaching positions in the South as a whole. Their numbers doubled during the 1880s as the number of male teachers declined, until women made up almost 60 percent of the teaching force. Between 1890 and 1900, more than 80 percent of all professional women in Georgia were teachers.[7]

In the late 1800s, a growing need to prepare young women for the workforce gave added momentum to the movement to improve female education. In 1860 there were only a few thousand female Georgians gainfully employed in occupations other than work on the family farm, and more than 92 percent of these were in cotton and woolen manufacturing. Postbellum industrialization and the rapid growth of cities quickly changed these figures. Between 1880 and 1910 the population of Atlanta more than quadrupled, that of Macon tripled, and the populations of Augusta, Columbus, and Savannah doubled. By the end of the period, one out of five Georgians lived in a city of twenty-five hundred or more, and another 11 percent of the population lived in smaller towns and villages. The economic development that drove urbani-

7. A. D. Mayo, *Southern Women in the Recent Educational Movement in the South,* ed. Dan T. Carter and Amy Friedlander, in Bureau of Education *Circular of Information,* no. 1 (Washington, DC: Government Printing Office, 1892; repr., Baton Rouge: Louisiana State University Press, 1978), xx–xxi, quote 6 (citations from the 1978 edition); Anne Firor Scott, *The Southern Lady: From Pedestal to Politics, 1830–1930* (Chicago: University of Chicago Press, 1970), 110–115; U.S. Census population occupation statistics, 1890–1930.

zation produced new jobs that attracted women from the countryside. Rural property ownership and management remained overwhelmingly male—little more than 5 percent of farmers, planters, and overseers were female—and women whose labor was not needed on family farms had few rural employment options aside from menial labor. As a consequence, women outnumbered men in all major cities, while the reverse was true of rural areas. Among those who migrated in search of work, most black women entered laundries and domestic service, and white women found employment as teachers, librarians, clerks, seamstresses, and textile mill operatives.[8]

Most white women concerned about equal access to educational and occupational opportunity regarded it as a particularly white issue. They were not especially bothered by the clustering of black women in low-status jobs associated with household labor; this aspect of the "natural order" was tolerable, and in some ways they depended upon it. Black women's wage labor in white homes and fields freed married club women to become social activists and enabled rural and urban single white women to aspire to something better. Furthermore, white reformers found it troubling that northern philanthropy appeared to be making more progress in improving the education of black women than the state of Georgia was in improving that of white women. Numerous secular and religious organizations helped to establish African American colleges in Atlanta after the Civil War, making the city a center of black higher education in the South. Black women had access to two coeducational colleges—Atlanta University, founded in 1867, and Clark University, established in 1879—as well as Spelman Seminary, a black female college supported in part by the Rockefeller Foundation. As white women struggled to improve their own options, Spelman gradually upgraded academic standards and gained a national reputation for the high quality of its teaching and nursing programs. More than one white female reformer was discomfited by this apparent narrowing of the gap of opportunity between

8. U.S. Bureau of the Census, *Thirteenth Census of the U.S. Taken in the Year 1910: Abstracts of the Census, Statistics of Population, Agriculture, Manufactures, and Mining for the United States, the States, and Principal Cities, with Supplement for Georgia Containing Statistics for the State, Counties, Cities, and Other Divisions* (Washington, DC: Government Printing Office, 1913), 569; and U.S. Census population statistics on occupations, 1890–1930. On the transformation of Atlanta, see Nancy MacLean, "The Leo Frank Case Reconsidered: Gender and Sexual Politics in the Making of Reactionary Populism," *Journal of American History* 78 (December 1991): 921–922.

black and white women, which they experienced as a decline in their own status. In 1901, when political activist Rebecca Latimer Felton addressed a joint session of the General Assembly on a number of educational reform issues, she pointedly remarked that she was pleading for the uplift of white girls "while schools and first-class universities are almost in the sound of my voice to provide colored girls with the higher education." Club women made a similar observation in 1912, when they asked opponents of coeducation to remember that "negro men and women in the State are being given that opportunity for higher education [for] which, so far, the white women of Georgia have pleaded in vain."[9]

The same social and economic changes that increased the need for female education produced the organizations that would lead the movement for reform. In the 1880s and 1890s, economic development and a growing urban middle class led to the proliferation of women's clubs in Georgia. At first these clubs were devoted mostly to cultural self-improvement, but a decided shift toward social activism occurred in November of 1895, when the Atlanta Cotton States and International Exposition became the setting for two momentous developments. The General Federation of Women's Clubs held its Biennial Council in the Woman's Building of the Exposition, and a group of Atlanta women attending these sessions decided that the time was ripe for the creation of a local organization devoted to the advancement of women. Much of the impetus came from club woman Rebecca D. Lowe. She recently had taken a trip to Europe and on the return voyage met Jane Cunningham Croly, founder of the New York women's club Sorosis. Lowe accepted Croly's

9. Amy Friedlander, "A More Perfect Christian Womanhood: Higher Learning for a New South," in *Education and the Rise of the New South,* ed. Ronald K. Goodenow and Arthur O. White (Boston: G. K. Hall, 1981), 79; Tera W. Hunter, "Domination and Resistance: The Politics of Wage Household Labor in New South Atlanta," *Labor History* 34 (Spring-Summer 1993): 205–220; first quote from Rebecca Latimer Felton, "Address before the Georgia Legislature, November, 1901," in *Country Life in Georgia in the Days of My Youth* (Atlanta: Index Printing, 1919; repr. New York: Arno Press, 1980), 190 (citations are to the 1980 edition); Cynthia Neverdon-Morton, *Afro-American Women of the South and the Advancement of the Race, 1895–1925* (Knoxville: University of Tennessee Press, 1989), 38–53; second quote as cited in Sara Bertha Townsend, "The Admission of Women to the University of Georgia," *Georgia Historical Quarterly* 43 (June 1959): 161. Other black colleges established in Atlanta with the assistance of private philanthropy included the coeducational Clark University (1879) and the male-only Atlanta Baptist Seminary, later Morehouse College (1879). Willard Range, *The Rise and Progress of Negro Colleges in Georgia, 1865–1949* (Athens: University of Georgia Press, 1951), 23–26.

invitation to attend a meeting of the club and returned home very impressed with its extensive program promoting equality for women. Lowe issued a call for all interested women to meet in her home during the Exposition to discuss forming a similar organization "to advance the education and general welfare of women along the broadest and most beneficial lines." "Atlanta is a large city," she noted, "but as yet its club life and interests are small among women." She found this puzzling "considering the great agitation felt on the subject in almost all other cities the size of Atlanta." Lowe asked Croly to speak to Atlanta women on female activism in New York and shocked some of her friends by also inviting the former abolitionist Lucy Stone. The two women's encouraging remarks paid off, however, and within a matter of weeks Lowe became the first president of the Atlanta Woman's Club (AWC).[10]

The Atlanta Woman's Club played a central role in the second critical development coming out of the Exposition—the creation of the state Federation of Women's Clubs. After creating the AWC, members immediately voted to join the General Federation, becoming the third Georgia club to do so. The other two Federated clubs were the Woman's Press Club of Georgia and Georgia Sorosis of Elberton, which was formed in July of 1892 by five women who also were impressed by the New York organization. Several founding members of Georgia Sorosis attended the Biennial Council meetings at the Atlanta Exposition and discussed with AWC members the possibility of forming a statewide group. It was not until a year later, in October of 1896, that representatives from women's clubs across the state finally convened in Atlanta to create the Georgia Federation of Women's Clubs. Sixteen women's organizations became charter clubs of the state Federation at that meeting, and delegates promptly voted Rebecca D. Lowe the first president. This act at once symbolized the importance of Atlanta leadership in female political activism and the significance of northeastern influences in Georgia's reform campaigns. Atlanta was a rapidly growing New South city with an unusual concentration of highly educated women, many of whom were alumni of northeastern colleges. As the connection with Croly and Sorosis indicates, leaders in the club movement tended to be well informed and well connected,

---

10. *Atlanta Constitution*, May 11, 1923; quotes from Corinne Stocker, first recording secretary of the AWC, "First Woman's Club Organized in Atlanta," Scrapbook 1, Atlanta Woman's Club Collection (hereafter AWC), Atlanta History Center Archives; "The Woman's Club Assured of Success," and "Atlanta Woman's Club," Scrapbook 1, AWC.

part of a national network of activist women. Lowe described her peers as "earnest, sensible, brainy women, with full purses and broad sympathies," who were "unwilling for Atlanta to fail to do her part in the work that women all over the world are interested in." [11]

The education of women activists directly shaped their campaign for reform by providing a rationale for their activism. In the late nineteenth century, higher education was a vehicle through which women could challenge the assumptions underlying the domestic ideal of womanhood, and many female educators and administrators considered advanced study the key to widening women's horizons economically and psychologically. However, the very concept of women's higher education was relatively new and there was no real consensus on its relationship to the domestic role. At first, college and marriage were considered mutually exclusive, but by the end of the century northeastern women's colleges began to move away from the "single female scholar" ideal and toward an effort to combine domesticity and career. Teaching and social work were two options that emerged as a compromise solution that allowed women to build a career and make public contributions without overtly challenging notions of womanhood. Even if many educated women never pursued a paid professional career or if they quit working after marriage, society could benefit from their intellectual talents and feminine virtues through their volunteer activism as public mothers and municipal housekeepers. The northeastern education of southern women acted as a conduit through which this particular configuration of separate spheres could permeate a culture in which domesticity had been shackled to (and hidden within) the household by the slave economy and its patriarchal infrastructure. Moreover, as one recent study has argued, the South's single-sex institutions facilitated organization by producing close bonds among female students that served as a basis for collective action in movements that challenged the status quo. [12]

11. Mrs. Clyde F. Anderson Jr., *A Walk through History* (n.p.: Georgia Federation of Women's Clubs, 1986); John H. McIntosh, *The Official History of Elbert County, 1790–1935* (1940; repr., Milledgeville, GA: Boyd Publishing, 1996), 315–316; *Atlanta Journal*, October 28, 1896; quotes from Stocker, "First Woman's Club Organized in Atlanta."

12. Barbara M. Cross, ed., *The Educated Woman in America: Selected Writings of Catharine Beecher, Margaret Fuller, and M. Carey Thomas* (New York: Teachers College Press, Columbia University, 1965); Roberta Frankfurt, *Collegiate Women: Domesticity and Career in Turn-of-the-Century America* (New York: New York University Press, 1977); Helen Lefkowitz Horowitz,

The larger concerns of the Atlanta Woman's Club are evident in Lowe's first press release, where she announced that equal educational opportunity for women of all classes would be one of the group's primary goals. In her initial organizing call to Atlanta women, Rebecca Lowe condemned the "fiscal injustice" of inferior pay for women and argued for the importance of educational equality. She assured female teachers and factory workers that club members would take up the cause of the "breadwinner" as if it were their own and invited working women to join what she insisted would be a thoroughly "democratic" organization. AWC members backed up these claims by weighing in on the side of female operatives in the debate over admitting women to the Georgia Institute of Technology. Georgia Tech was established in 1888 to train white men for administrative and engineering positions, to help them compete with educated northern men who came south to take part in the regional expansion of industry. There was public debate about the institution's exclusion of women from the beginning, but club women became particularly incensed when politicians funded the addition of a textile department in 1898 but took no steps to include female students, not even on a segregated or otherwise limited basis. Women comprised about 70 percent of operative labor in Georgia textile mills, yet they were being denied access to formal training and upward mobility in one of Georgia's fastest-growing industries. Rebecca Latimer Felton, who had argued for decades that the state was failing in its duty to educate poor white women, opened the charge by submitting an editorial to the *Atlanta Constitution* in which she excoriated men who would refuse the majority of textile workers an opportunity for occupational improvement simply because they were female.[13]

Alma Mater: Design and Experience in the Women's Colleges from Their Nineteenth-Century Beginnings to the 1930s (New York: Alfred A. Knopf, 1984); Barbara Solomon, *In the Company of Educated Women: A History of Women and Higher Education in America* (New Haven, CT: Yale University Press, 1985); Amy Thompson McCandless argues that the very conservatism of southern women's colleges that "made it difficult for Southern women to question tradition and to assert their individuality" also "created bonds of sisterhood" that facilitated their cooperation in civic improvement and reform campaigns. *The Past in the Present: Women's Higher Education in the Twentieth-Century American South* (Tuscaloosa: University of Alabama Press, 1999), 121, 156–158.

13. Robert C. McMath Jr., James E. Brittain, August W. Giebelhaus, Ronald H. Bayor, Lawrence Foster, and Germaine M. Reed, eds., *Engineering the New South: Georgia Tech, 1885–1985* (Athens: University of Georgia Press, 1985), 81–88; Passie Fenton Ottley, "Club Women in Educational Work," [Atlanta] *Southern Educational Journal* 12 (November 1898): 28–30; Rebecca

Journalist Isma Dooly, woman's editor for the *Constitution,* followed up on Felton's editorial by interviewing three AWC leaders for their opinions on the subject. Dooly was a native Atlantan whose own northeastern influence came from her education in a New York academy. She was a member of the AWC and a strong supporter of the Georgia Federation and used her position at the newspaper to give club women access to one of the state's most widely read periodicals. Her article provides an early example of the political importance of the new city and state federations in cultivating female leadership and publicizing particular issues. The club women who were interviewed—Rebecca Lowe, Sallie Chase Pattillo, and Ellen G. McCabe—agreed with Felton's assertion that the exclusion of women from the textile department constituted an unfair and discriminatory allocation of government funds, and they argued for a reversal of policy based on principle as well as economic considerations. In her statement, Lowe reiterated a commitment to promoting the interests of working-class women, this time as president of the Georgia Federation of Women's Clubs (GFWC). Pattillo and McCabe pointed out that many women had no choice but to be self-supporting and therefore needed proper training no less than men. Moreover, meeting the growing regional demand for skilled labor in an equitable manner would benefit the southern economy by improving workforce efficiency. Pattillo attempted to distance herself from women's rights rhetoric by arguing that educational equality was not so much an issue of women's "rights" as of simple "justice." McCabe agreed that equal education was a matter of economic justice, since if women were denied it, they "should be held ever to lower class of work and per consequence to lower compensation." But the justice women were demanding involved recognizing their rights as citizens, she argued, especially "the right to equal benefit from state aid." [14]

AWC leaders came to the defense of working women again the following year, 1899, when a member of the city Board of Education proposed radical

---

Felton's letter to the editor, *Atlanta Constitution,* September 10, 1898. Quotes from Stocker, "First Woman's Club Organized in Atlanta." On the relationship between club women and working-class women, see Georgina Hickey, *Hope and Danger in the New South City: Working-Class Women and Urban Development in Atlanta, 1890–1940* (Athens: University of Georgia Press, 2003).

14. Entries for Louise and Isma Dooly, *Women of Georgia* (Atlanta: Georgia Press Reference Association, 1927), 23, 139, 159; "Women Are a Unit for the Textile Education of Girls," clipping from *Atlanta Constitution,* September 11, 1898, Scrapbook 1, AWC.

changes in the curriculum of the Girls' High School. Judge Bloodworth introduced a resolution to abolish the business department of the school and to replace it with an industrial department to teach "cooking, cutting, fitting, sewing, and such other branches of industry as may be deemed advisable by the board." The changes, if adopted, were to take effect in September of 1899. Corinne Douglas, chair of the AWC business section, fired off an editorial to the *Constitution* condemning the proposal. According to Douglas, the Girls' High School was established in 1888 to prepare less privileged girls for "profitable employment." The business department, created in 1890, had successfully accomplished this by offering courses in stenography and bookkeeping. It had graduated 140 young women, a few of whom had become business teachers, while most found jobs in "offices of lawyers, insurance men, publishing houses, [and] manufacturing establishments." Douglas noted that whereas the city spent more than $54 annually on each student of the Boys' High School, a student at the female institution received funding of only about $34 per year. She complained that it was bad enough that no man had come forward to suggest correcting this disparity, but instead the board was considering "such a step backward." AWC members subsequently showed their support as a group by passing a resolution protesting the abolishment of the business department. Like many black leaders, they resented the introduction of industrial education when it came at the cost of other fields of study and narrowed opportunities for upward mobility.[15]

Club members' efforts in behalf of working women met with mixed results, as they repeatedly found themselves accepting compromise solutions. The Girls' High School lost its department and official program of study in business, but because of the protests of teachers and the AWC, the Board of Education agreed to retain faculty who would continue to offer business courses as electives. And while Georgia Tech did not become coeducational until 1952, women's campaign for admission did succeed in gathering public support behind the state college for women. Male supporters of Georgia Normal and Industrial College (GN&IC), founded only a year after Georgia Tech, intended it to be a female counterpart to the technical school for men. They hoped that the institution would address local economic concerns by matching white women who needed a means of self-support with industries

15. Clippings, Scrapbook 2, AWC.

in need of skilled labor. The college met the needs of many working women by providing training in clerical skills, bookkeeping, dressmaking, and other typically female industries, and graduates from its normal department contributed to higher standards of education in public schools. However, the services of the institution were aimed at the poorer classes of white women and in no way matched the caliber of education offered at the Georgia Institute of Technology and the University of Georgia. The women's college was founded as a two-year institution without the ability to grant degrees, and the only professional training it offered women was in education—a field already crowded with women and plagued by low pay and poor working conditions. Although organized women were grateful for the new college and regarded it as an important step in the right direction, they did not accept GN&IC as a substitute for full educational equality.[16]

Simultaneous with their efforts in behalf of working-class women, members of the AWC and the Georgia Federation of Women's Clubs led the movement to make the University of Georgia coeducational. The effort to gain women's admission to the university began in 1889, when the Colonial Dames and the Daughters of the American Revolution unsuccessfully petitioned the university's board of trustees. After the formation of the GFWC, the Federation assumed leadership in the campaign and helped to present five additional petitions between 1896 and 1912. Organized women considered the issue vital to statewide educational improvement as well as to equality of opportunity for women. The only state schools open to women before 1918 were junior colleges. They could attend the agricultural branch college in Dahlonega, the State Normal School in Athens, and Georgia Normal and Industrial College in Milledgeville, but all three institutions offered only a two-year course of study. Women who wished to obtain further education had to either choose from the few private women's colleges in Georgia that offered a four-year degree or face the daunting prospect of financing an education out of state, which was prohibitively expensive for most students. A prominent female educator presented the issue in terms that also were used in demands for racial integration. In 1898 State Normal School professor Celeste Parrish argued that Georgia's financial inability to provide an equivalent institution

16. Ibid.; *Speech of Hon. W. Y. Atkinson* (Atlanta: Constitution Publishing, 1889); Orr, *History of Education in Georgia*, 348–349.

for women required their admission to the university. It was a matter of justice and a patriotic necessity, she claimed, since the state was in dire need of better-qualified teachers.[17]

The university campaign hit close to home for female activists, because it involved making demands for women of their own class. In 1897 Rosa Woodberry, a founding member of the Woman's Press Club who was active in the GFWC, joined another young woman in presenting a separate petition to trustees requesting admission to the university. Both women were teachers in Athens, where the university was located. Woodberry headed the science department at Lucy Cobb Institute, an exclusive private girls' school, and fellow petitioner Susan Gerdine was an Atlanta doctor's daughter who taught in the public schools. The women wanted further training to improve their effectiveness as educators and resented the inconvenience of having to leave Athens to acquire it. They had already completed considerable work in the university physics and chemistry laboratories by permission of professors in those departments, but they needed official recognition of that work if they were to earn a formal degree. Their petition assured trustees that they were not seeking public attention and did not wish to do anything "that would detract in the slightest degree from the wise conservatism and womanliness of the southern woman." This stock phrase probably was intended to make the petition more palatable to trustees, since Woodberry soon made public remarks that belied its conciliatory tone. In an article in the *Constitution,* she advised club women that "we must not stress too much the appeals to gallantry and sentiment," since "expressions of gallantry have not always the force of argument, nor do appeals to sentiment carry with them the logic of facts." "The opening of the university to women is not a sentiment nor a privilege, but a right," she firmly concluded, "a civic duty that the state owes its women," and as such it was justifiable by legal and political principles and need not rest on appeals to chivalry.[18]

17. Thomas G. Dyer, *The University of Georgia: A Bicentennial History, 1785–1985* (Athens: University of Georgia Press, 1985), 170–171; Annie Laura Ragsdale, "The History of Co-Education at the University of Georgia, 1918–1945" (master's thesis, University of Georgia, 1948), 13–25; Townsend, "The Admission of Women to the University of Georgia," 156–169; Celeste Parrish, "Co-Education in the South," [Atlanta] *Southern Educational Journal* 12 (November 1898): 160.

18. Clippings, Scrapbook 2, AWC.

The petition of Woodberry and Gerdine illustrates how the educational concerns of club women were shared by female educators who found their opportunities for professional advancement curtailed by discriminatory practices. Women teachers found themselves stigmatized in the American educational community by the inferiority of southern women's colleges. The nation's premier organization for college-educated women, the Association of Collegiate Alumnae (ACA), accepted only members who were graduates from institutions belonging to the Southern Association of Colleges. Since most southern women's colleges were not accredited, this requirement effectively excluded a majority of southern alumnae. It must have been an especially frustrating predicament for Woodberry, who had completed course work at an accredited institution but could not get it recognized (she finally received her bachelor of arts in education from the University of Georgia in 1927, thirty years after her original petition). Female educators and educational reformers became increasingly convinced that southern women's particular needs demanded a regional approach to reform. In 1903 a group of women attending the summer session at the University of Tennessee acted on these concerns by establishing the Southern Association of College Women (SACW). They described their primary goal as "the advancement of the education of women in the South" and declared their intent to "work for the solution of educational problems which are distinctly southern." SACW members made it clear that they were in no sense competing with the ACA, but rather were motivated by the desire to create an organization that could utilize the abilities of college-educated women barred from the national group. The two groups later merged to form the American Association of University Women (AAUW).[19]

The Georgia membership of the SACW reveals the extraordinary extent of northeastern connections among the state's female educators. This is not surprising, considering that women who wished to move up in their fields had to go north for advanced degrees because of the lack of opportunity at home. In 1906 three-quarters of the state's SACW membership was educated in

19. "The Purpose and Policy of the SACW," *Fourth Annual Report of the Southern Association of College Women, 1906*, American Association of University Women (hereafter AAUW), Georgia Division Records, box 1, folder 1, GAH; Elizabeth Colton, "The Past and Future Work of the Southern Association of College Women," *High School Quarterly* 6 (July 1918): 224–225; entry for Rosa Louise Woodberry, in *Women of Georgia*, 63.

northeastern institutions, and not one member had earned a college degree in Georgia. Of the twenty-nine Georgians who were full members of the SACW, only six had college degrees from southern institutions, five from the top-ranked Randolph-Macon Women's College in Virginia and one from the University of Mississippi. The others were graduates of Vassar (7), the Woman's College of Baltimore (6), Wellesley (3), Radcliffe (3), Cornell (2), Smith (1), and the University of Nebraska (1). Only five of the Georgia members were married, reflecting the prevailing statistics on college women and marriage. According to a survey of ACA members conducted in 1895, female college graduates had a lower marriage rate than the general population, and graduates of women's colleges married even less often. The Northeast had the greatest number of women's colleges and the lowest marriage rate for graduates, while the South had the next lowest rate—28.4 percent—perhaps because so many southern women were educated in the Northeast and in female institutions. Ironically, institutional discrimination intended to shore up the old social order had, in effect, pushed southern daughters out of their region and into the seedbed of the women's rights and Progressive movements.[20]

The northeastern influences evident in Georgia's club movement and in the SACW provided a common sense of purpose among volunteer and professional women. Southern women were encouraged by the culture of northeastern female colleges to connect women's higher education with social service, and the SACW fulfilled this ideal by promoting quality education for women as part of a larger campaign for social improvement through Progressive reform. The group had three specific goals intended to address southern gender concerns: first, to interest more girls and women in attending college; second, to establish scholarships to facilitate women's higher education; and third, to categorize and standardize the levels of instruction in southern women's colleges and to provide prospective students with information on

---

20. The five married SACW members were all leading club women, as indicated by the SACW *Fourth Annual Report;* the marriage rate listed for the South is for female graduates twenty-five years of age or older, but the rate did increase for older groups, as college graduates tended to marry later in life—about half of all graduates of women's colleges married by the time they were forty, although this was still considerably less than the overall national marriage rate of 80 percent. Millicent Washburn Shinn, "The Marriage Rate of College Women," *Century* 50 (1895): 946–948; Marion Talbot and Lois Kimball Mathews Rosenberry, *The History of the American Association of University Women, 1881–1931* (Boston: Houghton Mifflin, 1931), 46–51.

what level of education was offered at each institution. Local SACW chapters pursued these goals by sponsoring a "College Day" for female high school seniors in their communities. Individual chapters simultaneously pursued Progressive reforms at the local level in conjunction with the corresponding campaigns of women's clubs. An overlap in leadership facilitated this dual purpose. Emily Garrett Boyd was a Vassar graduate from Atlanta who was elected president of the SACW in 1908 after serving as head of the Georgia chapter and as vice president of the ACA. She also was chair of the Georgia Federation's child labor and compulsory education committees and acted as chief lobbyist for the Federation on both issues. All of the state's SACW chapters fully supported these two campaigns as part of their effort to address problems in southern education. Because of the concentration of female leadership in Atlanta, its chapter was particularly active in GFWC campaigns, including those to improve rural education, black education, health care and nutrition for poor families, and the industrial working conditions of women and children.[21]

This confluence of educational reform goals and social service ideals can be seen in the activism of Frances Liggett Wey, an "outsider" who found a warm welcome among female activists in Atlanta. Wey was the granddaughter of abolitionists who left South Carolina for Ohio in the 1830s in opposition to the growth of slavery, and the daughter of missionaries who gave up a comfortable urban lifestyle to minister to the needs of poor whites and Indians on the western frontier. Wey's mother was determined to send her three daughters to Vassar but faced a constant struggle in coming up with the funding year after year. Frances had to work to earn her tuition and once had to postpone returning to school for a year when a fire destroyed her parents' house and all their belongings. In the late 1880s, after she married and moved to Atlanta, Wey's memories of her own difficulties led her to form a Vassar Club to assist young women in attending college. She tutored club members in preparation for college entrance examinations and solicited funds from Vassar alumnae and other friends to aid women unable to pay their own way.

21. Georgia chapters formed after 1919, when the SACW and the ACA merged to form the American Association of University Women, continued to engage in similar social reform work. "History of the Eleven Branches of the Georgia Division of the American Association of University Women," AAUW, box 20, folder 9-01; Talbot and Rosenberry, *The History of the AAUW,* 46–51.

In accordance with Wey's philosophy that "college education was a precious privilege and carried with it a special responsibility," the Vassar Club sponsored various social service projects, including a recreation room in Atlanta's night school for working children. She went on to become chair of Atlanta's first Board of Lady Visitors for Public Schools (created when women complained of exclusion from the city Board of Education) and a member of the first Georgia chapter of the SACW. She was most widely known, however, for her work with the state Federation's Student Aid Committee. She chaired the committee for twenty years, assisting hundreds of girls across the state who could not have attended college without financial assistance.[22]

The close working relationship enjoyed by Georgia women's clubs and the SACW illustrates how the southern reform movement actually benefited from the region's relative underdevelopment. In the South, the fields of social work and education were slow to establish credentials in training and experience, so that the line between professional and volunteer work remained blurred and the displacement of nonprofessionals by "experts" was delayed. Professional groups promoting female education actively recruited women's clubs as associate members and sought their assistance in reform campaigns. The SACW constitution stated that the first object of the association was "to unite college women in the South," and to this end the group established a system of affiliated memberships in which individuals and women's clubs could pay nominal fees into a scholarship fund and attend cooperative sessions at SACW meetings. In addition, the organization offered associate memberships to women who had completed two years of work at accredited institutions but had not yet earned degrees—a situation common among teachers who could attend college only during the summer. The SACW greatly benefited from the expanded organizational base created by such inclusive practices. In 1908 the GFWC changed its policy of providing scholarships only to Georgia institutions and formed the Student Aid Committee to assist the SACW in sending female high school graduates to colleges outside the South (a strategy for producing better-trained teachers). By 1920 Federated clubs were sponsoring students at Vassar, Columbia, Vanderbilt, and the University of Chicago. The Georgia Federation also assisted the SACW in fund drives to

22. Emily Harrison, *In Memoriam: Frances Liggett Wey, July 22, 1851–November 20, 1928* (Atlanta: Georgia Federation of Women's Clubs, n.d.), 4–14, 20–27, quote 13.

endow women's colleges, as in 1910 when club women worked diligently to provide Agnes Scott College in Atlanta with an endowment.[23]

Women's efforts to improve teacher training and raise southern educational standards were praised by the state's New South leadership, who recognized the economic value of such reforms, but their campaign for coeducation met with a much more chilly reception. The battle for access to the University of Georgia was perhaps the most difficult and bitter campaign waged by female activists, in part because it represented a frontal attack on the structural inheritance of antebellum elitism. Women who sought to throw wide the doors of the university were challenging the exclusivity of a state institution that had always served to perpetuate the privilege and power of a select few. From its founding in 1785, the university was intended to serve propertied white men, to give them the classical education that served as a basis for careers in politics and the professions. Almost 40 percent of all graduates between 1804 and 1860 became lawyers, while another 43 percent became physicians, clergymen, and planters. The university's reputation as an aristocratic institution was a source of long-standing animosity in the state. In the 1830s critics argued that it was undemocratic and elitist to maintain an institution of higher education when the state lacked a publicly supported elementary school system. The university established the College of Agriculture in 1872 in an effort to suppress continued charges of elitism, but the college failed to placate opponents. University officials refused to alter the liberal arts curriculum requirements for agricultural students, and the scarcity of public secondary schools meant that a majority of rural students were not prepared to begin such a course of study. The university's lack of commitment to meeting the needs of the larger population was evident to farmers, and by 1896

23. The quote on the SACW purpose is in the minutes of the Lexington meeting, SACW *Fourth Annual Report;* Joseph F. Kett, "Women and the Progressive Impulse in Southern Education," in *The Web of Southern Social Relations: Women, Family, and Education,* ed. Walter J. Fraser Jr., R. Frank Saunders Jr., and Jon L. Wakelyn (Athens: University of Georgia Press, 1985), 166–180. A similar example of collaboration between professionals and club women can be seen in the Southern Home Economics Association, which in 1921 encouraged the affiliated state association in Georgia to form a "home-makers' section" comprised of the home economics departments of women's clubs as a way to increase its visibility and widen the scope of its work. Edith Thomas to Mary Creswell, December 2, 1921, Georgia Home Economics Association Collection, box 1, folder 1, GAH.

there was only one student enrolled in the agricultural program. Rural leg-islators sought revenge by consistently opposing funding increases for the institution, effectively withholding resources needed for maintenance and expansion.[24]

A related source of opposition to coeducation was the university trustees' concern that their campus would be inundated by women if females were allowed to enroll, thereby diminishing the already scarce resources available to male students. National trends in coeducational institutions outside the South suggested that this was a very real possibility. Between 1870 and 1900, the number of women in colleges and universities nationwide increased from 11,000 to 85,000, and their proportion of the student population rose from 21 percent to 35 percent. By 1900 there were twice as many women in coedu-cational institutions as there were in women's colleges. A national backlash to this development is illustrated in part by the attempts of some private in-stitutions to use sex discrimination to boost their prestige as higher-quality alternatives to public colleges. Both the University of Chicago and Stanford took measures meant to restrict women's presence after female students be-came roughly half of the student population and were receiving more than half of all academic honors and awards. The president of the University of Chicago moved to segregate undergraduate classes in which large numbers of women were enrolled, and Stanford set a limit on female enrollment (three men to each woman) that was not lifted until 1933. Far from fulfilling the ex-pectations of coeducation critics by proving themselves physically and intel-lectually unable to withstand the rigors of high academic standards, women actually became victims of their own success. Leaders of the AWC and the Federated clubs spoke to these concerns by arguing that it was more likely that the average college-bound woman would show too little interest in the University of Georgia if it became coeducational, because she would believe a university education appropriate only for aspiring professionals (and pre-sumably most female students lacked such aspirations).[25]

As club women and female educators quickly came to realize, coeducation was an exceptionally volatile issue in the South. It cut to the heart of class, gender, and race relations and reflected the social turmoil accompanying

24. Dyer, *The University of Georgia,* 10–47, 128–136.

25. Frankfurt, *Collegiate Women,* 87–88; Solomon, *In the Company of Educated Women,* 56–59; clippings, Scrapbook 2, AWC.

transformations in the postbellum economy. There was widespread uncertainty about the future of the southern economy, about the ability of the South to compete nationally, and about the ability of dominant groups to maintain their status and authority. Farmers and planters saw the price of cotton fall below five cents per pound during the agricultural depression of the 1890s, and the rapidly rising tenancy rate threw into serious doubt the security of agriculture as a basis of white male economic independence. It became increasingly apparent that for those who must find new forms of support, and even for those who chose to remain in agriculture, education could be critical in determining who would sink and who would swim.[26] Many Georgians—black and white, male and female, rural and urban—hoped that government-funded educational opportunity would serve as a life preserver to keep them afloat, or even carry them upward on the crest of economic development. A heightened sense of competition for access to state resources emerged with a vengeance in the debate over coeducation and related curricular issues. Middle- and upper-class white men coveted the new positions in business and industry and the more prestigious jobs in the expanding system of public education. As Atlanta's female leadership recognized, sex-segregated colleges and sex-differentiated curricula ensured that men and women would be trained for different positions and that the inferior education of women would result in their assignment to lower-level and poorer-paying jobs.[27]

Men's concern for the relative economic position of women is evident in

26. Robert Preston Brooks, "The Agrarian Revolution in Georgia, 1865–1912" (Ph.D. diss., University of Wisconsin–Madison, 1914), 57–59. Professor A. C. Briscoe, president of Southern Business College, told the Georgia Teachers Association in 1896 that "the old feudal system" had been swept away by the Civil War, leaving the question of "What can the young man do to earn a livelihood?" *Proceedings and Addresses of the Thirtieth Annual Meeting of the Georgia Teachers' Association* [hereafter GTA], *1896* (Atlanta: GTA, 1897), 64–65.

27. Michael Fultz has made a similar case for the ways in which segregation and disparate standards in funding, curricula, and training doomed black teachers to inferior positions with low pay. "Teacher Training and African American Education in the South, 1900–1940," *Journal of Negro Education* 64 (Spring 1995): 196–212. For a detailed analysis of how this process worked in the field of public education, see Myra H. Strober and David Tyack, "Why Do Women Teach and Men Manage? A Report on Research on Schools," *Signs* 5 (Spring 1980): 494–503; and Myra H. Strober, "Toward a General Theory of Occupational Sex Segregation: The Case of Public School Teaching," in *Sex Segregation in the Workplace: Trends, Explanations, Remedies,* ed. Barbara F. Reskin (Washington, DC: National Academy Press, 1984), 144–156.

the way male supporters of a state college for women portrayed the purposes of female higher education. W. Y. Atkinson, who introduced the bill in the General Assembly that established Georgia Normal and Industrial College, tried to assuage opponents' fears by arguing that they would be bumped up, rather than down, the economic ladder by better-trained female workers. Blatantly appealing to Georgians' sentimental attachment to the concept of chivalry, he pleaded with legislators to acknowledge the disruptive impact of the Civil War on white women by providing for those who had no way to support themselves and their dependents. He portrayed improved educational opportunity as the only hope for poor white women who wanted to avoid menial labor and maintain their respectability. Despite Atkinson's own strong support for the institution (the idea for the college was sometimes credited to his wife), he felt the need to assure his colleagues that the women would not be too well trained, that the female college he envisioned would not be the equivalent of Georgia Tech or the university. He stressed that GN&IC would work "exclusively to the direct benefit of the poor and of those of small means" and made it clear that he did not expect women to be trained in the same industrial occupations as men. He promised legislators that preparing women for lower-level jobs in business and industry would be a "blessing," because it would allow the "men engaged in these pursuits to work at more manly employment."[28]

Educators and administrators associated with Georgia Tech were explicit in their belief that engineering and industrial trades could shore up the eroding occupational barrier that shielded white men's economic position from the competing labor of women and blacks. Professor William Perry characterized engineering as the only occupational alternative for white men who were pushed out of clerical work by the cheap labor of women but who lacked

28. *Speech of Hon. W. Y. Atkinson*, 4–8; Atkinson made his views on gender equality clear while serving as governor in 1895, when he refused to let the National American Woman Suffrage Association use the hall of the House of Representatives for their Atlanta conference. He claimed that allowing the group to use the hall was unconstitutional, which outraged Georgia suffragists, who noted that "white and Negro men had been permitted to do so for many and varied purposes." From an account of the history of woman suffrage in Georgia by Mary Latimer McLendon, *The History of Woman Suffrage*, ed. Susan B. Anthony and Ida Husted Harper (Indianapolis: Hollenbeck Press, 1902), 4:583; also see A. Elizabeth Taylor, "The Origin of the Woman Suffrage Movement in Georgia," *Georgia Historical Quarterly* 28 (June 1944): 63–79.

the capital to compete with the "large producer" in manufacturing. For men who faced an overcrowded field in the traditionally male professions of medicine and law and experienced decreasing opportunities "to rise to positions of control and independence" in business, engineering offered a new field "where competition is as yet little felt, and where the possibilities of accomplishment and reward are almost limitless." Lyman Hall, president of Georgia Tech between 1896 and 1906, made similar arguments in support of male industrial education. "Women have come forward as assistants and employees in every branch of business, at a smaller salary than married men can afford to work for," Hall noted, while industrial schools for blacks were turning out "skilled workmen who command good wages." He warned that unless southerners prepared "means for their own sons for the preservation of the prestige of their inheritance," white men would become the subordinate helpers to black workmen in the industrial trades.[29]

Men's and women's competing claims to state resources were an integral part of the battle to make the University of Georgia coeducational. University trustees and representatives of the student body initially responded to women's petitions by insisting that the institution lacked the funding necessary for the inclusion of women. They complained that classrooms already were overcrowded and the buildings in serious disrepair and that without substantial improvements it was not feasible to increase admissions. Attempting to put a chivalric veneer on their refusal, the men insisted that the poor condition of campus facilities rendered them unsuitable for female students. AWC leader Passie Fenton Ottley found this excuse especially galling, and she and other female activists effectively turned the notion of chivalry to their advantage. Ottley questioned the sincerity of Georgia men's claims to chivalry if they would give up their seats to women on streetcars but not in university classrooms. Even more pointedly, she challenged them to back up their oft-repeated assertion that southern women did not need the ballot because southern men could be counted upon to defend their rights. Other club lead-

29. William G. Perry, "Engineering Education in the South," in *SEA Journal of Proceedings and Addresses of the Seventeenth Annual Meeting Held Jointly with the Southern Association of College Women at Montgomery, Alabama, December 27, 28, 29, 1906* (Ashville, NC: SEA, 1906), 197–209, quotes 200; Lyman Hall, "Needs of the New South," in *Proceedings of the CES, the Sixth Session, Richmond Virginia, April 22nd to April 24th, and at the University of Virginia, April 25th, 1903* (New York: Committee on Publication, 1903), 136–142, quotes 140–141.

ers complained in the press that men who wanted to restrict female access to advanced training were simply trying to reserve office positions for themselves in selfish disregard of the unfortunate women who toiled in factories. Where was men's commitment to chivalry, club women asked, when the heaviest burdens were thrust upon the weakest?[30]

Simultaneous with their battle for admission to the university, Georgia women had to engage in a related struggle to broaden the curriculum available to female students. The single-sex institutions and the sex-differentiated curricula were flip sides of the same coin, two practices that helped confine working women to the bottom rungs of occupational and professional achievement. Between about 1900 and 1915, members of southern educational organizations frequently discussed the direction that reform of women's education should take. Southerners had to decide what aspects of antebellum education to retain, whether women's education would be the same as men's or different, and to what extent curricular emphasis would shift from culture to practicality. Arguments over curricula are especially revealing of gender conflict because they expose the concepts of womanhood that were at the core of various plans for a female course of study. Although the debate on these issues was similar to arguments concerning women's education in other parts of the country, southerners had an acute awareness of regional identity that shaped their analysis of change and agenda for reform.

One area in obvious need of reform was the holdover of the antebellum female academy curriculum, which many women educators believed to be excessively focused on fine arts and social skills. Professor Celeste Parrish, a founder of the SACW who accepted a position at the Georgia State Normal School in 1901, was one of the most vocal critics of the old female curriculum. She repeatedly argued to members of educational associations that an emphasis on the study of music, art, and elocution was inadequate and inappropriate for the needs of women in the New South. She asserted that the South's cultural fascination with the Southern Lady—a woman "noble in character, beautiful in person, gracious in presence"—served to discourage girls from seeking a college education. According to the Old South ideal of

30. Ottley, "Club Women in Educational Work"; Ragsdale, "History of Co-Education," 20–21; *Atlanta Constitution,* June 20, 1897; "Have No Room for the Girls," and Ottley editorial, clippings, Scrapbook 2, AWC.

womanhood embodied in the Southern Lady, moral purity and other admirable qualities of female character derived from women's removal from the competitive and corrupt public world. Parrish's concept of a higher education for southern women that met national professional standards appeared antithetical to this vision, since its end goal was development of rational thought and preparation for entrance into the workforce. Parrish acknowledged her own admiration for the genteel Southern Lady of the past, but she argued that such women were not prepared "for the work which the world needs now."[31]

Another common complaint regarding the antebellum inheritance of southern women's colleges was that their curricula continued to reflect the expectation that women would end their education at age eighteen to "come out" to society. Since this left only a few short years in which to complete female students' higher education, educators had to chose between studying a few subjects in depth or teaching many things superficially. In 1900 Nina Horner of Converse College complained to members of the Southern Educational Association (SEA) that too often the southern female curriculum was guilty of the latter; it tended to be broad but shallow, and its lack of intellectual rigor meant that students did not fully develop the mental discipline critical to character development and clarity of thought. "The southern girl of the twentieth century cannot and must not be a 'glittering generality,'" Horner protested. A female professor from Tennessee claimed that men regarded the products of inferior women's colleges with either indulgence or contempt. Low academic standards could be interpreted only as an "assumption or a confession of inferiority," she argued, and they would have to be raised if the intellectual abilities of women were to gain recognition and respect.[32]

The inferior curriculum of most southern women's colleges influenced many female educators to adopt the position that women's higher education should be modeled after men's, adhering to the same general course of study

31. Parrish, "Some Defects in the Education of Women," 69–70; Parrish, "The Education of Women in the South," 49–50.

32. Nina Horner, "Some Characteristics of a Good School for Southern Girls," in *SEA Proceedings, 1900*, 57–62, quote 60; Alice Lloyd, "Education for Southern Women," in *Proceedings of the Tenth CES, with an Appendix in Review of Five Years; Pinhurst, N.C., April 9, 1907* (Richmond, VA: Executive Committee of the Conference, n.d.), 220–228, quote 221.

and the same degree of difficulty. Two Georgia women who addressed the topic "Do Conventional Standards for the Education of Women Satisfy Present Demands?" at a Georgia Teachers' Association meeting argued that the sexual differentiation of curriculum was unnecessary and undesirable. Professor Pauline Pearce of Georgia Normal and Industrial College observed that education was developing into a scientific discipline concerned with the nature of knowledge and learning, and she passionately argued that a modern system of higher education must "reach the mass, disregard class, and draw no line between the sexes." Her partner in the discussion, Rosa Woodberry, the teacher from Athens whose petition for admission to the University of Georgia was rejected, expressed dismay that she should have to address the topic at all. Woodberry bluntly told Georgia educators, "I do not see why there should be a woman's education in contradistinction to a man's education." She argued that while the private and public social activities of men and women might be "appropriately differentiated" according to gender, "in education of the mind there is no sex."[33]

Some women educators who supported gender equity in academic standards and course of study had reservations about erasing all curricular differences. They accepted that gender difference was constructed and not innate and worried that the special qualities women derived from confinement in the home—compassion, understanding, and dedication to service—might eventually be lost if women received the same education as men and assumed similar economic roles. These women were joined by Progressive male educators in arguing that women's positive influence could be maintained through education for social work, a profession that would preserve humanitarian ideals in crucial counterbalance to the corruption and competitiveness of men.[34]

This embrace of higher education for women based on social need clearly

33. Pauline Pearce and Rosa Woodberry (misspelled as Woodbury in original text), "Do Conventional Standards for the Education of Women Satisfy the Demands of Today?" in *Proceedings and Addresses of the Thirty-Third Annual Meeting of the GTA, 1899* (Columbus, GA: GTA, 1899), 103–116, 198–202, quotes 104, 202.

34. Horner, "Some Characteristics," 61–62; Maggie W. Barry, "Training for Motherhood," 672–678; and B. C. Hagerman, "The Education of the Southern Girl," 97–105, both in *SEA, Journal of Proceedings and Addresses of the Twenty-Second Annual Meeting Held at Houston, Texas, November 30, December 1, 2, 1911* (Nashville, TN: SEA, n.d.).

reflects the influence of national trends in higher education and Progressive thought. One characteristic of higher education after the Civil War that distinguished it from earlier periods was the belief that it could prepare future leaders for a life of service to society, counteracting the excessive individualism of the industrial world and replacing prejudice and greed with the objective "Truth" as the basis of decision making. Social theorists and educators believed that women had a particular role to play in this process. Whether inherently female or a product of evolutionary change, the values they perpetuated in the home had to permeate society. Woman's role was no longer an individual one of responsibility to her own home and family but had become a "socialistic" one of responsibility to societal needs.[35]

The field of home economics, perhaps even more than social work, reflected this new emphasis on the use of formal education to enhance the social benefits of women's domestic role. The emerging fields of psychology and sociology produced a heightened appreciation for the social value of mothering through insights into the importance of early childhood development in the making of the adult. This motivated many southern professional women to advocate the inclusion of domestic science in the female curriculum, at either the secondary or the college level. In addition, educators and club women who sought to raise the standard of living among the rural and urban poor believed that improving sanitation and nutrition in homes could reduce the incidence of disease and bring about lower infant and child mortality rates. They regarded the home as the social center from which all else flowed; as primary caregiver, the mother was its most important occupant. The result of efficient housekeeping and informed, intelligent parenting would be a healthy, well-adjusted, and productive populace. Effective private mothering, no less than public mothering, had definite social benefits associated with it.[36]

35. Robert L. Church and Michael W. Sedlak, *Education in the United States: An Interpretive History* (New York: Free Press, 1976), 230–239; Grace Ruth Foster, *Social Change in Relation to Curricular Development in Collegiate Education for Women* (Waterville, ME: Galahad Press, 1934), 34–38; Rosalind Rosenberg, *Beyond Separate Spheres: Intellectual Roots of Modern Feminism* (New Haven, CT: Yale University Press, 1982), 32–41.

36. Jennie Ford of GN&IC, discussion on domestic science, in *SEA Proceedings, 1901*, 132–133; Carrie Belle Hyde, "The Training of Girls for Home-Making," in *SEA Journal of Proceed-*

Basing female education on a particular societal role was problematic in that it could result in a narrowed scope of study, and Georgia women came face-to-face with this problem in their campaign for coeducation. University of Georgia trustees finally gave coeducation serious consideration in 1918, when a dearth of male students and the importance of women's labor in the war effort added legitimacy to the campaign. At first the trustees expressed a preference for confining female students to the study of domestic science in the College of Agriculture, but the dean of the School of Education objected to this proposal and argued that a dire shortage of high school teachers necessitated admitting women to that department as well. The trustees reluctantly acquiesced to the dean's request but admitted women only at the junior and senior levels and pointedly excluded them from Franklin College, the liberal arts college that was the historic core of the university. A Franklin College professor had to walk across campus to the College of Agriculture to teach female students their required English courses in segregated classes. Women in the College of Education also attended segregated classes and could take only those fine arts courses that were required for their degrees. It was not until another decade had passed that female students were admitted to all programs on an equal footing with men.[37]

Male students joined the trustees in demonstrating a strong desire to limit the options of women at the University of Georgia. In the 1919–1920 school year, the second year of coeducation, they held a mass meeting in the university chapel to protest women's presence on campus. As a university administrator later related, the students were upset at proposals to admit women to Franklin College on equal terms with men. Most male students and faculty were opposed to coeducation from the onset, but it was only when it appeared that women would be allowed to escape their imposed exile in home

ings and Addresses of the Twenty-First Annual Meeting Held at Chattanooga, Tenn., December 27–29, 1910 (Nashville, TN: SEA, n.d.), 244–249; Celeste Parrish, "Child Study in the School and Home," in _SEA Proceedings, 1900,_ 260–273.

37. In addition to the limitations placed on female students, women faculty were limited to positions in the all-female programs of home economics and education until 1928, when pressure from the AAUW influenced the university chancellor to support the hiring of a female professor of journalism in the College of Arts and Sciences. Ragsdale, "History of Co-Education," 41–42, 83; Dyer, _The University of Georgia,_ 187–188.

economics and education that men's indignation became particularly aroused. Male students attempted to force women from the campus with a campaign of harassment that involved swearing and loudly debating female shortcomings in their presence and excluding them from social events. If the letter of one female student to the university newspaper is any indication, this type of behavior did not intimidate women into accepting the status quo. "A Woman in the College of Agriculture" argued that while most women may be inclined to take a course or two in home economics, it was no more likely that all women would specialize in that one field than it was that all men would become doctors or lawyers. A female student "may wish to develop along other lines," the writer argued, and "she demands recognition and opportunities for her capabilities." [38]

The battles over coeducation and curricular reform provide an example of how the intent of those implementing policy was largely what determined whether the end result of educational reforms would be discriminatory or egalitarian. In the case of women's educational reform, it was the underlying gender politics of the supporters of an endeavor that ultimately determined how conducive to women's advancement it would be. Progressive women regarded domestic science as an avenue of female advancement and social progress, but in the hands of men hostile to sexual equality, it became a road to segregated and inferior careers. It was a political reality with which African Americans were all too familiar, as they struggled against the racial politics of white officials who regarded industrial education as a training ground for laborers and servants rather than skilled, economically independent workers. And just as with racial politics, the impact of gender politics is illustrated most clearly in the "industry versus culture" debate. Most of the men who supported female industrial education saw it as an unfortunate necessity for poor women and a way to boost men to higher-status jobs; women regarded it as a key to female economic self-sufficiency and one step in the direction of occupational gender equality. Similarly, men who argued for a cultural emphasis in women's education used the antebellum female academy as the ideal,

38. Ragsdale, "History of Co-Education," 93–94; quotes in letter to the editor, *Red and Black*, May 8, 1919. For accounts of similar opposition to coeducation in other southern institutions, see McCandless, *The Past in the Present*, 86–101.

whereas women reformers wanted the kind of liberal arts education that served as a basis for graduate and professional training.[39]

Men who opposed equal educational opportunity for women usually drew upon the antebellum claim that white female dependency was a sign of regional cultural superiority. A speech presented at the annual meeting of the Georgia Educational Association (formerly the Georgia Teachers' Association, renamed to distinguish it from the black GTA) is representative of the classic southern argument against vocation-oriented female education. In 1910 South Carolinian D. B. Johnson addressed Georgia educators on the topic "Southern Ideals: Why They Should be Maintained in the Education of Southern Women." Johnson warned that if the South continued to emulate northern educational trends, ignoring the "splendid virtues and achievements of the old civilization because they cannot be measured by the new 'dollar' standard," the region would lose its "cherished ideals" and "moral degeneracy and intellectual degradation" would prevail. He envisioned a female education similar to that of the antebellum female academy, one that would recreate the Southern Lady of the Old South to stand in opposition to commercial and industrial development and the blurring of gender roles that accompanied it. The ideal product of this education was women who perpetuated Old South values and contributed to the improvement of the New South through their moral and educational influence on men and children.[40]

Southern men were not alone in fearing the impact of industrialization on gender relations and the family, although their arguments did contain certain regional peculiarities. Johnson and other male opponents of female industrial education portrayed it as an avenue through which economic relations might

39. Texas teacher Agnes Craig complained to southern educators in 1911 that men in charge of female industrial education often had an inferior education in mind, one purely manual and technical and devoid of academic content. *SEA Proceedings, 1911,* 548–556. African American educators tried to maximize white support for black education in the late nineteenth century by proclaiming their faith in the value of manual and industrial training, but they continued to provide the classic liberal education necessary to turn out teachers and ministers, especially since most black colleges could not purchase the expensive equipment needed for industrial education (in Georgia, Spelman Seminary was the only institution adequately equipped). Anderson, *The Education of Blacks in the South,* 66–77; and Range, *Rise and Progress of Negro Colleges,* 72–82.

40. D. B. Johnson, "Southern Ideals: Why They Should Be Maintained in the Education of Southern Women," in *Proceedings and Addresses of the Forty-Fourth Annual Meeting of the Georgia Educational Association* [hereafter GEA], *1910* (Macon, GA: GEA, 1910), 53–58, quotes 53–54.

corrupt the sanctity of the home, yet the Old South household they held up as a model of separate spheres was itself a business thoroughly permeated with the profit motive. While one might assume they intended to equate the separation of women from public life with their separation from the public marketplace, the illusion of separate spheres in the antebellum and postbellum households was just that, an illusion, and it served to obscure the relations of domination and subordination that characterized both. Similarly, framing their position as part of an "agrarian versus industrial" conflict allowed southern white men to remove the issue of educational equality to an abstract level in which gender relations was, at best, a subset of the larger—and by implication, more important—social structure.[41]

Despite the obfuscation of agrarian and patriotic appeals, relations of power were clearly discernible at times. In his speech to Georgia teachers, D. B. Johnson expressed not only opposition to female industrial education, but also opposition to any education that gave women aspirations that could not be fulfilled through a domestic role. Speaking for southern white men, Johnson stated, "We do not wish to produce the coldly intellectual woman— the mannish woman—without grace or heart or charm . . . the woman who in pursuit of scholarship for its own sake loses all interest in home, humanity, and social service." His preference was for an education that produced a woman with a "willingness and ability, forgetting self, to serve others." Apparently, women's subordination in the household made men inclined to see social service as a particularly feminine undertaking, as part of the process by which young women learned to subordinate their own needs to those of husbands and children. Women were to serve, and men were to be served. Many Progressive men dedicated their lives to social causes, but they did so from a

41. Ibid.; F. W. Gaines, "Should the Curricula of the Woman's College Be Broadened to Meet New Conditions Resulting From the Opening of Many Industries to Women during the War?" in *Proceedings and Addresses, Fifty-Third Annual Meeting, GEA, 1919* (Dalton, GA: GEA, n.d.), 45–47. For classic arguments in support of the "agrarian versus industrial" interpretation of southern social and cultural distinctiveness, see Donald Davidson, John Gould Fletcher, H. B. Kline, Lyle H. Lanier, Andrew Nelson Lytle, H. C. Nixon, Frank Lawrence Owsley, John Crowe Ransom, Allen Tate, John Donald Wade, Robert Penn Warren, and Stark Young, *I'll Take My Stand: The South and the Agrarian Tradition* (New York: Harper and Brothers, 1930; repr., Baton Rouge: Louisiana State University Press, 1977), esp. the essays by Ransom, Lanier, and Owsley.

distinctly different position, one economically privileged and politically en-franchised. Their right to pursue economic independence was a given, and they were not expected to choose between social service and realization of their potential. Johnson's words reveal how the ethic of social service as jus-tification for female higher education could have negative implications for women, making those who pursued a professional or scholarly interest "for its own sake" appear selfish and socially irresponsible.[42]

The social sciences and Progressive thought gave southern women a basis for rejecting such constructions of feminine social responsibility, allowing them to reconcile personal needs with commitment to service. Research in so-cial and individual psychology focused their attention on education as an en-vironmental influence that could restrict the development of personality and intellect, while Progressive thought encouraged them to believe that remov-ing such restrictions would benefit both self and society. In defending their right to equal educational opportunity, female activists often characterized a standard liberal education as an essential element of self-realization, self-determination, and intellectual development. In the words of one southern woman, "it is education which changes the equation between being and liv-ing," an equation that she believed to be profoundly human but not inher-ently gendered. Kentucky educator Irene Myers told her southern colleagues that industrialization and its social effects had cast into doubt traditional as-sumptions as to innate gender difference and that women needed a strong liberal arts component to their education if they were to discover what, if any-thing, was essentially female. "We have been checked by family, by religion, by sex-customs," Myers observed, "but these checks are loosening, and we shall ourselves have to prove what we are when the outside restraint has been removed." From this perspective, not allowing women a quality education hindered their progress as a sex while also denying society the benefits of their fully realized potential.[43]

42. Southern women often tried to reconcile women's desire for self-fulfillment with their obligation to service by arguing that their intellectual development was beneficial to home and family, as in the essay of SACW president Elizabeth A. Colton, "How Southern Colleges for Women Might More Effectively Fit Women for Their Life Work," *High School Quarterly* 4 (Oc-tober 1915): 45–48; D. B. Johnson, "Southern Ideals," quotes 54–48; and "The Education of the Southern Girl," in *SEA Proceedings, 1911*, 88–97.

43. Irene T. Myers, "Woman's Work in College," in *SEA Journal of Proceedings and Ad-dresses of the Twenty-Fourth Annual Meeting Held at Nashville, Tennessee, October 30, 31, Novem-*

In recognizing the psychological and social importance of education, women also came to recognize the ways in which the gender politics of education overlapped private and public relations. Professor Celeste Parrish, whose perspective was informed by her own experiences with familial and professional opposition to female intellectuality, developed the most comprehensive critique of the gender relations embedded in education. Orphaned as a child during the Civil War, she was raised in Virginia by two aunts and an uncle who regarded her intellectual ambitions as inappropriate for a girl. She used independent study to compensate for an inferior public school education and then proceeded to work her way through college by teaching. While Parrish benefited from the female networks of support in women's colleges, Virginia's sex-segregated institutions made it more difficult for her to earn a baccalaureate and pursue graduate studies. She frequently found herself a beggar at the table, having to entreat professors in male institutions to provide tutoring or correspondence instruction. The demands of her work schedule and the necessity of attending school outside the South also represented significant obstacles. In order to receive a degree from Cornell, she had to make a personal appeal to the president and faculty members to apply her summer school work to the one-year minimum residence required for awarding a degree.[44]

Celeste Parrish developed her comprehensive critique of education and southern gender relations between 1899 and 1901, just before she accepted the position of professor of pedagogy and psychology at the Georgia State Normal School. In papers delivered before the Conference for Education in the South and the SEA, and in articles in the *Independent* and the *Educa-*

---

ber 1, 1913 (Nashville, TN: SEA, n.d.), 314–315; first quote from Mrs. Charles A. Perkins, "Open Doors in Woman's Education," in *SEA Proceedings, 1900*, 81; similar arguments can be seen in Jane Addams, "The College Woman and the Family Claim," *Commons* 3 (1898): 3–7, repr. in *On Education*, ed. Ellen Condliffe Lagemann (New York: Teachers College Press, 1985), 64–73; and Charlotte Perkins Gilman, *Women and Economics* (Boston, 1898; repr. New York: Harper and Row, 1966). The role of education in reconciling individual and social needs is most thoroughly developed in John Dewey's *Democracy and Education* (New York: Macmillan, 1916; repr. New York: Free Press, 1966).

44. Celeste Parrish, "My Experience in Self-Culture," and Mary E. Creswell, "Personal Recollections of Celeste Parrish," both in Celeste Parrish Memorials, Hargrett Rare Book and Manuscript Collection, Special Collections, University of Georgia Libraries, Athens; *Dictionary of American Biography* (1934), s.v. "Parrish, Celestia Susannah."

tional Review, she outlined what she regarded as the central obstacles to southern women's educational and occupational advancement. At the heart of the matter, Parrish believed, was the inclination of men to see women "as things, not as persons; as means to an end, not as ends in themselves." Parrish argued that the "tendency of men to speak of women from their own standpoint," to discuss women's issues in terms of what men did or did not like, reflected the widespread belief among men "that women were created not to realize the highest and best which God has implanted in them, but to assist men in their self-realization, sometimes merely to amuse and please them." According to Parrish, it was this fundamental shortcoming among even "liberal and progressive" men that underlay support for a superficial cultural education for women. She admitted that she had once believed that if women demonstrated their intellectual capabilities they would overcome male opposition to equal access to higher education, but she had come to realize through experience that the "average man, unselfish as he may be in other respects, is hedonistic in his ethics in this field."[45]

Parrish considered men's desire to confine women to a supporting role extremely detrimental to women in academia. She argued that this bias motivated male educational leaders to encourage female college students to eschew the "mannish" course of intellectual achievement in favor of the cultivation of feminine traits aimed at pleasing men. Such male efforts conflicted with Parrish's attempts to impress upon her students the seriousness of college studies and the importance of mental discipline. She believed that one of higher education's greatest benefits for women was its ability to liberate them from the confines of the sex relation, "enabling them to meet men upon an intellectual basis." Parrish struggled to counteract the tendency of students to be obsessed with their sexual attractiveness by urging them to see that "their symmetrical development as individuals is far more important than increase in effeminacy, [and] that for them, as for their brothers, the capability of self-support is necessary to self-respect." However, according to Parrish, her hard work in this area was thwarted deliberately by men. The damage often came in the form of a commencement speaker who "exhorts these girls to make

45. First three quotes from Celeste Parrish, "The Womanly Woman," *Independent* 53 (April 1901): 775–778; Parrish, "The Education of Women in the South"; last two quotes from Parrish, "Some Defects in the Education of Women," 72, 76.

themselves more attractive, assures them that marriage is indispensable for them and solemnly warns them against wanting to do 'man's work' or being 'mannish' in any way."[46]

Parrish's training in pedagogical psychology, and more specifically her knowledge of childhood and adolescent development, encouraged her to see any self-serving efforts to manipulate or stunt the mental maturation process as an egregious affront to the basic human right of self-realization. She regarded early adolescence, the time when most girls were sent to boarding schools for secondary education, as a critical phase in psychological and intellectual development. It was during this phase that "passion for knowledge" and "ideals of vocation and personal consecration" should emerge. Parrish noted that adolescence was marked by certain excesses of emotion that could give rise to destructive behavior, but in her eyes the greater danger was that the "average girl will pass through it without awakening at all." And "if this should be her fate," Parrish argued, "life will never mean more to her than mere existence." Parrish identified the conservatism of southern communities and men's tendency to regard women as means to an end as exactly those factors that worked to ensure that girls' training for adulthood would prepare them to "vegetate rather than live." According to southern tradition, she complained, higher education for women was more concerned with "producing external grace and charm and . . . fitting them to entertain and amuse so-called society" than with "making possible for them the self-realization which is their birthright." Parrish argued that such training at the secondary level discouraged young women from even considering higher education beyond the academy.[47]

Parrish further argued that violations of women's right to self-realization continued after adolescence in the form of social pressure that worked to force them into the home regardless of individual abilities or inclination. Because of her knowledge of the importance of early childhood development, she had great respect for mothering, but she also realized that not all women would excel at it. It was illogical to assume that all females would be talented in the science of child study or the art of teaching. Although Parrish made the usual tributes to motherhood as the highest calling of women, she character-

46. Celeste Parrish, "Woman's Problems," *Independent* 53 (October 1901): 2582–2585.
47. Parrish, "The Education of Women in the South," last two quotes 52, all others 55–56.

ized it as only one of many worthy callings. She argued that remaining single (as she did) was not abnormal; what was abnormal was failing to acknowledge one's inherent strengths and weaknesses and make life choices accordingly. It was only reasonable and just that women who were not inclined toward motherhood be allowed to pursue any profession that fulfilled their individual potential. Parrish vigorously protested against the assumption that "all women must be married" and the practice of labeling the woman with an alternative aim a "crank."[48]

According to Parrish, compulsory marriage was only one aspect of the gender politics of the household that perpetuated women's subordination. She maintained that women were frightened away from any nontraditional pursuit such as graduate work or professional training by the warning that "men will not marry women who do that." Although Parrish disputed the accuracy of this claim, her foremost concern was its end result—the inadequate education of mothers in the home—and its practical implications for women's status. She had no dispute with a sexual division of labor that was voluntary, equitable, and efficient, but she despised the sexual division of intellectual functions that relegated all authority and discipline to the father and all kindness and love to the mother. A woman trained to persuade through charm and beauty rather than reason and intellect, Parrish believed, could do only harm to her children, and particularly to her sons. To her mind it was the "womanly strength and efficiency" that many people criticized as "mannishness" that produced the most effective mothering. "One may wonder," she speculated, "whether the mother who has relied upon 'beauty, sympathy, winsomeness, and soft, refined blandishments' will go on with her 'blandishments' when her young son begins to treat them with amused contempt." Parrish argued that women's humiliating intellectual subordination within the institution of marriage led sons to vice (liaisons with prostitutes) as a lack of respect for their mothers translated into a contempt for women more generally.[49]

48. Parrish, "Woman's Problems"; quotes from Parrish, "Some Defects in the Education of Women," 72, 75; Parrish, "Shall the Higher Education of Women Be the Same as That of Men?" *Educational Review* 22 (November 1901): 383–396.

49. Quotes from Parrish, "Woman's Problems"; Parrish, "Some Defects in the Education of Women," 74–75; Parrish, "Shall the Higher Education of Women Be the Same as That of Men?"

In her arguments for revision of southern gender relations, Parrish found an effective rhetorical tool in southern men's duty to recognize the sacrifices of white women during the Civil War. She rejected claims that the Old South represented the pinnacle of social and cultural achievement, at least in regard to women's status. She acknowledged that this was an unpopular position to take, given southerners' propensity to be "very sensitive with regard to any question concerning women" and to respond to any suggestions for change with a "defense of the older order which we have justly loved so much." However, Parrish felt compelled to point out that it was the experience of Civil War that proved that southern womanhood derived from internal qualities of character rather than the external and more superficial qualities of beauty and social pleasantness. Furthermore, it was the war itself that rendered the Southern Lady an outmoded and "defective" product of the past. Parrish argued that the "southern women who after the close of the Civil War bravely faced their changed conditions and worked hard to support little children left fatherless by the cruel fortune of war seemed to some very good people more womanly as they aged rapidly under the pressure of sorrow and toil than in the heyday of their youth and prosperity." "But," she drily added, "those who took that view were accustomed to think of women as rational human beings, not as mere instruments of man's passion or pleasure."[50]

As Parrish seemed to realize, the Civil War set a process in motion that was only beginning to reach fruition at the turn of the century, although the past refused to die an easy death. It was the roots of southern women's subordination in the gender politics of the plantation household—as well as an entire cultural mythology that developed around it as a salve to wounded southern pride—that continued to hold women back even after the household itself had disintegrated. While the southern debate over coeducation and curricular issues often mirrored national discussion on the topics, the subtext of regional distinctiveness in the historical foundations of gender roles was ever present. Many white men were bitter at the breakdown of the old order that had constructed their honor and privilege, even as they continued to describe it in terms of women's honor and privilege. Even young men born well after the Civil War echoed the underlying assumption that female (and black) subordination was their birthright. One of the University of Georgia students

50. Parrish, "The Education of Women in the South," 45; quotes from Parrish, "The Womanly Woman," 777.

who returned after World War I to find his "little island campus" inhabited by women complained that coeducation at the university would eradicate once and for all Georgia's "reputation of being one of the few remaining sections of the country where chivalry still exists." He accused women of betraying their men, of taking advantage of male absence during the war, and he asked them to "give us back our university."[51]

Parrish's insight regarding the intimate connection between the gender relations of marriage and the gender politics of higher education and the workplace helps to explain why women reformers were more successful at winning battles for poor women than in obtaining concessions for women of their own class. Middle-class and elite white men could not deny that many women had to work for survival and so were willing to grant them vocational training that would provide them with a modest income. White women in lower levels of business and industry would not compete with men on any equal basis and could even serve to boost them to higher positions, but in either case these women presented little economic threat. It was an entirely different matter when it came to conceding to middle-class white women the right of access to the institutions of higher education that boosted the privilege of white men. If this was allowed, Georgia men would lose out on two fronts: they would lose their ability to monopolize positions of economic and political leadership, and they would also lose the subordination of women within their own households that, according to Parrish, served to gratify their personal and emotional needs. Such an outcome represented both an economic and a psychological loss, and given the simultaneous decline of black dependency, it was one that southern white men were all the more reluctant to permit in women's struggle for emancipation.

51. "Give Us Back Our University," *Red and Black*, March 11, 1920, 6.

2

REFORMING RURAL PUBLIC SCHOOLS
Gender and the Creation of Southern Community

In the first decade of the twentieth century, southern women emerged as key figures in a movement designed to reconstruct the regional concept of community. Their campaign for the improvement of rural public schools—in actuality the attempt to institute the first modern school systems in the region—included efforts to impose on men a concept of citizenship that entailed a wider sense of civic responsibility than that associated with autonomous male heads of household in the antebellum South. Female reformers sought to transform the "community of men" into a "community of families," transcending the limitations of male-centered localism by replacing white male individualism with the greater social good as a basis for political decision making. This greater social good involved recognizing that the educational needs of children and the economic health of the state outweighed white men's authority over household dependents and the financial interests of property owners. In the end, what female activists wanted out of school reform—a new concept of fatherhood that defined the value of children in social terms and a new concept of the state that acknowledged its vested interest in the family—could not easily be imposed from without.

While the legal evolution through which the new relationships became formally defined and codified has been well documented, the agency of white women in pushing forward the changes has received less attention. An account of women's work in local school reform is critical to any understanding of how public support for change was generated, regardless of whether their activities resulted in effective legislation. Even though women's formal lobbying efforts helped publicize educational reform issues and pressured politicians into personal accountability, regional economic interests and conservative opposition to governmental interference thwarted most efforts at effective legislative reform. Georgia club women responded to these obstacles by expanding their work at the local level. By asserting the community interests of teachers and mothers, they were able to work with the very localism in politics that hindered state-level reform. Through their campaigns to provide financial and moral support for rural teachers, to organize parents and students, and to ensure an adequate source of funding for public education, female activists attempted to effect political change by gathering grassroots support in favor of a new relationship between family, community, and government.[1]

Efforts to establish public schools began as early as the 1850s under the governorship of Joseph E. Brown, but it was not until the end of the century that conditions were such that a full-scale movement could take root. Brown was an upcountry farmer and judge who gained much of his support from the "common man," leading some historians to argue that his advocacy of public education represented an early class-based challenge to the conservative planter aristocracy. These reform efforts were interrupted by the Civil War, and for several decades economic uncertainty and the white social and political backlash to Radical Reconstruction prevented significant progress on educational issues. Strong support of public education awaited the rise of an urban and rural middle class that could challenge the remnants of the old aristocracy who were intent on reestablishing the old order. By 1890 increased cotton production, the expansion of railroads, and industrial development facilitated southern economic recovery and produced a growing number of urban professionals who advocated Progressive reform. This urban middle class —including lawyers, doctors, ministers, editors, and businessmen—joined educators and the Georgia Federation of Women's Clubs (GFWC) in arguing

1. Peter Bardaglio, in *Reconstructing the Household: Families, Sex, and the Law in the Nineteenth-Century South* (Chapel Hill: University of North Carolina Press, 1995), 158–161, provides an excellent outline of the legal evolution of a new state authority over children in the post-bellum South, but his analysis of the motivations of child welfare reformers emphasizes a class-based desire for social hegemony and neglects the gender concerns of women. Recent works that recognize women's role in rural school improvement include Mary S. Hoffschwelle, *Rebuilding the Rural Southern Community: Reformers, Schools, and Homes in Tennessee, 1900–1930* (Knoxville: University of Tennessee Press, 1998); James L. Leloudis II, *Schooling the New South: Pedagogy, Self, and Society in North Carolina, 1880–1920* (Chapel Hill: University of North Carolina Press, 1996), 153–175; Judith N. McArthur, *Creating the New Woman: The Rise of Southern Women's Progressive Culture in Texas, 1893–1918* (Urbana: University of Illinois Press, 1998), 54–75; Anastatia Sims, *The Power of Femininity in the New South: Women's Organizations and Politics in North Carolina, 1880–1930* (Columbia: University of South Carolina Press, 1997), 89–109; and James L. Leloudis II, "School Reform in the New South: The Woman's Association for the Betterment of Public School Houses in North Carolina, 1902–1919," *Journal of American History* 69 (March 1983): 886–909.

that improvements in public education were central to helping their region catch up with the rest of the nation socially, politically, and economically. The increasing influence of a farming middle class of property owners (represented first by the Farmers' Alliance and later by the Farmers' Union) put additional pressure on political leaders to acknowledge the need for more democratic access to education.[2]

The educational problems that reformers sought to remedy were an inheritance of the Old South social structure and reflected the beliefs that schooling was a private rather than a public concern and that it was a prerogative more than a responsibility of fathers. Before the Civil War there was no public school system. Farmers who had the financial resources to pay tuition supported "field schools" that offered three years' study at most, while planters hired tutors or established private schools. Wealthy landowners also helped to fund "poor schools" (or "free schools") for children whose parents were unable to afford even the most basic education, but most rural whites shunned them because of their inferior quality and stigma as charitable institutions. The blacks and ordinary whites who dominated the first Reconstruction government laid the groundwork for a public school system in the constitution of 1868, and the second Reconstruction government passed additional educational legislation in 1870. However, with the return of Democratic rule in 1872 came a retreat from commitments to public education, and the 1877 constitution was the most conservative in Georgia history. Middle-class critics of this retreat from responsibility tended to view it as a product of antebellum attitudes as much as Redemption politics.[3]

2. Charles L. Flynn Jr., *White Land, Black Labor: Caste and Class in Late Nineteenth-Century Georgia* (Baton Rouge: Louisiana State University Press, 1983), 175–183; Edgar W. Knight, *Public Education in the South* (Boston: Athenaeum Press, 1922), 423–427; Mildred Thompson, *Reconstruction in Georgia: Economic, Social, Political, 1865–1872* (New York, 1915; repr., Atlanta: Cherokee Publishing, 1971), 119–120; C. Vann Woodward, *Origins of the New South, 1877–1913* (Baton Rouge: Louisiana State University Press, 1951), 107–141.

3. Numan V. Bartley, *The Creation of Modern Georgia* (Athens: University of Georgia Press, 1983), 79–80; Herbert T. Coleman, "The Status of Education in the South Prior to the War between the States," *Confederate Veteran* 15 (October 1907): 441–447, esp. 446; Charles William Dabney, *Universal Education in the South* (Chapel Hill: University of North Carolina Press, 1936), 1:246–250; Atticus G. Haygood, "The South and the School Problem," *Harper's New Monthly Magazine* 79 (July 1889): 225–231; Andrew Sledd, a professor at Emory University, blamed high illiteracy rates in postbellum Georgia on the ignorant and unruly behavior of poor whites, although he did consider their condition a result of slavery and the selfishness of the "aris-

The central problem with the educational legislation of the Redemption government was that it failed to establish an adequate source of revenue for public schools. In a reactionary backlash to the fusion governments, Democrats implemented "policies of retrenchment in public expenditures." The constitution of 1877 created a state educational fund from proceeds such as the poll tax and assessments on liquor sales and domestic animals, but the total was not adequate to fund even a three-month term for all counties. The Redemption constitution also hindered the ability of counties to supplement state funds by placing prohibitively strict requirements on local taxation for education. A county could not hold an election to approve a levy for its schools until two successive grand juries had approved the proposal; and once past this hurdle, it had to be approved by two-thirds of all qualified voters, not just two-thirds of those voting. The difficulty inherent in persuading jury members—propertied men who could afford private education for their children—to tax themselves to benefit others was compounded by the problem of getting voters from remote districts to the polling place. Only one county was able to fulfill these requirements. County boards of education had the legal right to buy land, build schools, and purchase furnishings, but they had no way to raise the money with which to do it.[4]

Georgia's funding system disadvantaged rural children when it came to secondary education, because the Redemption constitution also banned the use of state moneys for high schools. The superior tax base of municipalities and wealthy school districts enabled them to construct and operate high schools using only local taxation, but rural districts did not have the luxury of that option. Furthermore, rural communities were less likely than urban ones to have wealthy benefactors able and willing to pay for the construction of private or public high schools out of their own pockets. The dearth of rural high schools translated into diminished opportunities for higher education

tocratic oligarchy that ruled the antebellum South." "Illiteracy in the South," *Independent* 17 (October 1901): 2471–2474.

4. Louis R. Harlan, *Separate and Unequal: Public School Campaigns and Racism in the Southern Seaboard States, 1901–1915* (Chapel Hill: University of North Carolina Press, 1958), 219; James C. Bonner, Oscar H. Joiner, H. S. Shearouse, and T. E. Smith, *A History of Public Education in Georgia, 1734–1976,* gen. ed. Oscar H. Joiner, with introduction and epilogue by Claude Purcell (Columbia, SC: Georgia State Board of Education, 1979), 148–149; quote from Knight, *Public Education in the South,* 423; Dorothy Orr, *A History of Education in Georgia* (Chapel Hill: University of North Carolina Press, 1950), 216–225.

among the farming population. As the state school commissioner complained in 1903, there was nothing "to connect our common schools with the higher educational institutions in the state." Graduates of primary schools were not prepared to assume college-level work, and most lacked the resources to pay for remedial studies in college preparatory departments. This gap between elementary and higher education prevented rural students from attending the College of Agriculture at the University of Georgia (which had no preparatory department) and made a mockery of the populist function of land grant institutions. Georgians concerned about rural population flight knew that the search for better educational opportunities often motivated the migration of farm families, and so reformers advocated a constitutional amendment to allow the application of state funds to secondary schools.[5]

Inadequate funding of secondary education had a negative impact on quality of instruction in the countryside. A shortage of high schools resulted in a shortage of teachers, and especially a shortage of qualified teachers. On the one hand, most aspiring educators could not afford to attend normal colleges and had to rely on private or urban secondary schools for their training. Yet the absence of state funding and oversight translated into high schools of uneven quality, many of which used outmoded pedagogical methods and curricula. On the other hand, a majority of students who could pay for a normal school education had not attended high school and were not prepared to begin college-level work. This forced most four-year teachers' colleges to begin their courses of study with two years of high school–level instruction. Educational leaders fretted that inadequately prepared teachers only compounded the state's problems by failing to inspire in students an interest in learning. A State Normal School professor complained that teachers who relied on "the three R's" and rote memorization could not instill in students the "inspiration and aspiration" necessary to continue schooling especially when field work or factory labor put heavy demands on their time.[6]

5. Bonner et al., *History of Public Education in Georgia*, 157–158; Leland Clovis Thomas, "Some Aspects of Biracial Public Education in Georgia, 1900–1954" (Ph.D. diss., George Peabody College for Teachers, 1960), 21–25; W. B. Merritt, "Rural High Schools," in *Southern Educational Association* [hereafter SEA] *Journal of Proceedings and Addresses of the Fourteenth Annual Meeting Held at Atlanta, Georgia, December 30th and 31st 1903 and January 1st 1904* (Ashville, NC: SEA, 1904), 110–117, quote 111.

6. On problems regarding teacher training, see Ann Short Chirhart, "Torches of Light: African American and White Female Teachers in the Georgia Upcountry, 1910–1950" (Ph.D. diss.,

By 1900 federal and state statistics on public education contained plenty of evidence that Georgia's school system, and particularly its rural school system, was sadly lacking. More than 30 percent of the state's inhabitants were illiterate. More than 22 percent of children aged ten to fourteen years were illiterate, compared to a national average of just over 7 percent for the same age group. Georgia was ranked 46 in child illiteracy among the 50 states and territories. The average length of the state's school term was 112 days, two weeks longer than was typical for the rest of the South but more than a full month shorter than the national average. And as bad as the state's statistical averages were, they hid great disparities between urban and rural schools. In 1907 Georgia spent $3.77 per rural student for an average school term of 103 days, while municipal school districts spent $12.72 per student for terms of around 170 days. Constitutional restrictions on funding, combined with low population density and low per capita wealth, denied rural children the opportunity for self-development and advancement.[7]

Middle-class club women began the first organized efforts to address the serious problems facing the state's public schools. Even though historians often describe the activities of the Southern Education Board as the source of the "real" school reform movement in the South, women in Georgia and other southern states had school improvement campaigns well under way by the time the SEB began operation in 1902. The first circular issued by the GFWC upon its founding in 1896 proclaimed its intent to work "for the establishment of kindergartens, for better trained teachers, for better school houses, for a compulsory education law, for local taxation, for county high schools, for circulating libraries, and for the founding of mothers' clubs." The educational committee of each affiliated club formed subcommittees to address one or more of these concerns. In 1897 the General Federation of Women's Clubs encouraged local involvement in school reform when it asked

---

Emory University, 1997), 125–132; D. L. Earnest, "The Call upon Normal Schools," in *SEA Journal of Proceedings and Addresses of the Eleventh Annual Meeting Held at Columbia, S.C., December 26–29, 1901* (Knoxville, TN: SEA, 1902), 203–208, quotes 205, 208; Merritt, "Rural High Schools."

7. Bureau of the Census, *Supplementary Analysis and Derivative Tables: Twelfth Census of the United States, 1900* (Washington, DC: Government Printing Office, 1900), 341–344; Dewey W. Grantham, *Southern Progressivism: The Reconciliation of Progress and Tradition* (Knoxville: University of Tennessee Press, 1983), 258; Harlan, *Separate and Unequal,* 224.

state federations to conduct a study of the system of education in their regions. Emily Hendree Park, chair of the GFWC education committee, assumed the responsibility for this endeavor and worked closely with the state school superintendent in compiling a report on the status of public schools. Federation leaders met with county commissioners and other officials to publicize their work, asking for assistance in identifying problems and solutions.[8]

While the national Federation provided important impetus for Georgia women to engage in public school reform, their motivations lay in a complex and regionally distinct set of influences. The domestic role of southern women had been politicized by the Civil War, when that role was transformed into a patriotic commitment to service that transcended individual household concerns. Participation in a national network of women helped to fuse this regional gender identity to a Progressive ideology that justified female activism in pursuit of the greater social good. Beverly B. Munford, a Virginia reformer who worked with Georgians in regional organizations, was one of many women who claimed that female activism was rooted in the deprivations of the Civil War, when hardship taught southern women the need for sacrifice and endurance. Now that the war was over and the memorials built, she argued, loyal wives and mothers must assist in the "reconstruction" of the South through the development of public schools that would serve as the "basis of rural life, economic efficiency, and racial good will." Georgia women embraced this task and described their motivations in terms that reflected the Progressive ideal of public service. A GFWC representative speaking to educators on school reform declared that club women had organized out of a desire to shun "individual advantage" as a motivation for action in favor of collective efforts "toward the universal uplifting of the human race."[9]

8. Emily Hendree Park, "The Needs of Country Schools," speech from the Conference of Women's Work, Farmers' Conference, 1909, *Bulletins and Reports, State College of Agriculture, 1908–1912,* 248–256, quote 248, Andrew M. Soule Collection, box 6, University Archives, University of Georgia, Athens; Mrs. E. T. Brown, "How the Federation of Women's Clubs May Cooperate with the Teachers," in *Proceedings of the Thirty-Seventh Annual Meeting of the GEA, 1903* (Atlanta: GEA, 1904), 101–117.

9. Beverly B. Munford, "Report upon Women's Educational Work in Virginia," in *Proceedings of the Ninth Conference for Education in the South* [hereafter CES], *Lexington, Kentucky, May 2–4, 1906* (Richmond, VA: Executive Committee of the Conference, 1906), 39–41; other quotes from Brown, "How the Federation of Woman's Clubs May Cooperate," 101–102; also see Beverly B. Munford, "The Southern Woman's Work for Education: A Record and Interpreta-

The Georgia Federation of Women's Clubs consolidated its position as a state leader in school reform when members launched the rural "model school" campaign. In 1900 Federation members made plans to construct twelve new schools in rural areas across the state that would showcase the benefits of Progressive reform. Club women hoped that once surrounding communities could see the advantages of better buildings, curricula, and teacher training, they would want to adopt the innovations for their own schools. Federation president J. Lindsay Johnson sent letters to county school commissioners in which she pledged matching funds to any county interested in establishing a model school. More than fifteen sent immediate replies, with the largest cash amount offered by Madison County, where the Danielsville school opened in 1901. Shortly thereafter the Federation founded a second school in a remote district of Floyd County, where a "little village of 200 people" raised almost one thousand dollars to fund its construction. In 1903 the third model school opened at Cass Station in Bartow County, funded in part by a one-thousand-dollar donation from the Massachusetts Federation of Women's Clubs out of concern for the problem of child labor in the South. By 1905 the state school superintendent was singing the praises of the model schools, telling southern educators that "they have been greatly appreciated by the communities in which they are located" and that they had inspired parents and teachers to consider such things as the need for rural high schools and their own responsibilities to the "rising generation." [10]

As club women were instituting their model school program, Progressive men began to organize a separate campaign for educational reform. Social and economic concerns had been building since the late 1880s among politicians, philanthropists, educators, and urban professionals. Many educational reformers believed that the poor state of Georgia schools had to be remedied if southerners were to compete economically with other regions and achieve

---

tion," in *Proceedings of the Twelfth CES, Atlanta, Georgia, April 14–16, 1909.* Nashville, TN: Executive Committee of the Conference, n.d.) 132–139.

10. Eugene C. Branson, "The Real Southern Question," *World's Work* 3 (March 1902): 1888–1891; quotes from W. B. Merritt, "Model Rural Schools," in *Proceedings of the Eighth CES, Columbia, S.C., April 26–28, 1905* (New York: Committee on Publication, 1905), 39–40; Marguerite B. Sheffer, *Memorabilia of the Athens Woman's Club* (Athens: Athens Woman's Club, 1982), 3–4; reports on model schools, *Georgia Federation of Women's Clubs* [hereafter GFWC] *Yearbook, 1906–1907* (Atlanta: GFWC, 1907), 15–18.

a standard of living approaching that of the rest of the nation. In 1896 the president of the (white) Georgia Teachers' Association asserted that his organization was founded upon the belief that "the development of the intellectual resources of a state is prerequisite to the development of its material resources." This sentiment was echoed repeatedly by the northern and southern white men who began holding the Conference for Education in the South in 1898 and who formed the associated group, the SEB, in 1902. The northern philanthropists who funded the SEB were especially concerned with using education to create an efficient workforce as a means to stabilize the southern economy. An expanded system of public education could give rural children the skills for more efficient agricultural production or, alternately, the commercial and technical expertise necessary to assume positions in the growing industrial economy.[11]

Northern and southern educational reformers also feared race and class violence as a threat to property and political stability, and they shared a desire to use public schools to produce workers with internalized middle-class values as well as marketable job skills. In relation to their own communities, northern reformers regarded education as the key to assimilating immigrants who lacked "Anglo-Teutonic conceptions of law, order, and government." A New York minister attending the 1901 Conference for Education in the South dramatically claimed, "We have to choose between the standing army and the school house." Southern educators harbored similar hopes for the assimilation of rural poor whites into industrial society, but they had special cause for concern—the rise of reactionary racism and its associated violence, which was just reaching its peak between the mid-1890s and the early 1900s. Reformers were not above using appeals to race pride when seeking public support for reforms, and public schools worked to foster racial solidarity when they

11. James D. Anderson, "Northern Foundations and the Shaping of Southern Black Rural Education, 1902–1935," *History of Education Quarterly* 18 (Winter 1978): 371–396; address of Lyman Abbott, in *Proceedings of the CES, the Sixth Session, Richmond Virginia, April 22nd to April 24th, and at the University of Virginia, April 25th, 1903* (New York: Committee on Publication, 1903), 221–230; E. S. Richardson, "Training Boys and Girls for More Efficient Rural Life in the South," in *SEA, Journal of Proceedings and Addresses of the Twenty-Second Annual Meeting Held at Houston, Texas, November 30, December 1, 2, 1911* (Nashville, TN: SEA, n.d.), 123–134; presidential address of Joseph S. Stewart, in *Proceedings and Addresses of the Thirtieth Annual Meeting of the Georgia Teachers' Association, 1896* (Atlanta: GTA, 1897), 44–52, quote 45.

served as forums for ritualistic celebrations of the Lost Cause. However, racial violence disrupted business, discouraged outside investment, and increased the out-migration of black labor, leading some educators to call for moral instruction that would teach children respect for legal authority and the rights of property.[12]

Schools could not serve as a source of economic reconstruction and social stability until universal education was implemented, but this crucial step was blocked by the individualist bent of the traditional southern concept of white manhood. This individualism had its origins in an agrarian concept of republicanism that defined centralized power as a threat to freedom (at least that of white men). Populists modified the definition, for they needed the centralized power of the state to intervene in the economy in their behalf, but rural "traditionalists" persisted in seeing the state itself as a source of unwanted and illegitimate interference. In essence, traditionalists were defending their antebellum inheritance, the collection of autonomous households that constituted a community of white men. A logical result was a localism in rural politics that bred suspicion of reform efforts that came from outside. Rural white men regarded legitimate government as residing in local leaders who acted according to the wishes of male heads of households. Progressive reforms imposed from without, such as compulsory education and child labor laws, represented an attack on the basis of white male individualism, because they pro-

---

12. First quote from Ellwood P. Cubberly, *Changing Conceptions of Education* (Boston, 1909), 15–16, as cited in Lawrence A. Cremin, *The Transformation of the School: Progressivism in American Education, 1876–1957* (New York: Alfred A. Knopf, 1961), 68–69; Lyman Abbott address, in *Proceedings of the Fourth CES, held at Winston-Salem, NC, April 18–20, 1901* (Harrisburg, PA: Committee on Publication, 1901), 111–122, second quote 112. For evidence of scientific racism among southern white educators, see addresses of T. J. Jones of Hampton Institute and J. H. Phillips, superintendent of schools, Birmingham, Alabama, in *SEA Journal of Proceedings and Addresses of the Nineteenth Annual Session Held at Atlanta, Georgia, December 29–31, 1908* (Chattanooga, TN: SEA, n.d.), 118–128; James A. B. Sherer, "The School as a Check upon Lawlessness," in *SEA Journal of Proceedings and Addresses of the Fifteenth Annual Meeting Held Jointly with the Florida State Teachers' Association at Jacksonville, Florida, December 29, 30, 31, 1904* (Chattanooga, TN: SEA, 1904), 102–111. Joel Williamson calls the extreme version of scientific racism "racial radicalism," in *A Rage for Order: Black-White Relations in the American South since Emancipation* (New York: Oxford University Press, 1986), 71–83; Charles Reagan Wilson, *Baptized in Blood: The Religion of the Lost Cause, 1865–1920* (Athens: University of Georgia Press, 1980), 139–143.

posed the usurpation of the father's authority over the labor of his children at the same time that economic instability threatened white male property ownership.[13]

The problems of localism soon caused male reformers to realize that organized women could be a unique and valuable ally in the movement to improve public schools. Their maternal role gave women the moral authority to act on children's needs, and their ability to operate through informal channels of influence helped them to avoid the hazards of partisan politics and political opportunism that afflicted men. Men also recognized the value of the Georgia Federation as a network through which women across the state could be mobilized for work in their communities. Moreover, since women's clubs had been involved in both urban and rural school reform since the 1880s, members already were educated on problems and solutions. Thus, it was understandable when future governor Hoke Smith issued a call in 1902 for the "organization of the women of Georgia to help" in the movement for local taxation. Smith argued that "from no part of our people can such inspiration and service and moving power come as from you women of Georgia." The following year, a group of educational and political leaders met in Atlanta to form the Georgia Educational Campaign Committee, a state branch of the SEB. This group made a similar request for women's support. "Realizing the strong devotion of the women of the state to the welfare of the children," the men wrote in a press release, "we appeal to them to organize school improvement societies in every county and locality."[14]

Georgia club women responded to men's requests for their assistance by expanding the Federation's work already in progress, with added emphasis on getting public sentiment squarely behind legislative reforms. The men who

13. Bardaglio, *Reconstructing the Household*, 5–27. William A. Link has provided the most clear and concise discussion of the origins and nature of traditionalism in *The Paradox of Southern Progressivism, 1880–1930* (Chapel Hill: University of North Carolina Press, 1992), xi–xii. For an extended discussion of the antebellum southern social structure as a "network of households," see Elizabeth Fox-Genovese, *Within the Plantation Household: Black and White Women of the Old South* (Chapel Hill: University of North Carolina Press, 1988), 57–99.

14. Hoke Smith, "Popular Education as the Primary Policy of the South," in *Proceedings of the Fifth CES, held at Athens, Georgia, April 24, 25, and 26, 1902* (Knoxville, TN: Southern Education Board, 1902), 43–51, quote 51; remaining quotes as cited in Georgia Department of Education (hereafter GDE), *Thirty-Second Annual Report, 1903* (Atlanta: GDE, 1904), 33.

formed the Georgia Educational Campaign Committee were motivated in large part by the need to secure approval of a constitutional amendment, the McMichael Bill, which was to be submitted to a referendum vote in the fall of 1904. The bill proposed to make local taxation easier by eliminating the requirement of grand jury consent and by permitting approval by two-thirds of all who voted rather than by two-thirds of all eligible to vote. Male reformers needed women's help to build favorable public sentiment to gain the bill's passage and, since the measure was voluntary, to ensure that counties would enact local taxation once restrictions were loosened. Club women immediately responded by assisting in the planning and executing of dozens of rallies in Georgia counties designed to persuade rural property owners and parents that educational needs warranted self-imposed taxes. They usually timed the rallies to coincide with court sessions to guarantee a substantial audience. Male speakers provided figures in each county on local illiteracy rates (which were high) and the estimated additional cost per taxpayer should a school tax be imposed (calculated to be very low). As explained by a Virginia club woman who planned similar events in her state, women's role in this campaign was "to applaud the speakers, and, when the meeting is over, to gather up the fragments that remain in the way of public sentiment, and to focus them into educational associations and like forms of activity to work for the local schools."[15]

The whirlwind campaign of 1903–1904 was largely responsible for the ratification of the McMichael Bill and subsequent enabling legislation, but the victory created new problems that made reformers' second task—persuading rural Georgians to levy school taxes—more difficult. The legislation eliminated the requirement of grand jury approval, allowing counties to submit school tax proposals directly to the voters for approval, but it also contained critical loopholes. It allowed county boards of education wide discretion in establishing school districts, while also allowing local taxation on less than a countywide basis. One consequence was that county board members gerrymandered districts so that the counties' most valuable property, such as that

---

15. Walter B. Hill, "Local Taxation in Georgia," in *Proceedings of the CES, the Seventh Session, Birmingham, Alabama, April 26th to April 28th, 1904* (New York: Committee on Publication, 1904), 118–121; Sallie B. Hill, "Report of the Georgia School Improvement Club," in *Proceedings of CES, 1907,* 142–146; Beverly B. Munford, "Report upon Woman's Educational Work," 39–41.

containing railroad crossings, mills, or factories, was enclosed within their own districts' boundaries. According to laws that predated the McMichael Bill, municipalities and wealthy communities could and did create independent school districts encompassing the most valuable property, enacting local taxation to benefit only their own schools while still receiving state funds. Around 1900 thirty-five towns controlled one-third of the state's school funds and owned school property worth twice as much as the value of all rural schools and twenty times as much as the value of publicly owned rural schools. Because of lower property values, outlying rural districts could have approved the highest tax rate allowed by law and still not had enough funds to keep schools open more than a few months. This regressive system only strengthened rural-urban differences, making local taxation a hard sell for reformers.[16]

In the midst of the campaign for the constitutional amendment, Georgia women formed a new organization that would prove useful in overcoming rural opposition to local taxation. In July of 1904 a group of GFWC members and women educators met in Athens during the University of Georgia summer session to consider men's suggestion that they organize local clubs for school improvement. The women formally created the Georgia School Improvement Club (GSIC) the following month and announced their intention to establish clubs in every county to promote the improvement of schools' buildings and libraries. Sallie Barker Hill, the group's first president, emerged as one of the most important figures in the campaign to improve rural schools. Her husband, Walter B. Hill, chancellor of the University of Georgia and state representative of the SEB, died in 1905 in the midst of the campaign for local taxation. Although still in mourning, Hill agreed to assume her husband's duties as member of the Educational Campaign Committee, and she managed her multiple responsibilities by making the GSIC a branch of that committee. This move did not allow men to assume control of women's reform efforts, but rather enabled a closer collaboration between the

16. M. L. Brittain (Georgia state school superintendent), "My Brother's Keeper," in *Proceedings of the Fourteenth CES, Jacksonville, Florida, April 19th, 20th, and 21st, 1911* (Knoxville, TN: Executive Committee of the Conference, n.d.), 141–148; Harlan, *Separate and Unequal,* 211; Orr, *History of Education in Georgia,* 259–262; Bonner et al., *History of Public Education in Georgia,* 153–154.

two campaigns. Several Georgia Federation leaders also became members of the committee so that its membership no longer was exclusively male, and in January of 1908 the GFWC formed a subcommittee for school improvement work.[17]

The local, state, and regional networks of women's clubs quickly proved useful in getting the nascent school improvement movement off the ground. The extensive support of women in Federated urban clubs was critical to success in the early months of organization. In the first year of its existence, the Bibb County Improvement Club of Macon was able to enlist the help of nine women's clubs, including two history clubs, two chapters of the United Daughters of the Confederacy, the Vineville King's Daughters, and the Young Ladies' Hospital Auxiliary. They divided up responsibility for starting improvement clubs in local schools; and in areas where there were no women's clubs, they approached individual women for assistance. State leaders reached outward as well as inward, drawing upon the expertise and experience of women in other southern states who were attempting similar reforms. Hill corresponded regularly with female reformers from across the South and, along with GFWC representatives, attended the annual "women's meeting" at the Conference for Education in the South. The GSIC also joined the Women's Interstate Association for the Betterment of Schools in the South, which in 1907 could claim members in Kentucky, Alabama, Texas, and the Carolinas, in addition to Georgia.[18]

17. The Hills' extraordinary commitment to the cause of public education was reflected in the careers of their children: Parna was one of the first two women extension workers hired by the Georgia State College of Agriculture, Mary was a rural school teacher, and Walter junior served as state supervisor for Negro schools and was a strong advocate of black education; Sallie B. Hill, "School Improvement," press release for the Georgia School Improvement Club, ca. October 1904, Walter B. Hill Papers, Sallie Barker Hill Division (hereafter SBH), Hargrett Rare Book and Manuscript Collection, box 17, folder 3, Special Collections, University of Georgia Libraries, Athens; Harlan, *Separate and Unequal,* 217–221.

18. "The Report of the Work of the Women's Clubs of Macon, in Behalf of the Schools," in GDE, *Thirty-Third Annual Report, 1904* (Atlanta: GDE, 1905), 135–138; Sallie B. Hill, "Report of This Year's Progress of School Improvement Associations and Leagues in the Southern States," ca. 1907, SBH, box 22, folder 12; report of J. Lindsay Patterson, president of the Interstate Association for the Betterment of Public Schools, in *Proceedings of the Tenth CES, with an Appendix in Review of Five Years, Pinhurst, N.C., April 9, 1907* (Richmond, VA: Executive Committee of the Conference, n.d.), 108–115.

Under Hill's leadership, the GSIC began attempting to enlist the support of county school superintendents as a way to expand organization at the local level. Rural communities did not have the multiple social and civic clubs of Macon and other Georgia towns, and as reformers cast further afield they found fewer organized women upon whom to draw for assistance. Hill recognized the problems inherent in using urban strangers as advocates of rural reform and believed it absolutely essential that leadership in school improvement come from within the communities themselves. She argued that if reforms were to effect permanent change, they "must represent an evolution and growth from within individual communities, not a revolution working from without." The problem was to identify likely allies and encourage their activism at the grassroots level. In rural areas lacking social organizations, school administrators had to be relied upon to know which women had leadership qualities and a history of concern for community improvement. According to Hill's reasoning, county superintendents "come closest to the daily lives of our people living in the small towns and in the country" and thus were "more keenly in sympathy, perhaps, with their ambitions, purposes, wishes, and failings than others can be." Acting on this assumption, the GSIC circulated a bulletin announcing its purpose and aims and sent letters to superintendents "asking them to appoint three or more competent women who would be willing to undertake the work of county and district organization and promote the founding of local School Clubs." The campaign was slow to take off, but after two years Hill could boast the formation of seventy-six county committees and ninety-seven local clubs.[19]

One reason the GSIC organizing efforts proceeded slowly was that organization at the county level proved difficult. Hill had hoped that she could organize from the top down, starting with a countywide club comprised of the three women from different school districts who would then form local clubs in the surrounding communities. The success of this plan relied upon the full cooperation of county officials, who, after assisting in the selection of these women, needed to give them wholehearted support. As officials who traveled throughout the county inspecting schools, superintendents were in

19. Sallie B. Hill, "Report of State School Improvement Work," in GDE, *Thirty-Fifth Annual Report, 1906* (Atlanta: GDE, 1907), 273–275; quotes from Hill, "Report of the Georgia School Improvement Club," 143–144.

a good position to foster a favorable opinion among principals and teachers regarding women's reform work. They also had considerable political clout that could be exerted on civic and business leaders to support school improvement. However, while in some counties the superintendents proved to be the "best, most loyal, and appreciative" friends of club women, in others they showed a decided lack of enthusiasm. Hill complained that "without full cooperation and efficient work on the part of county officials and educational leaders in the counties, we cannot hope for substantial and lasting associations."[20]

Sallie Hill did not explain why some county officials were reluctant to help, but opposition could have come from multiple sources. Some men considered women's community activism a challenge to their own power and authority. Club women and their professional allies supported more stringent qualifications for administrative positions that emphasized formal training rather than political connections, and they opposed the manipulation of public assets through tactics such as gerrymandering that gained political leaders urban support at the expense of rural children. There were other political stakes involved as well. In 1909 the method of choosing county superintendents shifted from appointment by grand jury to election by popular vote. Once their positions became elective, men seeking office had to cater to the interests of the voters. In actuality they had to cater to the interests of wealthy landowners and their political powerbrokers, since most blacks had been unable to vote since the 1890s and many poor whites were disfranchised in 1908 by literacy and poll tax requirements. Although the beautification of schools and the creation of libraries did not appear on the surface to be political issues, women were open about their intention to use school improvement clubs to push forward the causes of local taxation and compulsory attendance. Since these reforms proposed a redistribution of wealth and a transfer of parental authority to the state, women's activism threatened property-owning men on both class and gender grounds.[21]

20. Quotes from Hill, "Report of the Georgia School Improvement Club," 143–144; Sallie B. Hill, "Report of the School Improvement Association," in GDE, *Thirty-Seventh Annual Report, 1908* (Atlanta: GDE, 1909), 402–415.

21. V. O. Key, *Southern Politics in State and Nation* (New York: Vintage Books, 1949), 119–123. Twenty thousand fewer white voters turned out for the 1910 gubernatorial primary than for the same two candidates in 1908, the last primary before the disfranchisement amendment took effect. Bartley, *Modern Georgia*, 153.

Opposition to local taxation also came from a desire to maintain the racial status quo. Distribution of state funds was on a per capita basis, with those counties containing the most school-age children receiving the most funds. Black Belt counties received a large proportion of their funds based on the African American population concentrated in that region of the state. School officials did not distribute the money fairly, however, but used the African American share to benefit whites. The superintendent from Jones County, in the heart of the Black Belt, wrote in his annual report of 1905 that "the district method of local taxation would not suit us, inasmuch as our rural white population in some districts is very sparse, while the Negro population is very dense." He explained that voters would support taxation at the county level, but only if local officials continued to control the funds and to ensure that "those who bear the greater burden of taxation" (i.e., property-owning whites) received the greater benefit. Officials and property owners outside the Black Belt shared a reluctance to spend any local money on black schools and feared that the movement for local taxation would be followed by a drive to cut or even eliminate the state's contribution.[22]

The school improvement movement provoked further opposition because of its advocacy of compulsory attendance laws and, by implication, child labor reform. Men and women pushing for regulation of child labor considered compulsory attendance an important way to control the employment of children in the fields. In Georgia the child labor legislation that ostensibly set minimum ages, maximum hours, and basic literacy requirements for juvenile workers did not apply to agricultural labor. This made a compulsory attendance law all the more important in rural areas, where it could be used to transfer children from the fields to the schoolhouse for at least three or four months of the year. Rural men were well aware of the relationship between the two issues and so had reason to distrust women's activism in local schools. Small-scale farmers struggling to hold onto their land in a time of low cotton prices and usurious borrowing rates resented attempts to check their control

22. According to calculations based on five black and five white counties, in 1908 black counties used state funds to spend $0.99 on each black child, while reserving $6.80 for each white student, and white counties spent $1.81 per black and $2.02 per white child. Harlan, *Separate and Unequal*, 235–237; E. W. Sammons, report for Jones County, in GDE, *Annual Report, 1905*, 78; *A Blow Aimed at the Common Schools of Georgia: Ratification of Two Proposed Constitutional Amendments a Scheme to Withdraw State's Aid to Public Education*, SBH, box 17, folder 2, pamphlet.

of children. A spokesman for Georgians who opposed mandatory schooling characterized it as a violation of a man's "claim upon his children," a measure "out of harmony with the true spirit and genius of our constitution." At the other end of the class spectrum, white landlords often required that share-croppers and tenant farmers work their entire families, and they regarded compulsory attendance as a threat to this important source of cheap labor.[23]

When county officials were less than forthcoming with their assistance, GSIC and GFWC members were forced to fall back upon the assistance of women's clubs. They did not abandon their efforts to gain the support of educational administrators, but supplemented that work with a campaign to build public pressure for reform from inside each county. Hill solicited lists of teachers from county commissioners so that she could send them GSIC literature. Local women's clubs wooed teachers, providing food and entertainment at their meetings and financial and moral support throughout the year. In what became known as the Tifton Plan, a Tifton library club made members responsible for one county school each, where they worked toward improvements such as individual drinking cups and medical inspections while enlisting the support of the teachers and parents in larger reforms. Tifton club women also got the local Chamber of Commerce, the United Daughters of the Confederacy chapter, and other business and social organizations to collaborate on public events to bring together teachers and the wider community. Club women in other towns duplicated this strategy, and the GSIC and the Educational Campaign Committee began a new public relations crusade. The groups distributed literature and swept the state with a series of speaking tours intended to create a more favorable climate for reform among "those backward counties, remote from cities and hardly yet touched by railroads."[24]

While club women continued to struggle with uncooperative male administrators, they found natural allies among the young women who worked

23. Elizabeth H. Davidson, *Child Labor Legislation in the Southern Textile States* (Chapel Hill: University of North Carolina Press, 1939), 201–202; J. N. Wall, "Has the Time Come for a Compulsory Attendance Law in Georgia?" in GDE, *Twenty-Ninth Annual Report, 1900* (Atlanta: GDE, 1901), 136–141, quotes 138.

24. Quote from Sallie B. Hill, "Report of the School Improvement Association," in GDE, *Thirty-Seventh Annual Report, 1908* (Atlanta: GDE, 1909), 407; W. T. Halliday to Sallie B. Hill, November 19, 1910; Edna M. Peterson to Sallie B. Hill, n.d., both in SBH, box 53, folder 5.

as rural schoolteachers. Until women's clubs stepped up their efforts to persuade parents and community leaders that educational improvements were necessary, rural teachers had few advocates to turn to. Most schoolhouses were one- or two-room cabins without water or electric lights, much less luxuries such as blackboards and maps. Conditions were not much better outside of work. Communities often lacked housing for teachers, so they had to board with various students' families in turn, commonly sharing a room or even a bed with one or more family members. Such living arrangements cast teachers less as professionals than as dependents, a position reinforced by low wages and strict rules governing their behavior. In south central Georgia, Bleckley County required its teachers "to be dressed properly at all times and to conduct themselves as ladies" and forbade dating except for approved outings on weekends. Given the numerous drawbacks to country life, it is not surprising that rural teachers tended to be teenage women fresh from high school who stayed only long enough to get additional training and find a better position.[25]

School improvement clubs and the associated committees of women's groups energetically tackled the problems of rural teachers and succeeded in bringing about local improvements as well as statewide reforms. At the local level, women raised funds to furnish schools with desks, teaching aids, and textbooks, and they solicited donations of books and money for school libraries. In Dublin club women raised the money to build a dormitory in the surrounding countryside for teachers who had no place to live. Organized women supported the campaign of female educators for the "teacher's cottage," urging rural communities to provide houses for their teachers for a nominal charge. The GFWC also lobbied for better pay for teachers and for a sounder method of funding their salaries. Since Reconstruction the state had not paid teachers their full salary until tax collection was completed in

25. Quote from Annette S. Winn, "Great Challenges of the Era," 311–316; and also see Corrie E. Smith, "Some of My Days," 521–527, both in *Reflections of Georgia Retired Teachers*, ed. Ruth Wynn Aultman (Macon: Georgia Retired Teachers Association, 1976); a study of public school teachers conducted around 1910 found that female rural school teachers (who comprised 68 percent of all female teachers) were the youngest and had the least experience of all teachers, male and female, and that they worked an average of two years in the country before finding employment elsewhere. Lotus Delta Coffman, *The Social Composition of the Teaching Population* (New York: Teachers College, Columbia University, 1911).

the fall, forcing teachers who worked in the spring and summer to borrow against their salaries. Interest payments reduced their already low pay by as much as 20 percent. Around 1905 the Bainbridge Woman's Club formulated a temporary plan by which counties would borrow the money for teachers' salaries. Club women's lobbying campaign for enabling legislation was successful, and by 1914 more than 80 percent of counties had adopted the plan. The GFWC then supported the movement for tax equalization, which presumably would have enabled the state to pay funds on time so that poorer counties would not have to spend scarce resources on borrowing rates. The state legislature finally passed an equalization bill in 1926, but it did not establish a source of funding until 1927.[26]

Since organized women believed that putting "better prepared teachers" in rural schools was the key to improving academic standards, they helped finance further training for teachers who could not afford it. Around the turn of the century, the average salary for a four-to-five-month school year was $150, and many rural teachers made even less. Although the state imposed mandatory attendance for annual county teachers' institutes in the 1890s, the expense involved was such a hardship for rural teachers that county superintendents refused to enforce the rule. Federated clubs solved this problem by assuming the costs of sending teachers to institutes and summer normal sessions. In addition, the clubs provided extensive financial assistance in the form of scholarships and loans to young women who wished to become teachers. Women in higher education contributed their skills to the cause as well. Club woman and State Normal School professor Celeste Parrish ac-

26. Emma Perry to Sallie B. Hill, December 7, 1909, SBH, box 22, folder 12; Lizzie Shed, "The Teacher's Cottage," *School and Home* 8 (June 1916): 10–11. For extensive evidence of women's support of teachers and schools, see annual district reports in the GFWC yearbooks. Using an example of a teacher from Columbus, Georgia, Patricia Smith Butcher argues that teachers were "natural allies" of the women's rights movement more generally because of the backlash against women's gains in academia and the professional workplace that took place in the 1890s and early 1900s, which included an attack on women as teachers. *Education for Equality: Women's Rights Periodicals and Women's Higher Education, 1849–1920* (Westport, CT: Greenwood Press, 1989), 62–66; M. L. Brittain, "Letter of Transmittal and Recommendations," in GDE, *Forty-First Annual Report, 1912* (Atlanta: GDE, 1913), 32; M. L. Brittain, "Recommendations," in GDE, *Forty-Third Annual Report, 1914* (Atlanta: GDE, 1915), 7–8; report on educational legislation, *GFWC Yearbook, 1910–1911* (Atlanta: GFWC, 1911), 41; report of the Committee on Legislation for 1913–1914, in *Proceedings and Addresses of the Forty-Eighth Annual Meeting, GEA, 1914* (LaGrange, GA: GEA, n.d.), 6; Orr, *History of Education in Georgia*, 278–279.

cepted a position as rural school supervisor for North Georgia in 1912 and literally worked herself to death trying to remedy the problem of, in her words, "untrained and very imperfectly educated" teachers. She visited hundreds of schools annually and held multiple teachers' institutes in every county in her territory, usually assisted by the unpaid labor of other highly trained female educators.[27]

Once they formed an alliance with schoolteachers, club women worked to create a bond of sympathy and common interest between educators and parents as a way to build public support for reforms. The GFWC proclaimed that mothers and teachers were concerned with the same process, the "education of the child," and Georgia's club women wanted to facilitate their effective communication and cooperation. The GSIC proposed that organization at the local level "should seek to make the pupils, parents, teachers, and friends partners in the work of bringing the school to the highest possible standard." School improvement clubs usually were headed by teachers, and the membership included club women and mothers; sometimes there were junior divisions for students. The clubs used "public meetings, lectures, entertainments, educational rallies," and any other possible occasion as means for getting the local population into the schoolhouse. When local adults were slow to participate, teachers organized the students into clubs and had them stage events for their parents. The Georgia Congress of Mothers and Parent-Teacher Associations did not enter this work until 1915. Celeste Parrish founded the Georgia chapter of the national organization in 1905, but for the first decade of existence, the group focused on urban schools. In 1915, at Parrish's request, state members obtained funding from the National Congress to allow domestic science teacher Elizabeth Holt to accompany Parrish on her visits to rural schools. During her summer of work, Holt established eighteen Parent-Teacher Associations and gave teachers information on how to organize additional cooperative groups.[28]

27. Celeste Parrish, report for 1917–18, in GDE, *Forty-Sixth Annual Report, 1917* (Atlanta: GDE, 1918), 24, 27 (Parrish died not long after filing this report); Orr, *History of Education in Georgia*, 252–253; Frances Liggett Wey, "Report of Student Aid Committee," *GFWC Yearbook, 1920–1921* (Atlanta: GFWC, 1921), 90–93.

28. First quote from Mrs. B. D. Gray, "School and Home Endorsed by the Federation of Women's Clubs," *School and Home* 9 (February 1917): 14–15; remaining quotes from Sallie B. Hill, Georgia School Improvement Club (hereafter GSIC), report for 1907–1908, SBH, box 22, folder 3; Mrs. John W. Rowlett, *History of the Georgia Congress of Mothers and Parent-Teacher As-*

As Sallie Hill noted, local work was a "slower method" of organization than the county-level plan. Rural club women and teachers were isolated from one another and had difficulty establishing broad programs of action. One effort at organization failed when the three women chosen to head the School Improvement Club found it impossible to meet with one another on a regular basis. They had to take individual action, visiting schools and teachers' institutes in their respective communities in an effort to recruit support among teachers. Teachers faced similar obstacles and often found themselves in the position of simply having to do what they could on their own. One teacher who accepted an appointment in a small town and found the schoolhouse woefully inadequate did not hesitate to make her opinion widely known. She went about the community saying "what she thought of a town which could support a bank and yet would allow its children to be housed in such a ramshackle structure," and through dogged persistence she was able to persuade residents to issue bonds for a new schoolhouse. Women activists usually relied on more subtle tactics, taking pains to give the impression that the idea for improvement came from the school neighborhood and reflected favorably upon parents and community leaders. For even if local work was frustratingly slow at times, if managed carefully it could avoid the impression that impetus for change was coming largely from outside the community.[29]

Southern men involved in educational reform agreed that local activism was vital to the success of the school improvement campaign. While historians have acknowledged the tendency of southern Progressives to look to the national arena for reforms when regional resistance proved formidable, they have given less attention to the simultaneous trend toward grassroots organizing. This trend gained momentum in the spring of 1904, when southern business interests seriously damaged the credibility of the SEB by accusing it of being northern-dominated, although many female reformers already were convinced that change must begin at the local level if it was to be successful. Samuel Chiles Mitchell, a professor at the University of Richmond and

sociations (1925); reports of Celeste Parrish and Elizabeth Holt, in GDE, *Forty-Fourth Annual Report, 1915* (Atlanta: GDE, 1916), 26–30.

29. Sallie B. Hill, "Report of School Improvement Association," March 27, 1909, Scrapbook, SBH, box 54, folder 2; Sallie B. Hill, GSIC report for 1907–1908, SBH, box 22, folder 3; quote from Sallie B. Hill, "Report of State School Improvement Work," in GDE, *Annual Report, 1906*, 274.

a regional leader in educational reform, confirmed the wisdom of the local approach when he argued that the strategy of the SEB and other regional groups to consider the "state as a unit" was inadequate to solve southern problems. The most profitable approach, he said, was to "consider singly the needs of the neighborhoods in these vast rural commonwealths" and to encourage the organization of local leaders who were in the best position to know and understand the needs of their communities. Like many other male reformers, Mitchell recognized the value of women's assistance in local organizing. He described school improvement clubs as "recruiting stations" that used schools to "energize democracy in the South" through the grassroots participation of citizens.[30]

Male reformers readily recognized that one of women's advantages in grassroots organizing was their ability to distance themselves from male power struggles. After the movement for local taxation met extensive rural opposition, men on the Educational Campaign Committee encouraged female members to conduct their activities independently of male leaders. One problem that arose was the controversy surrounding the Georgia College of Agriculture and its president, Andrew Soule. In the eyes of many country people, the College of Agriculture stood for the elitism in higher education that characterized the University of Georgia more generally, and Soule's autocratic demeanor did little to diminish this impression. Soule wanted to help in the campaign to improve rural living conditions, but his presence represented a dilemma for school improvement workers who did not wish to alienate country communities. State School Superintendent Jere Pound warned Sallie Hill that while she needed to "work in harmony with Dr. Soule," she should "avoid such entanglements as appearing to oppose those who are against him." Pound urged Hill to organize farm women in the communities

---

30. Samuel Chiles Mitchell, "The Task of the Neighborhood," in *Proceedings of CES, 1907,* 8–11. As William Link has noted in his account of the shift toward grassroots organizing in Virginia, in the spring of 1904 the publisher of the *Manufacturer's Record* accused the SEB of being part of a northern conspiracy to restrict child labor and interfere with race relations. *A Hard Country and a Lonely Place: Schooling, Society, and Reform in Rural Virginia, 1870–1920* (Chapel Hill: University of North Carolina Press, 1986), 111–115. Robert L. Church and Michael W. Sedlak argue that education became more local as a concern and as a reform project in the period between the two world wars, but they stress the conservative rather than Progressive factors that influenced the shift nationally at that particular time. *Education in the United States: An Interpretive History* (New York: Free Press, 1976), 344–360.

surrounding the District Agricultural Schools (agricultural and mechanical high schools built by the state around 1908 to address the lack of rural secondary education) and to work closely with the Farmers' Union. He was adamant that Hill should make it clear that her work was "independent of [Soule's] and different in character" and that she should show that she was "perfectly willing to work in harmony with all persons who have the uplift of country conditions as their purpose." [31]

While Pound's advice was useful, it is doubtful that female reformers needed encouragement either to distance themselves from the elitism of the University of Georgia or to practice diplomacy. They had their own grievances with the university, and the democratic ideals that underlay their struggle for equal educational opportunity contributed to their concern for the poor quality of schools available to rural children. Perhaps more importantly, the suppression of their formal economic and political power made them accustomed to using persuasion as a means of effecting change in home and community. Although the political activism of the GFWC represented an effort to bridge male and female spheres of influence, male reformers had an authority grounded in formal institutions that most club women lacked. This meant not only that women could operate outside the channels of partisan politics, avoiding the appearance of an overt challenge to rural male authority, but also that they had certain interpersonal skills that made them particularly well suited for grassroots organizing. Female reformers who claimed that their domestic role had given them commitment to service, modest expectations, and the tenacity to withstand setbacks were not so much using domesticity to justify activism as they were explaining how it facilitated activism. They were encouraging other women to see the value of these skills in political rather than purely personal terms. [32]

Women's particular approach to reform was shaped by their belief that their private domestic role was only the personal aspect of a larger social duty to protect children from neglect and exploitation. If they were to carry out this more comprehensive duty through reform, they had to persuade fathers to take a corresponding view of male parental duties; they had to convince

31. Jere Pound to Sallie Hill, April 27, 1909; May 5, 1909, SBH, box 22, folder 9; also see M. L. Brittain to Sallie Hill, September 24, 1910, SBH, box 23, folder 5.

32. Munford, "Report upon Women's Educational Work"; Brown, "How the Federation of Woman's Clubs May Cooperate."

men that fatherhood could not be defined only in terms of patriarchal authority and control, but that it entailed recognition of social obligations to community and state as well. Such a notion of fatherhood rejected the old basis of southern white male political identity and reconstructed men's citizenship based on a new relationship with the state. Middle-class men who promoted educational reform often acknowledged this shift in the conception of male citizenship when they argued that the state's need for educated citizens and workers superseded men's parental authority when rural fathers neglected their duty to educate their children. As men, however, they could approach farmers on common ground as voters or businessmen, so that the male struggles over compulsory attendance and local taxation were played out in the public arena as economic and political conflicts between town and country. For club women coming from a subordinate position, the struggles were much more personal and contained a dimension of gender reform specific to their own agenda as women.

Club women alluded to the gender reform inherent in school improvement work when they identified male individualism as a major obstacle to legislative reforms. In 1909, when state Federation leader Emily Hendree Park addressed rural club women on the topic "The Needs of Country Schools," she described a pending bill on compulsory attendance as a "compel-parents-to-do-their-duty law." She praised the farm woman as "an alert, patriotic citizen vitally interested in the welfare of the state," however, and targeted fathers as the responsible parties when children were kept from school. It was farm men who could not see that "it is a civic sin to allow our children to grow up in ignorance" and thus opposed compulsory attendance laws. Park noted that taxation measures often were rejected by county officials who claimed that "the farmers will howl if you talk about raising taxes." She questioned how this could be true, how rural men could fail to support local taxation when it only meant "giving advantages to their own children." With acerbic wit that revealed more than a little frustration and some cultural bias as well, Emily Park described the rural white man as an "obstinate, opinionated, self-willed angular sort of an individual." Claiming that a "bucking bronco is nothing to a Georgia cracker if you try to force him to go your way," Park argued that "lead him you may—after a time—so long, so long, but drive him, never." [33]

33. Park, "The Needs of Country Schools," quotes 249–252.

Sallie Hill also identified rural male individualism as an obstacle to school improvement, but her extensive work at the grassroots level encouraged a more sympathetic understanding of rural men's plight. In a report of her work for 1909, Hill suggested that the "dearth of local interest" that stymied local organizing efforts was attributable to the fact that the "average man in the country has an intense, hard-to-be-touched individualism." Describing the southern rural white male as "genial, kinly, the soul of hospitality," she observed that he had enjoyed an independent life for almost a century and so was "slow to change, wary of new ideas, and not easily converted to any scheme out of his usual order of living." Hill was optimistic that "tactful and intelligent women, when they go about it in the right spirit," could persuade rural men to see the growing importance of education in the New South and the need for cooperation in preparing their communities to meet the challenges of the future. School improvement work must go beyond improving buildings, equipment, and grounds, she argued, to "reach the hearts of the people who should be most vitally interested in the welfare of their own children," bringing to them "new thoughts, better living, and a broader comprehension of the privileges and obligations of citizenship."[34]

The "right spirit" to which Hill referred was an approach to reform in which female activists met rural opponents with respect and willingness to compromise. The early efforts of the GFWC to establish the model school program illustrated this approach very well. Some parents initially opposed the schools' curriculum, which combined manual arts with traditional academic training, because they feared club women were trying to impose an inferior education on their children. Carrie Hyde, teacher at the Danielsville school, complained in 1903 that "in the country districts we hear such expressions as these: 'I don't take much stock in the *model* work'; or, 'the *work*'; by *model* meaning *manual*." GFWC representatives met this challenge by modifying their plans in accordance with local wishes without abandoning their original aims altogether. They knew that the key to acquiring local support was diplomacy and compromise, and thus they discontinued the industrial department of the Madison County model school until the teachers and parents could be convinced of its value. Similarly, club women reported that

34. Hill, "Report of This Year's Progress of School Improvement Associations and Leagues in the Southern States," SBH, box 22, folder 12.

at the Bartow County school the "one aim of the teachers has been to corre-
late the two branches, literary and industrial, very closely, thus gaining the
approval of patrons who at first failed to look with favor upon the industrial
work."[35]

The cooperative approach and underlying ideals of women's reform efforts eventually won the support of many rural parents and communities.
Rural Georgians were not necessarily opposed to industrial education and the
Progressive ideal that education should "fit the individual to environment."
The Southern Farmers' Alliance and the Farmers' Union were staunch supporters of agricultural and industrial education, and populists had long argued that a purely classical education was elitist. What agrarian groups opposed was a strictly vocational approach that might hinder upward mobility
and the development of rural leadership; they advocated instead a combination of classical and industrial studies that would provide an "ample, inclusive, generous education." Most female leaders were committed to just such
a plan. While many club women were subject to the same class biases present
in the national movement for industrial education, GFWC and GSIC leaders
were influenced by Progressive pedagogy and their own experiences as women
to see education as an interactive process that enabled self-determination.
Convinced of their sincerity, the state and national presidents of the Farmers'
Union sent letters to the GFWC in 1910 "heartily commending the efforts of
the Federation" and pledging their support. Local chapters of the organization began drawing upon the expertise of Sallie Hill and the GSIC in establishing curricula and training teachers in new public schools.[36]

35. Carrie Hyde, "Model Rural Schools," in *Proceedings of the Thirty-Seventh Annual Meeting of the GEA, 1903* (Atlanta: GEA, 1904), 93–100, quote 93, emphasis in original; reports on
model schools, *GFWC Yearbook, 1906–1907*, quote 15–16.

36. Munford, "The Southern Woman's Work for Education," 137; first quote from Emily
Hendree Park, "The Educational Work of the Georgia Federation," *Southern Woman*, March 25,
1901; for a similar view, see Julia A. Flisch, "The Purpose and Results of Education," *Southern
Woman*, March 25, 1901; Charles Simon Barrett, *The Mission, History, and Times of the Farmers'
Union* (Nashville: Marshall and Bruce, 1909), 26–27, 88–89; second quote 26; Lucy Lester Willet, "President's Report," *GFWC Yearbook, 1910–1911*, 9–15; third quote 14; Kate B. Snipes to Sallie B. Hill, January 22, 1910, SBH, box 23, folder 1. On the class biases of white southern women
in regard to industrial education, see Joan Johnson, "'This Wonderful Dream Nation!': Black
and White South Carolina Women and the Creation of the New South, 1898–1930" (Ph.D. diss.,
University of California–Los Angeles, 1997), 363–366. On national trends in industrial educa-

Organized women's strategy of using education to reconstruct southern community was well conceived when it came to issues of gender and class, but its clarity faltered when it came to addressing how African Americans would fit into this new community. Clearly, female reformers were dedicated to gender reform. They wanted to make men more like women, exhibiting a greater commitment to service and self-sacrifice, and they wanted to make women more like men in the sense of enabling them to pursue their interests and talents in higher education and the workplace. Their belief that Progressive pedagogy could empower rural children, fitting them for rural life while also developing their potential to do otherwise if they wished, represented a commitment to egalitarian reform that could cut across class lines and at least partially bridge the gap between town and country. When it came to crossing the color line, however, both the obstacles and the stakes were much higher. Whether because of their own racial conservatism or the volatile state of race relations at the turn of the century, club women generally endorsed an approach to black education that could be characterized as noblesse oblige. They were willing to address whites' moral duty to provide schooling for black children, but they did not openly challenge the discrimination in educational funding that grew even worse during the campaigns to improve public education, crippling black efforts to achieve economic independence.

Organized women's silence on the issue of racial discrimination in public education is not surprising considering that race relations reached a nadir during the early campaigns for school improvement. Even though the poll tax and the white primary had virtually eliminated the black vote, the collapse of the People's Party in 1896 led to a renewed attack on black political influence. Populist leader Tom Watson remained obsessed with the idea that antireform Democrats were using white fears of black dominance to stay in power. This concern led him to support the 1906 gubernatorial candidacy of Progressive Hoke Smith, who waged a campaign based on "purification of the suffrage" through complete black disfranchisement. The contest between Smith and rival Clark Howell, editor of the *Atlanta Constitution,* was marked by incredibly racist rhetoric. Atlanta newspapers' sensational and irresponsible treatment of alleged attacks on white women by black men only exacerbated racial

tion, see Cremin, *The Transformation of the School,* 26–33; and Rush Welter, *Popular Education and Democratic Thought in America* (New York: Columbia University Press, 1962), 277–282.

tensions, resulting in the Atlanta riot of September 22, 1906, in which whites attacked and killed scores of blacks. The African American middle-class community of Brownsville, which contained Clark University and Gammon Theological Seminary, was a primary target of violence.[37]

The fires of racial animosity were further fueled by opponents of educational reform who used racial tensions to protect their economic and political power. Elite whites who did not want to fund education for the masses, factory and mill owners who were concerned about the connection between compulsory attendance and child labor restrictions, and landlords who wished to fully exploit white and black tenant families did not hesitate to play the race card. Critics of compulsory attendance and local taxation claimed that the reforms would benefit African Americans more than whites because black parents exhibited a greater willingness to send their children to school. In 1900 political leaders who opposed the use of state money for black education proposed a constitutional amendment mandating that the state fund be racially divided, with whites and blacks receiving an amount proportionate to each race's contribution in taxes. Since blacks paid roughly 3 percent of the state's property taxes but comprised 46 percent of the population, the measure would have been disastrous for their impoverished rural public schools. W. E. B. Du Bois and other African American leaders sent a memorial to the legislature declaring that the bill would "depopulate the fields and plantations and fill the cities," while also setting an ominous precedent as an "entering wedge of discrimination" that could be used in the future to divide funds according to ethnicity or class.[38]

Men who used racial divisiveness to stir up opposition to educational re-

37. Ray Stannard Baker, *Following the Color Line: American Negro Citizenship in the Progressive Era* (Doubleday, Page, 1908; repr., New York: Harper and Row, 1964), 3–25 (citations are to the 1964 edition); Charles Crowe, "Racial Violence and Social Reform—Origins of the Atlanta Riot of 1906," *Journal of Negro History* 53 (July 1968): 234–256, quote 237; Mark Bauerlein, *Negrophobia: A Race Riot in Atlanta, 1906* (San Francisco: Encounter Books, 2001); Barton C. Shaw, *The Wool-Hat Boys: Georgia's Populist Party* (Baton Rouge: Louisiana State University Press, 1984), 183–202; C. Vann Woodward, *Tom Watson: Agrarian Rebel* (New York: Macmillan, 1938), 320–333.

38. "The Negro Common School, Georgia," *Crisis* 32 (September 1926): 248–264, quotes 250; Alton DuMar Jones, "Progressivism in Georgia, 1898–1918" (Ph.D. diss., Emory University, 1963), 240–241; John Michael Matthews, "Studies in Race Relations in Georgia, 1890–1930" (Ph.D. diss., Duke University, 1970), 289.

form were playing to the same fears evident in the national debates over immigration, race suicide, and international competition. Evolutionary theory had convinced many white Americans that races and nations were engaged in a battle for control of resources and that their very survival hinged upon success. Southern whites saw themselves as the underdogs, squeezed between hardworking southern blacks on one side of them and wealthy northern capitalists on the other. Education, with its potential to adapt individuals to shifting economic needs and opportunities, was one resource they were determined to configure to benefit themselves. Although white Georgians frequently used physical violence to maintain the social order (at times leading the nation in lynchings), limiting black access to education—a quieter form of oppression—had greater long-term implications. Educational discrimination long outlasted the reliance upon vigilante violence as a tool of control, and the impact on black political influence was tremendous. African American leaders frequently complained that whites deliberately used the impoverishment of black schools as a way to disfranchise black voters on the basis of the literacy requirement. As one white Georgian acknowledged, "knowledge is wealth, and it is power," and those who had access to the right kind of education were destined to become the new leaders of the region.[39]

In this racially oppressive climate, it was the most conservative female reformers who felt free to publicly comment on black education. In the two years following the Atlanta riot, GFWC president Mary Ann Lipscomb informed Federation convention delegates that the inappropriate education of African Americans was responsible for the deterioration of race relations and that educating the black child for "his proper place in the South" was the answer to the problem. After Reconstruction, southerners had allowed northern philanthropists and missionaries to assume responsibility for black schools, she explained. As a result, blacks spent time in "richly endowed universities"

---

39. Quote from J. O. A. Clark, *The Races and Their Future: A Plea for Their Education* (Macon, GA: J. W. Burke, 1889), 28–31; Lyman Hall, "The Needs of the New South," in *Proceedings of the CES, the Sixth Session, Richmond Virginia, April 22nd to April 24th, and at the University of Virginia, April 25th, 1903* (New York: Committee on Publication, 1903), 136–142; as late as 1940, the state spent $35 on the education of each black child, compared to $142 for each white child. Numan V. Bartley, Kenneth Coleman, William F. Holmes, F. N. Boney, Phinizy Spalding, and Charles E. Wynes, *A History of Georgia*, gen. ed. Kenneth Coleman, 2nd ed. (Athens: University of Georgia Press, 1991), 327; *The Common School and the Negro American*, Atlanta University Publications, no. 16 (Atlanta, 1911), 115–119.

studying "Latin and Greek and Higher Mathematics," preparing themselves for places in society that did not exist. Lipscomb argued that although one generation of blacks had been ruined by heightened expectations and "with their little learning will continue to be dangerous," white southerners had to look to the future. "Every nation must of necessity have its working population," she bluntly concluded, and giving blacks an appropriate education in industrial education "is the duty of the South today."[40]

Lipscomb's reaction to racial violence was not unusual for a daughter of wealthy slave owners who had grown up on a plantation. Her sister, Mildred Lewis Rutherford, was state historian for the United Daughters of the Confederacy and one of the region's most ardent defenders of the Lost Cause. After the Atlanta riot, many whites of Lipscomb's generation and class background argued that the escalation of mob violence was an indication that the social order had become unbalanced and distorted by the inappropriate ambitions of educated blacks. Mobs descended upon Clark University intending to attack students, only to find it closed. The black president of Gammon Theological Seminary, one of the most respected African American leaders in the city, was denied his request for protection of the two campuses. Instead, white police assaulted and injured president J. W. E. Bowen and arrested black college students and professors. Rather than condemning white vigilantes and officers for targeting productive and law-abiding citizens, white conservatives urged disfranchisement, domestic and industrial training, more restrictive segregation, and temperance for Georgia blacks. In this latter demand they were supported by members of the Women's Christian Temperance Union, the Atlanta Anti-Saloon League, and the Businessmen's Gospel Union. The obvious implication was that racial violence was the fault of blacks rather than whites and that only a return to the older order could remove the conditions conducive to murderous assault.[41]

40. Mary Ann Lipscomb addresses, GFWC Yearbook, 1908–1909 (Atlanta: GFWC, 1909), 7–16, first four quotes 13–14; and GFWC Yearbook, 1907–1908 (Atlanta: GFWC, 1908), 8–10, fifth and sixth quotes 10. Conservative whites often blamed vigilante justice on blacks' refusal to stay in their place, as in the case of Allen D. Candler, governor of Georgia during the worst years of racial violence, who condemned lynching while blaming it on blacks' unreasonable expectations of democratic political participation. W. Fitzhugh Brundage, Lynching in the New South: Georgia and Virginia, 1880–1930 (Urbana: University of Illinois Press, 1993), 201–204.

41. Baker, Following the Color Line, 13; Crowe, "Racial Violence and Social Reform"; John Dittmer, Black Georgia in the Progressive Era, 1900–1920 (Urbana: University of Illinois Press,

Conservative women who promoted black educational reforms tended to cast their activism in terms of the old order, even though it was very much a product of the new. Regional and state leaders often claimed that their concern for black education was simply an extension of their antebellum role as plantation mistresses and a reflection of their natural concern for blacks as "a weaker and less developed people." In her annual address of 1908, Lipscomb made a plea "in behalf of Uncle Remus, whom Joel Chandler Harris has immortalized, and his unfortunate people." She argued that southern whites had abandoned their obligations to blacks, removing their beneficial influence, and as a result the "relations between the colored race and Southern people have become strained and changed." Deftly sliding from old social structure to new, Lipscomb claimed that the solution to this problem lay in the authority of the state, in its obligation to provide more schools for black citizens and to enforce compulsory attendance for both races. She also called for white women to involve their clubs in activities to uplift black Georgians. Noting that a white women's club in Athens had opened a child-care facility for the children of black working mothers, Lipscomb declared such activities "a move in the right direction" that "will bring practical results."[42]

Not all club women were as conservative as Mary Ann Lipscomb, but the need for unity of purpose among reformers and the strength of reactionary racism made the open expression of more moderate positions difficult, to say the least. Such considerations compelled Sallie Hill to make private arrangements to fund black school improvement work. She corresponded regularly with Alice Dugged Cary, an African American teacher at Morris Brown Institute in Atlanta who was active in the State Federation of Colored Women of Georgia and participated in both urban and rural educational reform. Cary spoke before black women's groups on organizing for school improvement and during the summers visited numerous counties to hold teachers' institutes and form school improvement clubs. She also visited homes and churches, helped to place teachers and principals in rural schools, and col-

---

1977), 128–131; Tera W. Hunter, *To 'Joy My Freedom: Southern Black Women's Lives and Labors after the Civil War* (Cambridge, MA: Harvard University Press, 1997), 125–126.

42. First quote from Mary Cooke Branch Munford, "Woman's Part in the Educational Progress of the South," in *The South in the Building of the Nation* (Richmond, VA: Southern Historical Publication Society, 1909), 10:638–645, quote 638–639; Mary Ann Lipscomb address, *GFWC Yearbook, 1908–1909*, quotes 12–14.

lected books with which to create libraries. Hill was able to obtain modest funding for Cary's work from George S. Dickerman, a general field agent of the John F. Slater Fund and associate secretary of the Southern Education Board. Dickerman requested that Hill keep his financial contributions a secret from other members of the SEB to save him "embarrassment." Northern reformers such as Dickerman and the members of the General Education Board found their efforts to publicly address the needs of black education in the rural South thwarted by southern-born men on the SEB who were concerned about the "excited state of public sentiment" on the race question. Sallie Hill understood the need for discretion, and in respecting Dickerman's request for secrecy was able to avoid further conflict within the ranks of her fellow educational reformers.[43]

Organized women and female educators who openly expressed a desire to use educational reform to benefit both races found themselves constrained by the ways in which the gender and race hierarchies reinforced one another. Celeste Parrish, whose intelligence and assertiveness often struck southern men as inappropriate for a woman, was accused of advocating social equality of the races shortly after her arrival in Georgia. She assumed the chair of the Department of Psychology and Pedagogy in the Georgia State Normal School in the fall of 1901 and in mid-April of 1902 made remarks in a discussion with her freshman class that became the center of a statewide controversy. Parrish advised her students that southern whites should accept responsibility for the educational advancement of blacks, and she used her own involvement in black teachers' institutes as an example of the sort of work that should be done. Asked if she would consider teaching in a black school, Parrish replied

43. Report on Cary's work, SBH, box 22, folder 3; G. S. Dickerman to Sallie B. Hill, May 5, 1908; and Dickerman to Hill, May 8, 1909, SBH, box 22, folder 9; Mrs. S. H. Knight to Alice D. Cary, May 8, 1910, SBH, box 23, folder 4; Alice D. Cary to Hill, February 27, 1911, SBH, box 23, folder 9; quote from Louis R. Harlan, "The Southern Education Board and the Race Issue in Public Education," *Journal of Southern History* 23 (May 1957): 189–202; William J. Breen, "Black Women and the Great War: Mobilization and Reform in the South," *Journal of Southern History* 44 (August 1978): 421–440; Hunter, *To 'Joy My Freedom,* 136, 213–215. For a less flattering view of northern philanthropists and reformers that stresses their class-based economic motives, see Anderson, "Northern Foundations and the Shaping of Southern Black Rural Education"; Sallie Hill's son, Walter Hill Jr., while serving as state supervisor of black schools, was openly disgusted with white neglect of black education, as evidenced by his frankly critical reports filed annually with the State Board of Education.

that she would "if her white girls did not need her." When a female student spoke up to say that *she* would never consider teaching blacks, Parrish informed her that if that was her attitude she "ought to be made to stop teaching." Normal School president Eugene C. Branson was angered when he heard of the remarks and called Parrish into his office to account for herself. He apparently was unsatisfied with her reply, and relations were so strained between the two that more than a year later Parrish requested an inquiry by the Normal School's board of trustees to clear her of any wrongdoing.[44]

Parrish withstood efforts to remove her from her position, but the dispute revealed the constraints that Georgia's race politics imposed upon female reformers. Newspapers incorrectly reported that she advocated sending white women from State Normal to teach in black schools. All white Georgians knew that this statement was tantamount to promoting social equality, a phrase connoting the free mingling of white women and black men that could lead to miscegenation. If proved, such an accusation would have ended Parrish's effectiveness as a reformer. As W. E. B. Du Bois wrote in an essay on race relations in Georgia, whites committed to interracial cooperation did not dare think of social equality, much less "whisper it aloud," because "it would spoil everything; it would end their crusade." This prohibition was stronger for white women than for men, for as Du Bois also noted: "Every Negro question at times becomes a matter of sex. Voting? They want social equality. Schools? They are after our daughters. Land? They'll rape our wives. Continually the secrecy, the veiled suggestion, the open warning pivot on sex; gossip rages and horrible stories are spread." Parrish's respectability, her authority as a Progressive educator and a reformer, and indeed her very ability to earn her livelihood hinged on her ability to accommodate a white supremacist ideology that connected white racial dominance with the "purity" of white womanhood. Fortunately for Parrish, educators and students rose to her defense, arguing that she was only "expressing a generous Christian interest in a backward race" and had said nothing that "would have offended the ear of a well informed, refined southern gentleman."[45]

Women operating at the local level faced additional obstacles that limited

44. *Macon Telegraph,* December 15, 17, 1903.

45. Ibid.; W. E. Burghardt Du Bois, "Georgia: Invisible Empire State," *Nation,* January 21, 1925, 63–67, quotes 66–67; last two quotes from *Athens Daily Banner,* December 17, 1903.

their ability to engage in interracial reform. The Farmers' Union limited its membership to whites and by 1910 exhibited the nativist and racist characteristics that one historian has termed "reactionary populism." Reactionary populism, which combined attacks on "big capital" with racism, nationalism, and a "militant sexual conservatism," gained its impetus from white men's perception of their own growing social and economic insecurity. R. F. Duckworth, president of the Georgia Farmers' Union, appealed to racist and xenophobic fears in rallying support for his organization at a state conference in 1907. Claiming that the "State of Georgia is populated almost exclusively with men of pure Anglo-Saxon blood," he assured his audience that the Farmers' Union would "stand as a bulwark" against the "pauper and criminal element from the crowded centers of Europe" and the "more worthless Mongolian from the Orient," whose immigration threatened the inheritance of southern white men. Prejudice was just as easily turned toward blacks, as rural men's heightened sense of vulnerability played out in destructive rituals that discouraged interracial school reform. In several counties, newly constructed black schools mysteriously burned, and in one case the replacement school burned as well. Hostility to nonwhite advancement forced racially moderate women to appeal more to white than biracial uplift to avoid discrediting their reform movement and even provoking violent retaliation against blacks.[46]

The hostile racial environment made local women's clubs hesitant to approach rural blacks, or at least reluctant to report their interracial activities, until after World War I. One exception was Sallie Hill, who occasionally spoke before African American groups on school improvement work and secretly helped to fund their separate activities. Despite Mary Ann Lipscomb's admonitions that club women should step up their work with blacks, the district reports of Federated clubs reported almost no interracial activity prior to the GFWC resolution against lynching in 1917. The 1915 lynching of Leo

46. For more on reactionary populism, see Nancy MacLean, "The Leo Frank Case Reconsidered: Gender and Sexual Politics in the Making of Reactionary Populism," *Journal of American History* 78 (December 1991): 917–948, first three quotes 930; remaining quotes from "Immigration Is Rapped Hard: Farmers' Union Declares against Foreigners Coming to U.S.," *Atlanta Constitution,* July 26, 1907; "The Negro Common School, Georgia." On the culmination of reactionary populism in the rise of the Klan in the 1920s, see Nancy MacLean, *Behind the Mask of Chivalry: The Making of the Second Ku Klux Klan* (New York: Oxford University Press, 1994).

Frank, a white Jewish man most likely innocent of the charge of killing a young white woman, and the acceleration of mob violence at the end of the war pushed organized women into taking a public stance on the issue. At their annual convention in November of 1917, GFWC delegates complained that "lynching substitutes the violent passions of the mob for orderly processes of the courts of justice, thus creating in the minds of our people disrespect for the law." Declaring it "in the power of the enlightened women of the state to create a public sentiment in favor of law and against the continued blight of mob violence," club women registered their "unqualified condemnation of lynching as a means of punishment for crime of any character" and announced their support of legislation to address the problem.[47]

By 1917 a number of factors had worked together to generate public opposition to racial violence, providing a space in which white women could more easily and safely address the educational needs of blacks. According to one study of lynching in Georgia, these factors included business concerns regarding disruption of the economy (especially the loss of labor from black migration northward), the social gospel influence in organized religion, the rise of racial liberalism in academia, and the persistent efforts of organizations such as the Commission on Interracial Cooperation and the National Association for the Advancement of Colored People. What had to develop at the grassroots level was an understanding that mob violence no longer was a legitimate expression of community will and that the authority to mete out justice appropriately resided in the state.[48] Women's school improvement work contributed to the development of this understanding through its promotion

47. Isaiah Blocker (president of the black Georgia State Teachers Association) to Sallie B. Hill, January 31, 1911, SBH, box 53, folder 5; even Hill sometimes eschewed interracial reform efforts when other educational leaders believed that the time was not right, such as when the state school superintendent agreed that she should not go to a black school in Savannah, telling her, "There is no reason why you should take the chances" involved. Jere Pound to Hill, January 13, 1909, SBH, box 22, folder 8; minutes of the twenty-first annual meeting, *GFWC Yearbook, 1917–1918* (Atlanta: GFWC, 1918), 12–13; Brundage, *Lynching in the New South*, 208–230. For different perspectives on the Leo Frank case, see Leonard Dinnerstein, *The Leo Frank Case* (Athens: University of Georgia Press, 1987); and Robert Seitz Frey and Nancy Thompson-Frey, *The Silent and the Damned: The Murder of Mary Phagan and the Lynching of Leo Frank* (Lanham, MD: Madison Books, 1988).

48. Brundage, *Lynching in the New South*, 208–244.

of a concept of white male citizenship that was more communal than individualist-oriented. Whatever their position on race relations, female educational reformers challenged white men's authority to act as a law unto themselves when they supported a more inclusive notion of democracy and a more activist role for the state. The household no longer represented the extent of "community," and its head no longer was its only member with a direct tie to government interests.

As public condemnation of racial violence grew, so did organized white women's involvement with black school reform. From about 1917 through the 1920s, local white women's clubs increasingly included the black community in their school improvement activities, working to upgrade furnishings and equipment in black as well as white schoolhouses. They solicited donations of books and domestic science equipment and sometimes paid for improvements with their own funds. In 1920 one club sponsored sixteen black schools in addition to thirty white schools. Club women also gave lectures at schools and assisted black teachers and mothers in forming their own organizations, such as civic clubs or Parent-Teacher Association chapters. As the beautification campaign spread to rural black schools, local white clubs assisted in that endeavor as well, giving demonstrations and providing supplies for the external improvement of buildings. In the late 1920s, the GFWC launched a program aimed at abolishing illiteracy among the rural adult population. When the chair of the Department of Education summarized the activities of district clubs in 1930, she noted that in the campaign against illiteracy, "many opportunity schools for white and Negro were sponsored by the individual clubs" and that "many of these were not only taught but financed by the club women themselves." Much had changed since 1903, when Celeste Parrish found her job jeopardized by the modest assertion that southern educators should take an active interest in improving black education.[49]

White women's black school improvement work reveals the limitations of localism, since racial inequalities increased rather than declining or remaining constant between 1900 and 1925. Two legislative reforms supported by orga-

49. Presidential address of Louise Frederick Hays, *GFWC Yearbook, 1920–1921*, 29–39; Department of Education report, *GFWC Yearbook, 1929–1930* (Atlanta, GFWC, 1930), 170–171; also see annual district reports in the GFWC yearbooks for specific examples of local women's clubs' work with black schools.

nized women—local taxation and compulsory attendance—were used at the local level to benefit whites exclusively. As more and more counties and districts approved local taxes, state funds decreased as a proportion of total appropriations for public schools. Although the dollar amount of state funding rose by 36 percent between 1918 and 1926, it declined as a proportion of total school moneys from 42 to 21 percent. Local officials who had control of allocations used their new financial resources to extend the white school term, raise white teachers' salaries, and improve white educational facilities and services. In his first year as state supervisor for black schools, Sallie Hill's son, Walter B. Hill Jr., complained about the injustice of taxing black property owners for the construction of white schools. As a result of discrimination at the local level, blacks' education lost ground in relation to whites' in many areas. For example, in 1900 the average black teacher made three-quarters of an average white teacher's salary, but in 1925 the black teacher received only half of a white teacher's pay. Their lack of access to advanced training confined most black teachers to the lowest rung on the professional ladder, so that rural black education remained substandard.[50]

Local school officials bowed to the wishes of whites in refusing to apply compulsory attendance law to blacks, fulfilling the prophecy of educational reformers who argued that the regulations were never intended for African Americans from the beginning. Many male educational leaders sought support for compulsory attendance legislation (finally passed in 1916) by openly claiming that "in the actual execution of the law, white officials would be more zealous to enforce it among the whites than among the blacks." The Georgia Department of Education's annual report for 1925 showed that this was in fact the case. During that year, officials served 1,102 warrants to recalcitrant white parents and put 12,806 white students back into school but did not take a single action in black communities. Although this and other forms

---

50. Report of Walter B. Hill Jr., in GDE, *Forty-Ninth Annual Report, 1920* (Atlanta: GDE, 1921), 78–87. A small number of blacks (especially men) benefited from the opportunities for professional advancement that opened up with the creation of public high schools, but the vast majority remained clustered at the elementary level, where racial disparities in pay were the greatest. GDE, *Fifty-Ninth Annual Report, 1930* (Atlanta: GDE, 1931), 281; also see summary of public school statistics contained in GDE, *Annual Report, 1900,* and in the report for 1925, in *Fifty-Fourth and Fifty-Fifth Annual Reports, 1925–1926* (Atlanta: GDE, 1927).

of discrimination lessened slightly in the late 1920s in response to the persistence of black migration out of the state, impoverishment and the indifference of white administrators continued to cripple the ability of black public schools to meet the educational needs of African Americans.[51]

The conservatism and limitations of white women's interracial approach appear to support an interpretive emphasis on the continuity of southern race relations, when in fact very real changes had taken place. Those club women who characterized their role as that of "public mistress" obscured the dramatic differences between their antebellum benevolence and postbellum activism. Their care of white and black "family" in the plantation household had taken place under the ultimate authority of the master. Their efforts to improve New South public schools, however, took place among white women acting more or less as independent agents and African Americans who were members of their own autonomous households. Women's appeals to the older order and their efforts to generate support for reform from below served to obscure the Reconstruction origins of the socially activist state, making the concept somewhat more palatable to southern whites. Organized women's overtures to black communities, however patronizing they may have been at times, provided rural blacks with at least some access to resources in an otherwise hostile and sometimes violent social climate. It remained for African Americans to more directly subvert the social order by utilizing white assistance in their quest to gain the credentials of social respectability, using education to co-opt white middle-class markers of gender identity and social status.[52]

51. Quote as cited in Walter B. Hill, "Negro Education in the South," in *Proceedings of CES, 1903*, 212–213; GDE, *Annual Report, 1915*, 243.

52. Recent scholarship interprets African Americans' embrace of domestic science and industrial education—exactly those types of training white Georgia women thought most appropriate for blacks—as a strategy for race uplift with deliberate reformist implications. This was especially true of black women, who sought to use education to co-opt white female gender roles, thereby improving their status and that of the black family. See, for example, Johnson, "This Wonderful Dream Nation," 446–478; Beverly Washington Jones, *Quest for Equality: The Life and Writings of Mary Eliza Church Terrell, 1863–1954* (New York: Carlson Publishing, 1990), 19–29; Audrey Thomas McCluskey, "Mary McLeod Bethune and the Education of Black Girls," *Sex Roles* 21, nos. 1–2 (1989): 113–126; Sandra N. Smith and Earle H. West, "Charlotte Hawkins Brown," *Journal of Negro Education* 51, no. 3 (1982): 199–202; and Carol Ortman Perkins, "Prag-

Despite the persistence of racial discrimination, women's school improvement work had a significant positive impact on public education in Georgia. Efforts to beautify schoolhouses and to upgrade the quality of education taught in rural areas stimulated public interest and pride among members of those communities. Residents who were proud of their local schools were more likely to approve local taxation, which in turn allowed further improvements. The number of county tax districts grew from 1 in 1904 to 27 in 1911 and to 56 in 1917. Although this last number represented only about 40 percent of Georgia counties, there were more than fifteen times as many district tax systems. Even communities that failed to enact local taxation often realized increased public support for schools that translated into higher enrollment and attendance figures. In 1908 79 percent of white children and 57 percent of black children of school age were enrolled in school. In 1920 these figures had increased to more than 94 percent of white and almost 72 percent of black school-age children. Although compulsory attendance laws required only twelve weeks of school attendance, the rural school term increased from an average of 100 days in 1900 to 150 days in 1925. The increases are all the more impressive when the weakness of compulsory attendance laws is taken into account. The 1916 bill lacked enforcement provisions and contained numerous loopholes, most notably the one allowing school boards to make exemptions for any reason they considered legitimate. Even after subsequent legislation in 1918 established truant officers, local officials were notoriously reluctant to enforce the law.[53]

Increased rural support for public schools in the absence of legal coercion signaled a definite change in attitudes toward the place of education in family and community, but not all of the change can be attributed to organized women. Community leaders and rural parents had reasons of their own for embracing reform. Local leaders believed that better schools could stem rural-to-urban migration, attract outside investment, and encourage eco-

---

matic Idealism: Industrial Training, Liberal Education, and Women's Special Needs—Conflict and Continuity in the Experience of Mary McLeod Bethune and Other Black Women Educators, 1900–1930" (Ph.D. diss., San Diego State University, 1986).

53. GDE, *Annual Report, 1908*, 559–560; Report of the state school superintendent, in GDE, *Forty-Seventh Annual Report, 1918* (Atlanta: GDE, 1919), 18–19; GDE, *Annual Report, 1920*, 480–486; Harlan, *Separate and Unequal*, 231–233.

nomic development. Rural families were attracted to the school improvement club activities because they provided entertainment and opportunities for socializing with neighbors. The democratic structure of the clubs also served as an avenue for parental influence that at least partially offset the loss of community control accompanying reforms. Furthermore, as the mechanization of agriculture slowly but steadily reduced opportunities for community social events, boys' and girls' clubs and school-related sports stepped into the gap by offering opportunities for friendly competition. Beginning in 1913, educational reformers began sponsoring statewide academic and athletic contests for high school students that were held at the University of Georgia the first week in July. According to their sponsors, the contests inspired entire communities to take an interest in the training of student scholars and athletes, and they were so popular that within a few years they were extended to the upper primary grades.[54]

Despite their hard-won successes at the local level, female activists continued to face economic and political impediments to large-scale reform. In battling the infamous rural male individualism, women found it easier to convince rural fathers to put the educational needs of children ahead of immediate financial gain when the families had the means to do so. The obvious pride of many rural parents in their improved schools suggested that poverty and isolation often underlay their initial disinterest more than a simple lack of concern. But in this campaign as in others, women's struggle with male individualism involved not just poor men resentful of outside intrusion, but men of their own class as well. State legislators dragged their feet on the issue of an equalization fund, which would have narrowed the educational gap between the wealthiest and the poorest communities, and after creating the fund in 1926 they failed to provide it with an adequate source of revenue.

---

54. On the connections between the mechanization of agriculture, rural social events, and Progressive reform, see Ted Ownby, *Subduing Satan: Religion, Recreation, and Manhood in the Rural South, 1865–1920* (Chapel Hill: University of North Carolina, 1990); Bonner et al., *History of Public Education in Georgia,* 188–189. Georgians approved a referendum to include high schools in the public school system in 1912, and the statewide competitions were so successful in building public support for the institutions that Georgians went back to the polls in 1919 and ratified a constitutional amendment to make county taxation for high schools mandatory. Bartley et al., *A History of Georgia,* 324.

Politicians also bowed to pressure from rural elites and industrialists in doggedly refusing to adequately enforce compulsory attendance laws. As the work of rural school reform increasingly professionalized and became the responsibility of educators employed by the state Department of Education, female reformers turned to new strategies designed to improve access to education and alleviate the hardships of country life.[55]

55. In 1911 the state legislature created within the Georgia Department of Education three new supervisory positions dedicated to the improvement of rural education, and although the primary responsibility of the new agents was to organize and conduct teachers' institutes, they also were charged with the "authority to aid the teachers and schools in every way possible." GDE, *Fortieth Annual Report, 1911* (Atlanta: GDE, 1912), 26. The legislature simultaneously created a Division of Negro Education in the GDE but did not provide funding for a state agent, so that black schools did not have the benefit of the teachers' institutes and a bureaucratic advocate until 1913, when the General Education Board agreed to pay the salary for such a position. GDE, *Forty-Third Annual Report, 1914* (Atlanta: GDE, 1915), 13–14; also see Josie B. Sessoms, Ella A. Tackwood, Rebecca E. Davis, Maenelle D. Dempsey, Ethel W. Kight, Madie A. Kincy, and Susie W. Wheeler, *Jeanes Supervision in Georgia Schools, A Guiding Light in Education: A History of the Program from 1908–1975* (Athens: Georgia Association of Jeanes Curriculum Directors and Southern Education Foundation, 1975), 22, 24–26.

{3}

REFORMING THE COUNTRYSIDE
Women, Blacks, and Cooperative Extension Services

During their campaign for the improvement of rural schools, Georgia women developed a better understanding of the underlying structural causes of poverty and inequality, and their discoveries led them to engage in a wider program of rural uplift. They sought fundamental changes that would enable rural communities to afford local taxation, longer school terms, better school facilities, and higher teacher salaries. They had to surmount the problems of a system of agriculture in which farmers produced tremendous wealth but retained little of it owing to exploitative tenure arrangements and an excessive reliance upon cotton. The problem was a self-perpetuating one that threatened to bleed the countryside of its population, since poverty resulted in poorly funded schools and, in turn, inadequate schools encouraged the migration of farm families to wealthier communities and towns. The campaign that organized women developed in response to these issues reflected their belief that the costs associated with the structure of the agricultural economy fell disproportionately on women and children. Club women and female educators wanted to improve the viability of farming through crop diversification and greater self-sufficiency, but they also sought to raise rural women's status and standard of living by increasing female educational and cash-earning opportunities.[1]

In pursuing their program of rural uplift, female activists once again had to face the pervasive politics of gender, this time in the form of institutional barriers to the redistribution of public resources through extension work. They continued to rely upon the relatively autonomous network of local women's clubs mobilized in support of school improvement work, but the severity of rural economic woes propelled female reformers into an increased

---

1. Mrs. A. H. Brenner, "Report of the President," and Mrs. Stewart D. Brown, "The Aim of Rural Co-Operation," *Georgia Federation of Women's Clubs* [hereafter GFWC] *Yearbook, 1929–1930* (Atlanta, GFWC, 1930), 22–28, 225–226; Dolly Hawthorne, "The Economic Surplus of Georgia; What It Is," *Educational Monthly* I (June 1915): 115–19; Epsie Campbell, "Rural, Consolidated, and Vocational Schools, *GFWC Yearbook, 1929–1930*, 172–176.

reliance upon male-dominated institutions. Institutionalized extension services appeared the most promising solution to the problems of the rural household, as they afforded access to public funds and the expertise of home economists who shared a desire to improve educational opportunities for women. However, agricultural institutions perpetuated the gender divisions of labor and knowledge that relegated home extension work to subordinate status. Federal and state support for extension services was critical, yet the gender and racial hierarchies embedded in the agencies that oversaw such work constricted women's ability to reach their goals. Despite these barriers, female reformers persisted in their attempts to realize the democratic promise embodied in extension services, stretching limited resources to maximize their benefit to girls, women, and families in rural communities throughout Georgia.

Club women's expanded agenda for rural reform was evident at the Georgia Federation of Women's Clubs conference in 1910. When GFWC president Lucy Lester Willet delivered her annual address, she informed delegates that the most important work facing them in the following years would be the "betterment of our Georgia rural homes." Willet noted that the Georgia College of Agriculture and eleven new district agricultural schools were beginning to address the needs of rural children—the future adults—through club work and vocational training, but there still were no official programs to assist rural women. After presenting a sad picture of "pale-faced, weary" farm women "living in isolation with few creature comforts," Willet urged the club women convened in Athens to assume responsibility for meeting the needs of the rural home. The Federation was lobbying to add household extension teaching to the institute work of the state College of Agriculture, but in the meantime women's club members needed to step forward and help solve the "problems of household sanitation, ventilation and management, the care, feeding and clothing of children, and how to fight tuberculosis, the typhoid fly, [and] the mosquito."[2]

2. Mrs. Hugh M. Willet, "President's Report," *GFWC Yearbook, 1910–1911* (Atlanta, GFWC, 1911), 9–15, quotes 11–12; one reason farm women were the last to have their needs addressed by state agencies was that the early extension programs targeting rural men met with resistance, leading officials to conclude that children would be a more receptive audience than adults. Kathleen C. Hilton, "'Both in the Field, Each with a Plow': Race and Gender in USDA Policy, 1907–1929," in *Hidden Histories of Women in the New South*, ed. Virginia Bernhard, Betty Brandon,

Willet's speech reflects southern women's alarm at the destructive impact of the postbellum cotton economy on home and family. On the surface, the concerns and strategies she outlined do not appear unique to the region, but echo similar statements made by participants in the national Country Life Movement. Concerned about rural population flight, Country Life reformers in other regions also identified poor living conditions as evidence of public neglect of the needs of farm families. Like southern club women, they publicized the problems of women in rural households and lobbied to establish public funding for educational remedies. However, in some ways the situation facing female reformers in the Deep South was unique. The persistence of monoculture after the Civil War and the postbellum rise in farm tenancy exacerbated the subordination of women and the home to the market economy and discouraged subsistence production for the family. Even after slavery was abolished, the one-crop economy was perpetuated on multiple small farms, where it paid the wages of sharecroppers and the rent of tenants and represented practically the only hope of moving upward into property ownership. Furthermore, the dominance of cotton—a substitute for cash and a basis for credit—continued to suppress the development of local markets for alternative agricultural and domestic products.[3]

The persistence of monoculture presented new problems for rural white women, who increasingly found their lives dominated by exploitative relations that previously had been more applicable to black women. The Civil War and emancipation set a process in motion that shifted some of the work

Elizabeth Fox-Genovese, Theda Purdue, and Elizabeth Hays Turner (Columbia: University of Missouri Press, 1994), 115–116.

3. On the Country Life Movement, see David Danbom, *The Resisted Revolution: Urban America and the Industrialization of Agriculture, 1900–1930* (Ames: Iowa State University Press, 1979); Katherine Jellison, *Entitled to Power: Farm Women and Technology, 1913–1963* (Chapel Hill: University of North Carolina Press, 1993); and Mary Neth, *Preserving the Family Farm: Women, Community, and the Foundations of Agribusiness in the Midwest, 1900–1940* (Baltimore: Johns Hopkins University Press, 1995). For an overview of various and conflicting perspectives on the historical reasons for the persistence of monoculture and the rise of tenancy, see Harold D. Woodman, "Sequel to Slavery: The New History Views the Postbellum South," *Journal of Southern History* 43 (1977): 523–554; and for a broader discussion, Harold D. Woodman, "Economic Reconstruction and the Rise of the New South, 1865–1900," in *Interpreting Southern History: Historiographical Essays in Honor of Sanford W. Higginbotham,* ed. John B. Boles and Evelyn Thomas Nolen (Baton Rouge: Louisiana State University Press, 1987), 254–307.

of cotton cultivation from blacks to whites. In the South as a whole, whites cultivated 40 percent of the cotton crop in 1876 as compared to 10 percent in 1860. One reason for the shift was the dramatic increase of cotton cultivation in the upcountry. Indebted farmers, assisted by the expansion of railroads and the greater availability of commercial fertilizers, turned to cotton as the most lucrative crop. Another important factor was the freed people themselves, many of whom migrated to urban areas or withdrew female and child labor into their own households after the war. There was less black agricultural labor available to white farmers, leaving them more dependent upon the labor of female family members. The amount of cotton a small-scale farmer could produce was determined not by how many acres he could plow but by how much cotton his family could hoe and pick. This equation was especially important for sharecroppers and tenants, who had to maximize use of family labor in their pursuit of advancement. White women who previously had worked outdoors solely to benefit themselves and their families now found their labor profiting landlords. In Georgia the proportion of all farmers who owned their farms declined from about 55 percent in 1880 to less than 34 percent in 1910. Even though more than 42 percent of white farmers owned the land they tilled, whites made up an ever-increasing proportion of tenants.[4]

Among both black and white farm families, postbellum conditions siphoned resources away from the home. Although most farming couples preferred to engage in some subsistence production, there were numerous forces militating against this. Landlords who leased land in exchange for a share of the crop knew that the larger the crop, the greater their profit, and some of them pressured farmers who they believed were not working their families as

4. Robert Preston Brooks, "The Agrarian Revolution in Georgia, 1865–1912" (Ph.D. diss., University of Wisconsin–Madison, 1914), 25, 57–58, 70; Eric Foner, *Reconstruction: America's Unfinished Revolution, 1863–1877* (New York: Harper and Row, 1988), 393–394; Steven Hahn, *The Roots of Southern Populism: Yeoman Farmers and the Transformation of the Georgia Upcountry, 1850–1890* (New York: Oxford University Press, 1983), 141–152; Idus A. Newby, *Plain Folk in the New South: Social Change and Cultural Persistence, 1880–1915* (Baton Rouge: Louisiana State University Press, 1989), 49; Rebecca Sharpless, *Fertile Ground, Narrow Choices: Women on Texas Cotton Farms, 1900–1940* (Chapel Hill: University of North Carolina Press, 1999), 2–15. Women's labor also was important in tobacco cultivation. Laura F. Edwards, *Gendered Strife and Confusion: The Political Culture of Reconstruction* (Urbana: University of Illinois Press, 1997), 148–149; and Dolores Janiewski, *Sisterhood Denied: Race, Gender, and Class in a New South Community* (Philadelphia: Temple University Press, 1985), 27–29.

hard as they could. One observer noted that tenant gardens rarely contained more than "a row or two of cabbage and perhaps some string or lima beans and sweet potatoes," adding that "sometimes the labor is pushed so hard by the landlord that no time is allowed for this work." Cash tenancy, which was on the rise in Georgia in the late nineteenth and early twentieth centuries, allowed rural families more flexibility. However, it was common even for more independent tenant farmers to dedicate all of their resources to cotton-growing as a strategy for advancement, a sort of all-or-nothing proposition that could lead to property ownership if good cotton prices held. If prices did not hold, the household would be in even greater debt from buying subsistence needs on credit. Whatever the tenure arrangement, husbands and wives worked side by side in the fields in an effort to build a more secure future. Women performed domestic work for their families in the evenings and on weekends when their obligations to cotton cultivation were fulfilled. Even if they could manage a small garden, oftentimes families were unable to meet their basic food needs because they lacked the resources necessary to make the initial investment in chickens or a cow. This lack of resources had the additional drawback of limiting women's ability to contribute to household income through the sale of surplus goods.[5]

The concerns of federal and state officials regarding the dominance of cotton production in the South distinctively shaped women's strategies for rural reform. In a speech entitled "The General Scheme for Carrying on Extension Work with Women," Bradford Knapp, head of the Office of Extension Work in the South for the U.S. Department of Agriculture, outlined the reasons why his department took a different approach to home demonstration work in the South: "With 84.9 per cent of all the women in America working habitually in the fields . . . located in the Cotton States, our problem has been

5. Brooks, "The Agrarian Revolution in Georgia," 57; Newby, *Plain Folk in the New South*, 26–32; quote from T. J. Woofter Jr., "Migration of Negroes from Georgia, 1916–1917," in *Negro Migration in 1916–1917*, U.S. Department of Labor, Division of Negro Economics (Washington, DC: Government Printing Office, 1919), 87; also see Charles S. Johnson, *Shadow of the Plantation* (Chicago: University of Chicago Press, 1934). In regions with better-developed and more diversified local markets, the status of farm women's subsistence production increased along with their cash-earning opportunities. For example, see Joan Jensen, *Loosening the Bonds: Mid-Atlantic Farm Women, 1750–1850* (New Haven, CT: Yale University Press, 1986); and Nancy Grey Osterud, *Bonds of Community: The Lives of Farm Women in Nineteenth-Century New York* (Ithaca, NY: Cornell University Press, 1991).

to restore time-honored industries, to add to family incomes, to emphasize production and income, and from these to lead out into the better home and all its attractive features." Knapp argued that the poor standard of living prevailing in the rural South necessitated this no-nonsense approach to home extension services. The only way to get women out of the cotton fields was to provide alternative sources of income, preferably ones that would keep them closer to the home and benefit the family as a whole. Although Knapp, like USDA officials more generally, endorsed a strict sexual division of labor on the farm, he hoped that women's successful productive efforts in truck gardening, dairying, and poultry raising would persuade rural men to take a more favorable view of crop diversification in their own work.[6]

Club women also regarded home demonstration work as a way to reclaim rural women's labor for their families, thereby raising standards of living and enabling farm households to adopt middle-class standards of female respectability. Urban female reformers believed that just as industrialization had rendered much of their own productive labor obsolete (and as mechanization was lightening the burden of farm men), so should farm women's work be freed from onerous tasks and redirected to meet the intellectual and emotional needs of their families. This reform goal was common among activists in the Country Life Movement, who regarded the primitive conditions prevailing in farm homes as evidence that rural women were not sharing equally in the benefits of social and economic progress. Such concerns were intensified among white reformers in the South because of the regional race politics of agricultural labor. Part of the legacy of slavery was a persistent tension between the agrarian ideal of the industrious yeoman's wife and the plantation ideal of the genteel Southern Lady. Heavy manual labor, and especially female field labor, was associated with slavery and blackness. For white women it carried a double stigma of lowered class and race status that many rural women felt very acutely. One club woman reported that when she and her husband drove past two "poor Georgia girls" chopping cotton in the countryside, "their pride and humiliation seemed to overcome them, and they jerked their

6. Bradford Knapp, "The General Scheme for Carrying on Extension Work with Women," speech given to the Association of American Agricultural Colleges and Experiment Stations, Chicago, Illinois, November 11–16, 1919, Leila R. Mize Papers (hereafter LRM), box 1, folder 10, University Archives, University of Georgia, Athens.

bonnets over their faces." Such sights gave southern female reformers even greater impetus to improve educational and respectable cash-earning opportunities for rural women.[7]

Organized women's public advocacy of home economics extension work began in earnest in 1908, when the Georgia College of Agriculture officially established agricultural extension services but made no provisions to include work with women. Club women knew that the college was hosting a farmers' conference in January of 1909, and they issued a call for farmers to "bring their wives to this meeting." With Sallie B. Hill presiding, female educational reformers and domestic science professionals presented lectures and demonstrations to farm women in hopes of arousing interest in home economics extension work. The Georgia Federation of Women's Clubs also formulated a bill to create an appropriation of five thousand dollars in each of the years 1910 and 1911 to add home extension teaching to the College of Agriculture's farmers' institutes. According to the Federation's Committee on Educational Legislation, lobbying efforts were "brilliantly unsuccessful," because, in their words, legislators believed the work was "a fad among city women attempting impractical things, or a mistaken kind of mission crusade to the women of the country." Undeterred, female reformers held another series of women's meetings at the farmers' conference in 1910, at which time GFWC president Lucy Willet presented an impassioned plea to rural women to organize and voice their concerns publicly. Attempts to establish home extension work were unsuccessful, however, until the General Education Board (GEB) agreed in 1911 to contribute funds to the USDA and the Georgia College of Agriculture for this purpose.[8]

7. D. Harland Hagler, "The Ideal Woman in the Antebellum South: Lady or Farmwife?" *Journal of Southern History* 46 (August 1980): 405–418; quote as cited in Mary Beth Barnett Lewis, "A History of Home Economics at Georgia State College for Women from 1891 through 1943" (master's thesis, University of Georgia, 1943), 23; Jellison, *Entitled to Power*, 1–5; Sharpless, *Fertile Ground, Narrow Choices*, 159–163.

8. First quote from *History of Home Economics in Georgia* (Atlanta: Standards Committee, Georgia Home Economics Association, 1933), Georgia Home Economics Association Collection, box 3, Georgia Department of Archives and History; second quote from "Report of Committee on Educational Legislation," *GFWC Yearbook, 1910–1911*, 52–55. Work with rural men actually began in 1903, after the legislature approved funding for farmers' institutes in each of the state's forty-four senatorial districts. "Report of the Director of Farmers' Institutes, 1908," *Bul-*

The setbacks women faced in the early stages of their campaign for home extension services set the tone for what was to follow. They continued to face male opposition or, at best, indifference to the work and had to maintain constant pressure on their political representatives to ensure continued funding. At first, philanthropic and federal assistance appeared to solve their problems. In addition to GEB support, the Smith-Lever Act of 1914 provided federal matching funds to any state or county with farm and home demonstration agents, and the USDA greatly increased funding for home economics services during World War I. However, the withdrawal of federal funds after the war and the agricultural depression of the 1920s led state legislators to tighten the purse strings once again. In 1921 they failed to appropriate the necessary funds for Smith-Lever programs, resulting in the loss of a large portion of federal money available for extension services. Every year thereafter, the GFWC urged its members to engage in lobbying efforts to prevent this from happening again. The chair of the Home Demonstration Work Committee, urging women to make extension funding an issue at the polls, asked for "the cooperation of every club woman in creating a sentiment in favor of this appropriation . . . by the next election day."[9]

In the eyes of many female reformers, politicians' reluctance to fund home extension services was symptomatic of a larger problem—men's lack of appreciation for the value of women's work in the home and on the farm. Club women believed that male reluctance to share private and public resources showed a deliberate disregard for the importance of women's role as producers of future citizens and their position as partners on family farms. Some of the state Federation's most prominent leaders were farmers and farm women who were determined to remedy the neglect of rural women. One such club woman was Lulu M. Farmer, a widowed farmer and Country Life reformer who had managed the Georgia populist newspaper the *Daily Press* in her youth. Speaking as chair of the GFWC committee on home demonstration

letins and Reports, State College of Agriculture, 1908–1912, Andrew M. Soule Collection (hereafter AMS), University Archives, University of Georgia, box 6.

9. Mrs. Ira E. Farmer, A Home Demonstration Agent in Every County Committee report, *GFWC Yearbook, 1921–1922* (Atlanta: GFWC, 1922), 116–117, and *GFWC Yearbook, 1922–1923* (Atlanta: GFWC, 1923), 124–125; quote from Mrs. Ira E. Farmer, Home Demonstration Work Committee report, *GFWC Yearbook, 1923–1924* (Atlanta: GFWC, 1924), 119; Resolution Number 8, passed by the Biennial Council of the GFWC, Atlanta, May 11, 1923, LRM, box 1, folder 1.

work, she argued that "if the farmer is the backbone of America, as we hear every election year, the farm women are the ribs and the farm home is the great heart of it and without them we can have no national life." Since the "farm and the farm home are one and inseparable," Farmer concluded, any campaign for rural development had to take into consideration the needs of farm women and children. Other reformers, such as Rebecca Latimer Felton, held farm men accountable for the neglect of home and family. More than a decade before the emergence of extension services, Felton argued that the economic problems of overproduction and low cotton prices could be solved and poor living standards raised if only farmers would acknowledge the value of domestic life by dedicating more resources to production for home use.[10]

Women's interrelated complaints regarding male heads of household and male-dominated institutions are indicative of their belief that the gender hierarchy in rural households was itself in need of reform. At the national level, reformers identified male abuse of authority as a central reason for women's discontent with rural life. When Theodore Roosevelt's Country Life Commission conducted a survey of farm households in 1908, many farm women complained that their husbands assumed control of household income and used it to finance improvements in the fields and barn, ignoring such basic needs as running water that could lighten the workload in the home. Progressive men and women interpreted their remarks as evidence that the values of the marketplace had invaded the rural home and degraded the status of farm wives. The cash economy had devalued their subsistence work, yet they had no separate sphere to highlight the intangible value of contributions in the home. Female reformers hoped that instruction in domestic science might address this problem. The introduction of more efficient and scientific methods of work could remove the heaviest burdens of labor from the home

10. "Speakers Urge Women to Work with Campaign," clipping from *Americus Times,* March 3, 1917, Agricultural Rallies Scrapbook, 79, Nellie Peters Black Papers (hereafter NPB), box 11, Hargrett Rare Books and Manuscript Collection, Special Collections, University of Georgia Libraries, Athens; Mrs. Harper Tucker, "A Farm Woman's Creed," LRM, box 1, folder 5; resolution in support of the Fess Bill for amendment of the Vocational Education Act to increase appropriations for the teaching of Home Economics, *GFWC Yearbook, 1920–1921* (Atlanta: GFWC, 1921), 21; Lulu M. (Mrs. Ira) Farmer, "The Woman and the Home in Rural Development," *Georgia Magazine* 2 (September 1926): 12; *Atlanta Constitution,* January 5, 1895; LeeAnn Whites, "Rebecca Latimer Felton and the Wife's Farm: The Class and Racial Politics of Gender Reform," *Georgia Historical Quarterly* 76 (Summer 1992): 354–372.

and thereby facilitate the transformation of farm woman into housewife. Urban women presumed that this process would benefit rural women as it had them, by encouraging companionate marriage and public recognition of female moral authority in home and community.[11]

Georgia's female reformers were concerned with more than just remaking farm women in their own image. Nellie Peters Black was one Federation leader whose experiences in farming led her to challenge the sexual division of labor in other ways. Black had been greatly influenced by her childhood summers on the family farm in Gordon County, where her father, Richard Peters, experimented with new crops and techniques. His success at introducing new breeds of livestock and imported varieties of peach trees led a correspondent with the *Southern Cultivator* to argue that he deserved the "thanks of all the South for his demonstration that we can make a living without cotton." After Peters's death in 1889, Black (whose husband had died three years earlier) agreed with her siblings' proposal to hire two men to manage the farming enterprise. When it began to operate at a loss, however, she decided that she could do better on her own. Black continued in her father's tradition of innovation when she assumed control of the farm in 1897, but she found that despite her enthusiastic and intelligent approach to farming, she was not taken seriously because she was a woman. After tiring of the constant need to explain and justify her vocation, she began presenting herself as a man on paper, signing all of her farm correspondence "N. P. Black, manager." This experience provoked her to think about the implications of the sexual division of labor for rural women, and she later used the rural uplift campaign as a public platform through which to address the issue.[12]

Black's public involvement in agricultural reform began with a letter to an Atlanta newspaper in November of 1914, in which she complained of the lack

11. Rachel Ann Rosenfeld, *Farm Women: Work, Farm, and Family in the United States* (Chapel Hill: University of North Carolina Press, 1985); Jane Knowles, "'It's Our Turn Now': Rural American Women Speak Out, 1900–1920," in *Women and Farming: Changing Roles, Changing Structures,* ed. Wava G. Haney and Jane B. Knowles (Boulder, CO: Westview Press, 1988), 303–318.

12. "Nellie Peters Black, 1851–1919," NPB, box 1, folder 1, clippings; handwritten account by Nellie Peters Black, Agricultural Rallies Scrapbook; letter to editor, *Southern Cultivator,* October 1856; and "Life of Richard Peters, City's Great Pioneer," *Atlanta Journal,* July 18, 1919, Nellie Peters Black Scrapbook, NPB, box 1, folder 1, clippings.

of markets for locally grown feed and food crops. She claimed that local deal-
ers refused to buy her "perfectly good" oats and baled hay because they preferred "western oats" and "western hay." Friends advised her to market fruits,
vegetables, and dairy products, but she discovered that these products could
not fetch a fair price anywhere in the state outside of Atlanta. She even had
difficulties getting livestock to market. The law prevented her from shipping
dressed hogs until a government official inspected them, but the only inspec-
tor lived in Atlanta and could not make regular trips to her farm in northwest
Georgia. Black asserted that it was useless to preach to farmers about the need
for diversification when they had no assurance of acceptable prices or available markets and the state could not provide adequate support services. Such
complaints had been voiced in the press for years, but the lively tone of Black's
letter and the novelty of public debate with a woman farmer helped to spark
a flood of responses from farmers and reformers across the state. Not all letter writers agreed about whom to blame for agricultural woes or the first steps
that should be taken to remedy them, but they concurred with Black that
something needed to be done.[13]

Nellie Peters Black's participation in this ongoing debate in the press
brought her to the attention of male agricultural reformers and led to the formation of a partnership between club women, agriculturalists, and businessmen. In December of 1914 the secretary of the College of Agriculture Extension Department invited Black to speak at a joint conference of the Georgia
Breeders Association, the Georgia Live Stock and Dairy Association, and the
State Horticultural Society. In her address, "The Producer's View of the
Marketing of Georgia Grown Farm Crops," Black argued that farmers needed
to work toward diversification for both subsistence means and market sales,
so that they would have a two-edged buffer against poor cotton prices. After
suggesting that the College of Agriculture provide farmers with more instruction on the marketing of products, Black capped her speech with a proposal for a series of rallies to be held in each congressional district during the
winter and spring. Soon after the conference, she met with the state's top
agricultural officials to discuss how the rallies might be organized and con-

13. Nellie Peters Black, letter to the editor, *Atlanta Constitution,* November 29, 1914; *Atlanta Constitution,* December 2, 16, 1914; *Madison Madisonian,* December 11, 1914; *Macon Daily
Telegraph,* December 18, 1914, all clippings from Agricultural Rallies Scrapbook, NPB.

ducted. The final plans made provisions for Georgia Federation club women to share the platform with representatives from the state Department of Agriculture, the Georgia College of Agriculture, the experiment station, and the Georgia State Fair. The GFWC was the lone women's organization among the ten associations that participated in determining the content of the public meetings.[14]

The agricultural rallies held from 1915 through 1917 brought considerable publicity to the campaign for rural uplift and provided Black with an opportunity to address rural men on the place of women in agriculture. The rallies attracted hundreds of men, women, and children to meetings in schools and courthouses, where speakers addressed them on topics such as farming methods, crop diversification, civic improvement, public health, poultry raising, and cooperation between rural and urban schools. Black's speeches tended to combine instructional talks on practical farming methods and crop diversification with appeals to rural men on the importance of treating their wives as equal partners. Farm men needed to allow their wives to invest money in gardening and poultry raising, she argued, instead of monopolizing household resources for cotton production. Furthermore, they should share resources with children by allowing them to keep the profits realized from agricultural clubs. Black also announced that club women "feel that agriculture as a study and as an occupation for women is most desirable," and she made a point of including examples of successful women farmers in her speeches on diversification. At a rally in Newnan, she pointed to a woman who "had raised twenty pounds of Irish potatoes from three potatoes she had planted, and forty gallons of sorghum syrup from 25 cents worth of seed," and announced to the audience, "This shows what women can do."[15]

---

14. Nita Black Rucker, "History of Agricultural Rallies Told by Mrs. Rucker," *Atlanta Constitution*, September 20, 1925; Guy W. Firor to Nellie Peters Black, December 15, 1914, Agricultural Rallies Scrapbook, NPB; "Georgia's Farm Problem Stated in Nutshell by Mrs. Nellie Peters Black," Agricultural Rallies Scrapbook, NPB, clipping.

15. *Rome Tribune Herald,* February 27, 1915; *Macon Daily Telegraph,* March 24, 1917; first quote from Black, letter to the editor, *Valdosta Times,* March 17, 1915; second and third quotes from *Atlanta Constitution,* March 7, 1915; all clippings from the Agricultural Rallies Scrapbook, NPB. Also see Isma Dooly, "Current Events from a Woman's Point of View," *Atlanta Constitution,* November 12, 1916, NPB Scrapbook, clipping.

Club women's cooperation with male reformers in the agricultural rallies was an anomaly in the campaign for rural uplift, since the economic foundations of male political culture and the gender hierarchy of agricultural institutions constricted their ability to make common cause. Because Nellie Peters Black was a farm manager whose initial public activism centered on business concerns, she was able to form an alliance with groups of men who were interested in promoting rural economic development. Just as the male educational reformers sought women's assistance in the rural school improvement campaign, agricultural experts valued the Federation's network of club women and their connections to community leaders who could be called upon for help. When it came to the gender concerns of female activists, however, agricultural experts were less interested in cooperation. The Georgia College of Agriculture paid lip service to the needs of farm home and family while institutionalizing a gender hierarchy of knowledge that benefited male agricultural experts at the expense of female home economists. Ironically, the same male control of financial resources and technology that subordinated women in the farm home was replicated in state institutions and other agricultural agencies.

Home economics professionals in the Georgia College of Agriculture and Georgia Federation members became inseparable allies in rural reform because they faced common obstacles in their efforts to improve the status of women. Domestic science had a difficult start in the state, and as in so many other branches of educational reform, the reasons were at least partially rooted in the antebellum social structure. Much of the opposition was similar to that faced by professionals throughout the nation—critics charged that homemaking was a personal matter better learned in the home and that formal instruction in domestic science was either a frivolous waste of time or an attempt to turn rural and working-class girls into servants. Leaders in the national movement countered with the argument that the social importance of the home necessitated making the domestic arts a learned profession like any other, which they hoped would prevent the deterioration of women's status as productive functions left the home. However, in the South there was little cultural basis for an ideal of white womanhood defined by domestic productivity. Domestic work was definitively black, and in the New South many advocates of home economics did indeed intend for it to be an inferior education that merely reproduced a black servant class. This link hindered white women's ability to use recognition of the value of their own domestic work as a lever to force white men to share resources.[16]

In Georgia these obstacles fused the campaign for expansion of women's extension services to the larger struggle for gender equality in higher education. The career of Mary E. Creswell, the most prominent domestic science professional in the state, shows the parallel nature of these movements. Creswell, who was born in Pennsylvania but moved to Georgia as a small child, graduated with first honors from one of the multitude of small private schools in the state. She then attended the Georgia State Normal School under the tutelage of Celeste Parrish. Like Parrish, Creswell had difficulty completing her baccalaureate degree because of the state's limited opportunities for women. She attended summer schools at the University of Chicago and was one of a handful of female students who sidestepped the University of Georgia's exclusion of women by arranging to be privately instructed by a sympathetic professor. In 1911 Creswell became the first female member of the College of Agriculture faculty when she was hired to supervise extension services for women and girls. At that time the state had no four-year degree program to train her workers, who had to settle for course work at one of the two-year institutions open to women. It was not until 1918 that the College of Agriculture, in response to the wartime need for professionals trained in food conservation and preservation, created a home economics department with a course of study leading to the bachelor of science degree. Creswell headed that department and the following year received the college's first B.S. in home economics.[17]

16. Although they were addressing class more than race, Catharine E. Beecher and Harriet Beecher Stowe pointedly remarked that "manual labor has been made dishonorable and unrefined by being forced on the ignorant and the poor," so that "especially has the most important of all hand-labor, that which sustains the family, been thus disgraced." *The American Woman's Home: Principles of Domestic Science* (New York: J. B. Ford, 1869; repr., New York: Arno Press, 1971), 21 (citation is to 1971 edition); Epsie Campbell, "Eight Years of Vocational Home Economics in Georgia," Mary E. Creswell Papers (hereafter MEC), box 1, folder 4, University Archives, University of Georgia, Athens; Jane Bernard Powers, *The "Girl Question" in Education: Vocational Education for Young Women in the Progressive Era* (Washington, DC: Falmer Press, 1992), 13–21, 87–92; Hagler, "The Ideal Woman in the Antebellum South."

17. Mary E. Creswell résumé, MEC, box 1, folder 1; Rose Harrold dedication to Mary E. Creswell, *Georgia Agriculturalist* 9 (October 1930): 3; *Athens Banner-Herald,* clipping on Cres-

It was no coincidence that the first baccalaureate awarded to a woman by a college on the University of Georgia campus was in home economics, because both club women and educators used home demonstration work to push for greater access to higher education. Both groups believed that a central purpose of the extension service canning clubs was to increase educational opportunity among rural girls and women. For extension workers this goal served several purposes. Creating a desire among rural girls for an agricultural education added momentum to the movement to admit women to the College of Agriculture, providing pressure from below while club women and home economics professionals exerted pressure from above. In turn, home economics experts were generating demand for their own services, thus improving employment opportunities and increasing the need to create a formal degree program to train home demonstration workers. In this way canning clubs proved to be the linchpin in the effort to break down the "chivalrous attitude" that was keeping women out of the College of Agriculture and the University of Georgia. Official recognition of the economic value of domesticity further benefited club women as mothers and as reformers by more firmly establishing their own expertise in the field as justification for their social activism.[18]

The emphasis on production and income in southern women's extension work fitted well with Georgia women's concern for increased educational opportunities. The girls' clubs, the first effort at demonstration work with women, were firmly centered on the production, processing, and marketing

---

well retirement, ca. 1945, Mary E. Creswell folder, Georgia Biography Vertical File, Special Collections, University of Georgia Libraries, Athens; Report of the President of the Board of Trustees, Georgia State College of Agriculture, June 14, 1918, from *Reports, Board of Trustees, College of Agriculture, 1917–1918,* 4:6–7, AMS, box 4. Creswell was able to get her informal study with a University of Georgia professor accepted for course credit at the University of Chicago. Thomas G. Dyer, *The University of Georgia: A Bicentennial History, 1785–1985* (Athens: University of Georgia Press, 1985), 172.

18. Form letter to "Georgia Club Girls Who Are Completing the 4-Year Program of Work" from the "State Girls' Club Agent," LRM, box 1, folder 1; "Women in the College of Agriculture," ca. 1918, MEC, box 1, folder 5, clipping; address of Lucy Lester Willet, GFWC president, at the Conference for Women held at the annual Farmers' Institute at the College of Agriculture in Athens, Georgia, January 1910, from *Bulletins and Reports,* AMS; "Women of Carroll County Form Council to Revolutionize Rural Life of Section," March 23, 1924, LRM, box 1, folder 6, clipping.

of food items. The clubs therefore naturally emphasized scientific agriculture and formal knowledge and instruction. In the first year of participation, girls had one-tenth-acre plots of tomatoes and in successive years were allowed to expand to three vegetables and to perennial fruits; by their fourth year of club work, girls could choose some specialty crop grown specifically for the market. In their third year, canning club members could join a poultry club as well. At the urging of Mary Creswell, demonstration workers and their local supporters established club contests shortly after the program was launched. In 1912 Creswell supervised the creation of a girls' short course in agriculture and domestic science at the College of Agriculture, and she instructed club workers to offer scholarships to the course as contest prizes. "The value of short courses for farmers has been so clearly demonstrated," she announced, "that no lengthy explanation should be needed to convince those interested in educational progress of the value of a similar course for girls and women." The GFWC provided invaluable assistance in this project, as women's organizations across the state began sponsoring local girls' clubs and made raising the funds for their scholarships a top priority.[19]

Home extension workers and club women further used girls' clubs as a tool for promoting women's education by having club members start "Go-to-College funds" with the proceeds from sales of poultry, produce, and canned goods. A bank account was set up for each individual girl for the purpose of funding her high school and college education. In 1919 the Home Demonstration report for the Extension Division showed that there were almost 100 girls attending college on scholarships awarded for club work, and an additional 95 girls were paying for most or all of their school expenses with money earned through club work. Four years later, Lois Dowdle, state agent of girls' clubs, claimed that 760 girls had established Go-to-College funds and that 656 girls were in high school and 146 in college as a result of their club work. Both black and white girls participated in the educational funds, although there is no racial breakdown available for these figures. As the agricultural clubs evolved into 4-H Clubs in the 1920s, they retained the emphasis on encouraging female education. In 1924 one black club member wrote

19. Quote from Mary E. Creswell, "The Organization of Girls' Clubs," *Bulletin* of the University of Georgia, vol. 12, no. 5 (January 1912), from *Bulletins and Reports,* AMS; Mary E. Creswell, "Georgia Now Has 28 Canning Clubs," *Atlanta Constitution,* Women's Edition, June 4, 1913; Mary E. Creswell, "Home Economics Extension," LRM, box 1, folder 8.

to an Extension Division professor that she had "sold enough eggs and fryers to get a part of my school clothes for going to college," and she hoped that the sale of her 265 cans of tomatoes would "pay at least two months' board." Club sponsors continued to hold contests for the express purpose of "provid[ing] means of establishing and increasing 'Go-to-College' funds."[20]

Since educational institutions in Georgia had little financial aid available for female students, the loans and scholarships offered by women's organizations had the potential to make a tremendous difference in the lives of rural women. No doubt one applicant to the GFWC Student Aid Foundation spoke to the fears, if not the reality, facing women needing assistance to attend college when she said, "If I cannot get this money from you, I shall have to hoe cotton all my life." Better-off students were no less thankful for loans that freed them from dependency on male relatives. Katherine Lanier, who became Extension Service district agent in Savannah after completing her bachelor's degree, credited the Student Aid Foundation with helping her through a critical time in her life. The death of her father left Lanier and her mother and sister heavily reliant upon monthly payments from her brother, who chafed under the responsibility. He had his own family to maintain and criticized Katherine for furthering her education rather than staying home to help provide for her mother. Lanier later claimed that without the Federation's support and assistance during this time of difficulty she would have "fallen by the wayside." In other instances, helping the daughter also meant helping the entire family. Lucy Wood Floyd, the first 4-H Club member to enter the home economics degree program, used Federation aid to earn her bachelor of science degree. She then became a home demonstration agent, repaid her loans, and helped her family to purchase a farm and stock. In addition, she helped a sister through college who also went into home demonstration work.[21]

20. Georgia State College of Agriculture (hereafter GSCA), Extension Division, *Annual Report of Extension Service, 1920–1921*, vol. 10, no. 4, bulletin 243 (July 1921): 28; *Homecon Tattler*, Georgia State College of Agriculture, May 1925, LRM, box 1, folder 2; first quote from GSCA, *Service Bulletin: A Monthly Statement of Negro Extension Work*, November 1924, 4; second quote from description of girls' 4-H Club garden contest, LRM, box 1, folder 5.

21. First quote from Report of the Student Aid Foundation, *GFWC Yearbook, 1916–1917* (Atlanta: GFWC, 1917), 41–43; Leila Mize, "Influence of Home Demonstration Work on the Lives of 4-H Club Girls" (1928), LRM, box 1, folder 9; second quote from Emily Harrison, *In Memoriam: Frances Liggett Wey, July 22, 1851–November 20, 1928* (Atlanta: Georgia Federation of

Girls' agricultural clubs met the objectives of demonstration workers and club women: they proved to be an avenue for female higher education and economic independence while also providing a source of professionally trained workers for rural Georgia. All six of the assistant agents hired from the 1929 graduating class of the College of Agriculture were former 4-H Club girls, and the director of home demonstration work asserted that "our group of 4-H Club girls in college grows larger each year and is furnishing an important group from which to draw new workers." A survey of women graduates from the College of Agriculture between 1920 and 1925 reveals that approximately 40 percent were employed as extension workers, while about 60 percent were engaged in teaching home economics at the high school and college levels. In all, 85 percent were working in Georgia. Just as the club women who provided scholarships had hoped, after receiving an education many women returned to their communities as home economics teachers and demonstration agents. The graduates often said their gratitude for the help received from county agents, teachers, and club women motivated them to give something back to their communities.[22]

Even though most graduates remained in the state, the development of home economics departments and home extension services across the South meant that Georgia women also could use their training as a stepping stone to further personal ambitions. Despite the limitations of the separate spheres philosophy that shaped the structure of agricultural education and extension services, a home economics education afforded many women an occupational and geographical mobility that they otherwise would not have had. At the time of the College of Agriculture alumni survey in 1925, 10 percent of the graduates surveyed were teaching home economics in a southern state other than Georgia, all but one at the college level. It is likely that some women found their rural communities too restrictive and provincial when they returned from college, while others valued professional advancement and chose to pursue opportunity wherever it took them. According to the survey, Edith Robertson of Dalton, Georgia, had served as home demonstration agent in

Women's Clubs, c. 1929), 42–43; family correspondence, Katherine Lanier Clarke Papers, box 8, folder 1, Hargrett Rare Book and Manuscript Collection.

22. Alumni survey from *Homecon Tattler;* GSCA, Extension Division, *Georgia Extension Service Report, 1929,* vol. 18, bulletin 393 (January 1930): 21–22.

Georgia for one year, then headed the Home Economics Department of Greensboro High School in North Carolina for a year, and was currently serving in her third year as home demonstration agent in South Carolina with plans to pursue graduate study at Columbia University in the summer. One of Robertson's fellow graduates from the class of 1920, Ora Hart Avery, was state supervisor of home economics in Virginia and supervised sixty-seven schools, three teacher-training institutions, and evening schools in five cities with an enrollment of twenty-five hundred.[23]

While both black and white women used extension work to promote female education and community improvement, the two groups did not have equal access to the system of state services. White club women often attempted to gain recognition for the importance of domestic labor by presenting the family as the basic building block of the community and emphasizing the need for educated and healthy women to raise future citizens. They were, in effect, calling upon a gendered concept of citizenship that justified access to state resources. They had at least some grounds on which to make this appeal, given their race and class ties to the white men who controlled Georgia politics. African American women faced a much more difficult task in attempting to use their domestic importance as a basis of public authority. The black domestic labor with which whites were most concerned was that performed for white families, and white employers' determination to maintain the upper hand in relations with black servants precluded public recognition of its value. This denial of independent black womanhood reflected the continuation of the bitter contest for control of black family labor that took place during Reconstruction, when African Americans claimed the work of their women and children for their own homes and fields. In rural Georgia, the dispute involved black farming families' attempts to claim resources—white land and black labor—for their own improved standard of living and upward mobility. It was not just about the transferal of wealth, but also about the overthrow of a social hierarchy that underpinned the production of wealth.[24]

23. Alumni survey from *Homecon Tattler*.

24. Leila R. Mize, "The Woman of Power," LRM, box 1, folder 1; Mrs. Harper Tucker, "The Home Demonstration Council, Its Opportunities and Achievements," LRM, box 1, folder 2; Brooks, "The Agrarian Revolution in Georgia," 19–53; Charles L. Flynn Jr., *White Land, Black*

The numerous arguments advocating black household dependency that continued to float about postbellum Georgia acted to thwart effective rural reform by obscuring the extent to which the issues at hand were about class as well as race. The attempts of rural elites to assert control over black labor dealt a considerable blow to the independence of white households as well as black. After emancipation, planters succeeded in pushing through a series of laws designed to redefine property rights as based in land rather than labor, which intentionally cut freed people off from sources of subsistence support. These statutes prohibited squatting, hunting on Sunday, gathering fuel or foodstuffs from land without the owner's permission, and similar activities that had the potential to increase the independence of poor families. This trend continued after Reconstruction, as Democrats who regained control of state government in 1872 passed additional laws eliminating open range and public access to private lands for hunting and fishing. All of these measures threatened the economic independence of poor-to-middling whites, who already faced worsening conditions from increased population pressure on the land, greater economic competition from cheap manufactured goods, and growing indebtedness. White and black farmers persistently fought tenure arrangements that limited their autonomy, but this did not necessarily protect their families from a heavy burden of labor and ever-shrinking sources of support. Black and white women's parallel campaigns to improve the rural home reflect the class- as well as gender-based nature of the problems facing farm women and children.[25]

The reaction to the rise in independent tenure arrangements in Georgia is

---

Labor: Caste and Class in Late Nineteenth-Century Georgia (Baton Rouge: Louisiana State University Press, 1983), 58–63. Other works that include a discussion of the contest over black family labor and to varying extents address the related assignment of different gender roles to blacks include Foner, *Reconstruction;* Jacqueline Jones, *Labor of Love, Labor of Sorrow: Black Women, Work, and the Family, from Slavery to the Present* (New York: Vintage Books, 1985); and Leon L. Litwack, *Been in the Storm So Long: The Aftermath of Slavery* (New York: Vintage Books, 1979). Tera W. Hunter provides a thorough and insightful account of the white struggle for control of black domestic labor in Atlanta in *To 'Joy My Freedom: Southern Black Women's Lives and Labors after the Civil War* (Cambridge, MA: Harvard University Press, 1997).

25. Flynn, *White Land, Black Labor,* 122–125, 136–144; Joseph P. Reidy, *From Slavery to Agrarian Capitalism in the Cotton Plantation South: Central Georgia, 1800–1880* (Chapel Hill: University of North Carolina Press, 1992), 215–17, 221–22.

particularly revealing of how race was used to obscure the class origins of the attack on household independence. Landlords benefited from perpetuating the dependency of their white and black tenants, because successful tenant farmers would buy land and remove their labor to their own farms. Property owners who had direct oversight over tenants and croppers were better able to manipulate changing circumstances so as to maximize profit to themselves and prevent the loss of their labor. They actually preferred using sharecropping and share tenancy for this reason, even though cash tenancy removed much of the element of risk from the landowner through rents that were fixed and not tied to crop prices. As cash tenancy increasingly became the tenure arrangement of choice for white and black Georgians, rising from 13.4 to 28.2 percent of all farms between 1880 and 1910, landlords cast about for a way to slow the trend. The only way they could openly attack independent farm households and maintain the appearance of white solidarity was to present the issue as one of black inferiority. Not surprisingly, several studies conducted in Georgia between about 1910 and 1923 purported to show that black sharecroppers made a higher per acre profit than independent black tenants, farming more efficiently when landowners directed all phases of the work and provided all equipment—the most dependent arrangement possible.[26]

In spite of, or rather because of, the commonalties of black and white tenure arrangements, analysts of Georgia's agricultural problems persisted in portraying the issues in terms of a natural black dependency. A study of black farmers in four north central counties in the early 1920s specifically addressed the issue of family labor and claimed that independent black households were characterized by a particular inefficiency. The author, Donald Dewey Scarborough, noted that the labor of women and children was widely used in the "light labor" on farms of black landowners. He found that, in comparison to their white counterparts, black owners input more than four times as much

26. U.S. Bureau of the Census, *Thirteenth Census of the U.S. Taken in the Year 1910: Abstracts of the Census, Statistics of Population, Agriculture, Manufactures, and Mining for the United States, the States, and Principal Cities, with Supplement for Georgia Containing Statistics for the State, Counties, Cities, and Other Divisions* (Washington, DC: Government Printing Office, 1913), 644; Brooks, "The Agrarian Revolution in Georgia," 63–65; Donald Dewey Scarborough, "An Economic Study of Negro Farmers as Owners, Tenants, and Croppers" (master's thesis, University of Georgia, 1923), 13–16.

value from family labor but realized only 57 percent of the income. Scarborough used these figures as proof for his assertion that the independent labor of black women and children should be eradicated, yet in pointing to lower income among black farm families he failed to see as relevant his own findings that they usually had inferior soil, livestock, and implements with which to work. He stated that one of the purposes of his study was to determine "whether in general it is well for all interests for him [the black farmer] to have complete control of the factors of production with which he works." Implicit in the study's conclusions was the assumption that black farm families' inefficiency justified replacing their labor for themselves with labor for whites. This represented not only an attack on the black family as an autonomous unit, but also an attack on independent households that used family labor as a strategy for advancement.[27]

The more racially progressive white educators in Georgia sometimes were willing to acknowledge the class politics of rising tenancy rates, but the power of Democratic landowners and the racist origins of the extension program itself limited their ability to use agricultural extension work to attack the problem. Early attempts at extension work were limited mostly to farm owners, because landlords opposed interference with their tenants that might lead to decreased profits. In the words of one Georgia educator concerned with rural reform, extension workers "could only reach the plantation tenant by permission of the landlord and most of these were unsympathetic with diversification and production for home use." Georgia senator and former governor Hoke Smith, coauthor of the Smith-Lever Act of 1914, which officially established federally funded cooperative extension services at state land-grant colleges, made it quite clear in his promotion of the bill that it was intended to benefit primarily white farmers. Furthermore, he successfully defeated an attempt to amend the bill so that black land-grant colleges would be ensured an equitable share of funding and the right to administer their funds independently. Since black farmers made up almost 40 percent of all farmers in Georgia, restricting the resources available for their assistance effectively limited the ability of extension services to advance the interests of farmers as a class.[28]

27. Scarborough, "An Economic Study of Negro Farmers," quotes 17–18, 8.

28. Thomas J. Woofter Jr., *Southern Race Progress: The Wavering Color Line* (Washington, DC: Public Affairs Press, 1957), 50; *Farm Demonstration Work: Speeches of Hon. Hoke Smith of*

When gender is added to the mix, it is clear that the interlacing of race and class politics in rural reform had negative implications for both black and white women. Black motherhood remained almost invisible in rural extension work, as officials who allocated state and federal funds treated the black household as a nonentity. To have recognized black and white mothers as standing on common ground would have been to humanize (or "deracialize") the issues at hand, bringing into sharper relief the evidence that suggested rural problems were less about the moral and intellectual inferiority of a race than they were about a system of land tenure that exploited black and white farmers alike. Instead, the refusal of state agencies and officials to recognize the common needs of motherhood worked to obscure what could have been a powerful basis for biracial alliance among club women and demonstration workers. White women benefited from the denial of black womanhood to some extent, since most of the federal funds allocated to women's work were reserved for them and brought greatly increased educational and career opportunities. Nonetheless, they also lost the opportunity to form a unified front with black women in support of a fair division of resources between field and home; race (and the class politics of race) worked to obscure the gender interests they had in common. White women were able to win some recognition of the importance of domestic needs in programs for rural improvement, but racialized, constricted notions of motherhood contributed to officials' ability to continue to marginalize extension services for women and children.

The invisibility of the black household was due in part to the structure of extension services, in which work with black women and children began as little more than an afterthought. Services targeting black women were extremely understaffed, reflecting the double burden they faced as citizens who lacked both race and gender privilege. Despite the relentless lobbying of club women and home economists, state funding had always favored men. When

Georgia in the Senate of the United States (Washington, DC: Government Printing Office, 1914), 13–15; R. Grant Seals notes that the debate over the Smith-Lever Act was the first time that Congress openly acknowledged discrimination in regard to black land-grant colleges, although the outcome of the debate was merely the continuance of discriminatory policies begun under the Hatch Act. "The Formation of Agricultural and Rural Development Policy with Emphasis on African-Americans: II. The Hatch-George and Smith-Lever Acts," *Agricultural History* 65, No. 2 (1991): 12–34.

the United States entered World War I in the spring of 1917, the extension division employed 148 white male agents and 68 white female agents. State officials authorized the hiring of an additional 48 white women, but only after receiving increased federal funding for work in food conservation and preservation. The black extension workforce, however, remained constant and its services continued to focus almost exclusively on work with men. Before 1920 there were never more than two black home demonstration agents employed by the Extension Division for the entire state of Georgia, while there were about fifteen black male county agents. The reports filed by the head of black extension work reflected the understanding that women's work was to be subordinated to the work with male farmers. Reports for 1918 and 1919 described the county farmers' club as the "agricultural center" of communities, while the clubs for women and children were labeled "auxiliaries" or "branches of the farmers' clubs." Although the disparity in funding and staffing between the work for black men and the work for black women gradually disappeared during the 1920s, in that decade white home demonstration agents consistently outnumbered black female employees by more than four to one.[29]

Within the division of home economics more generally, treatment of black home demonstration agents showed that they were not considered the equals of white agents either as women or as professionals. A particularly blatant example is contained in extension records, which almost invariably neglected to include "Miss" and "Mrs." before the names of black agents, whereas all white women were accorded such titles of respect. Even the official reports of the Extension Division usually omitted "Mrs." when referring to married black women. This deliberate symbol of subordination was compounded by the structural subordination of black women to their white co-workers. Black women agents had to report to the white women working in their counties, and the language of Extension Division reports makes it clear that this was not a conference of equals. The 1923 report explained it in this way: "In each county the Negro *worker* reports weekly to the white *home demonstration*

29. GSCA, Extension Division. *Annual Report of Extension Service, 1917–1918*, vol. 7, no. 3, bulletin 157 (July 1918); GSCA, Extension Division. *Annual Report of Extension Service, 1918–1919*, vol. 8, no. 6, bulletin 184 (July 1919); GSCA, *Annual Report of Extension Service, 1919–1920*, vol. 9, no. 2, bulletin 216 (July 1920).

agents for instructions. The latter are thus able to help place proper empha-sis upon the most important aspects of work." Such terminology constructed a barrier between white and black women, branding black womanhood as an inferior form of domesticity that did not warrant public recognition or respect.[30]

Ultimately, it was the migration of black Georgians to other states that created a more favorable climate for the recognition of black family needs. The alarm was raised initially at the end of World War I, when somewhere be-tween thirty-five thousand and fifty thousand black Georgians left the state. Among all the southern states, only Mississippi and Alabama suffered greater losses. Whites were especially concerned about the loss of domestic servants and field laborers and widely debated the extent to which blacks were leaving in search of better social conditions (less racial discrimination in education, transportation, and housing) or in search of economic opportunity (greater occupational choice and better pay). Newspaper editors and state officials publicly lamented the poor treatment of blacks, the legislature threw a few more dollars at black rural education, and observers claimed a new spirit of racial goodwill, as in the case of an Albany farmer who "laid aside his whip and gun, with which it is reported he has been accustomed to drive his hands, and begged for laborers." However, these gestures were not enough to pre-vent another flood of migration in the 1920s. The postwar economy went into a slump, as cotton prices could not recover their wartime high and overpro-duction resulted in steadily declining profits. Georgia lost an additional 35 percent of its black farmers between 1920 and 1925, the largest decrease of any southern state.[31]

30. Employment record of home demonstration agents for 1924–1925, LRM, box 1, folder 1; also see list of agents in each annual report of the state Extension Division; quotes from "Work of Negro Agents," in GSCA, Extension Division, *Annual Report, 1918–1919,* 24–25, and GSCA, Extension Division, *Annual Report, 1919–1920,* 68; quote from GSCA, Extension Division, *Annual Report of Extension Service, 1922–23,* vol. 12, no. 6, bulletin 290 (July 1923): 42, emphasis added.

31. Pete Daniel, *Breaking the Land: The Transformation of Cotton, Tobacco, and Rice Cul-tures since 1880* (Urbana: University of Illinois Press, 1985), 18–19; H. A. Hunt, "Negroes Leav-ing the South, and Why," *School and Home* 8 (December 1916): 8–9; Thomas J. Woofter Jr., *Ne-gro Migration: Changes in Rural Organization and Population of the Cotton Belt* (New York: W. D. Gray, 1920); also Woofter, "Migration of Negroes"; W. T. B. Williams, "The Negro Exo-dus from the South," in *Negro Migration in 1916–1917,* 93–113, quote 96.

The rural economic hardships of the 1920s and the initiative of migrating blacks finally forced white southerners to acknowledge that it was they who were dependent upon blacks rather than the other way around, and their dependency necessitated concessions. Local political and educational leaders had to recognize the economic importance to the state of black labor and black land ownership, and in attempting to address African American concerns they had to address the needs of the black family. The loss of black labor also forced white women to take a franker look at their own dependency on black domesticity. One study of black migration claimed that the loss of the "best trained domestic servants" caused "more acute suffering . . . than the loss of the men laborers," resulting in "a real hardship for wives and daughters, from whom have come the loudest complaints against the migration of the Negroes." Urban women who were impacted by this loss not only had to acknowledge the value of black women's domestic work for whites; they also had to admit the costs paid by black families. They had to see black womanhood; it no longer could be invisible.[32]

Beginning in 1920, black club women and racially liberal white female activists were able to use economic and labor concerns to push forward public accountability for the many forms of exploitation that diminished the integrity and independence of black families. That year, members of Atlanta's newly established Commission on Interracial Cooperation (CIC) encouraged urban white women to work cooperatively with black female leadership. The Woman's Missionary Council of the Methodist Episcopal Church, South, responded by creating a commission to study the problems of black families and to develop a strategy for interracial cooperation in addressing them. Carrie Parks Johnson, a Georgia native and a Decatur minister's wife, was both chair of the Methodist commission and the first director of women's work for the CIC. At the request of Lugenia Burns Hope, one of Atlanta's most prominent black club women, Johnson and a group of Methodist women attended the biennial conference of the National Association of Colored Women at Tuskegee Institute in July and subsequently worked with the CIC to organize a regional interracial women's conference. Participants of the conference, which was held in Memphis in October, issued a set of resolutions that were derived from a list of grievances drawn up by black female leaders. White

32. Williams, "The Negro Exodus from the South," 99.

women endorsed improvements in child welfare services and educational and housing standards for blacks and decried lynching and racial discrimination in travel, the courts, and the press. Perhaps most surprisingly, they also accepted "responsibility for the protection of the Negro women and girls in our homes and on the streets."[33]

It would be hard to overemphasize the symbolic importance of women's efforts at interracial cooperation. The Memphis resolutions acknowledged white culpability for destructive influences on black families, including both the labor exploitation and sexual exploitation of black women. White women had to recognize this latter problem as yet another outcome of white male individualism and privilege that was appropriately part of their task of remaking white manhood. Equally importantly, in associating respectable white women with interracial work, reformers such as Carrie Parks Johnson chipped away at the connections between female sexual purity and racial segregation that long had prevented effective cooperation between the two groups. In addition to forging a path for interracial public welfare reforms, the leadership of Johnson and Lugenia Burns Hope also set the stage for the founding of an interracial women's campaign against lynching. Club women were among the minority of Georgians who had the courage to speak out against the rise of the Second Ku Klux Klan, and they continued to provide leadership in the campaign against racial violence after the Klan's decline, through activism in the CIC and the Association of Women for the Prevention of Lynching.[34]

The Memphis conference and female activism in the CIC directly contributed to the development of interracial alliances at the local level by legitimating white women's recognition of the needs of the black household. An examination of the complaints of departing blacks concerning the poor quality of life in rural areas led to the inescapable conclusion that home demon-

33. For the most thorough account of interracial cooperation among Atlanta's black and white organized women, see Jacquelyn Dowd Hall, *Revolt against Chivalry: Jessie Daniel Ames and the Women's Campaign against Lynching* (New York: Columbia University Press, 1974), esp. 80–106; *Southern Women and Race Cooperation: A Story of the Memphis Conference, October 6 and 7, 1920*, Neighborhood Union Collection (hereafter NU), box 10, folder 31, Atlanta University Center Woodruff Library, Archives and Special Collections, booklet.

34. Nancy MacLean, *Behind the Mask of Chivalry: The Making of the Second Ku Klux Klan* (New York: Oxford University Press, 1994), 29–31; "Campaign Is Launched Here against Mob Law in the State," clipping from *Atlanta Constitution*, January 15, 1931, NU, box 10, folder 34.

stration work was especially needed by this group of Georgians. Black farmers had always comprised a majority of the state's sharecroppers, and during the hard times of the early 1920s black cash tenancy practically disappeared. This meant that an ever-increasing number of rural black women and children were suffering the most extreme form of subordination to the market economy, one that deprived families of virtually all subsistence production. Furthermore, black farm households realized shrinking profits from cotton cultivation in the 1920s, not only because of low prices, but also because they planted less acreage owing to the boll weevil infestation. The extension services that the Georgia College of Agriculture offered to men could ameliorate this latter problem, but increased yields only contributed to the problem of overproduction. Women's extension work, with its emphasis on increasing diversified production for the market and for home use, training in nutrition and sanitation, and support for rural education and social services programs, appeared to be exactly what rural blacks needed (and in fact had always needed) to improve their standard of living.[35]

As club women began to assume a leadership role in interracial cooperation, their activism encouraged the development of a more cooperative attitude among local whites. During the 1920s white club women in small towns took unprecedented steps in working with black club women and rural teachers, conducting home demonstrations and contributing domestic science equipment to black schools. White female extension workers had begun making tentative overtures to the black community during World War I, when African Americans' expressed desire to participate in war work motivated white agents to assist them in organizing clubs, demonstrations, and fair exhibits designed to encourage crop diversification and increased subsistence production. As the postwar agricultural depression set in, white extension workers stepped up these activities and worked more closely with the black agents in their region. White home demonstration agents intervened when local officials tried to cut funding for blacks, providing "aid wherever possible in securing contracts" for black agents and "helping to maintain interest on the part of the county officials." In the summer of 1924, Camilla Weems, the

35. Williams, "The Negro Exodus from the South," 98–99; John William Fanning, *Negro Migration*, Phelps-Stokes Fellowship Studies no. 9, *Bulletin of the University of Georgia* 30 (June 1930): 19–28.

black state supervisor for African American home demonstration work, made note of the new cooperative spirit that had emerged among local businessmen. When seven short courses were organized for black children in five counties, white merchants and boards of education responded with generous donations of food and hardware. In Weems's words, "There seemed to have been a feeling of good will and helpfulness," as "the white people as well as the colored people were willing and glad to do what they could to make the short courses what they should be." [36]

Despite the emergence of a more cooperative spirit among many white rural reformers, the work of white and black club women continued to be segregated. The state Federation's main publicity campaign for rural improvement in the 1920s, the "Made in Georgia Week" celebrated in late May, focused primarily on the white community. Begun early in the decade, the purpose of the campaign was to promote the "Live-at-Home" philosophy of local and regional self-sufficiency by encouraging crop diversification. This was one of the Federation's most far-reaching efforts, since it represented the "pooling of resources" of a variety of organizations, including the Parent-Teacher Association, the Georgia College of Agriculture, the State Manufacturing Association, and the Georgia Association (a commercial interests group). Two women from the state Extension Division—Mary Creswell, director of home economics, and Lois Dowdell, director of canning clubs—sat on the Federation's campaign advisory committee. As part of the celebration, white women's clubs across the state held "made in Georgia dinners" and sponsored displays of manufactured goods, agricultural exhibits, curb market exhibits, canning club exhibits, baby shows, flower shows, and the wearing of

36. First two quotes from GSCA, Extension Division, *Georgia Extension Service Report, 1928,* vol. 17, bulletin 375 (January 1929): 28. Also see district reports in GFWC yearbooks and home demonstration reports in the Georgia State College of Agriculture annual reports of extension service and Georgia extension service reports for 1914–1930; Weems quote from "Report of Negro Home Demonstration Work," in GSCA, Extension Division, *Service Bulletin: A Monthly Statement of Negro Extension Work,* July 1924, 3; see also the *Monthly Statement* for August and October 1924 and for March 1925. In a typical fashion, many whites who commented on improved race relations in areas of the state that had suffered great losses in the black population attributed the change in attitude to the fact that whites felt less threatened than before by the presence of blacks; such comments did not acknowledge white dependency on black labor or the simple fact that a black body on a farm was far better than no body at all.

Georgia-made clothing. Club women used these events to raise public awareness of the many items that could be produced and purchased locally and that
more often than not were imported from outside the South. Although black
farm families had the "live at home" philosophy preached to them by their
own extension agents and benefited from the development of markets for locally produced goods, GFWC members made little attempt to include representatives of the black community in their own planning and execution of
"Made in Georgia" activities.[37]

Another important development of the 1920s, the organization of County
Home Demonstration Councils, also perpetuated racial segregation of extension services at the grassroots level. Local white and black club women
who helped to initiate home demonstration work in their communities by
sponsoring girls' clubs went on to organize women's demonstration clubs,
representatives of which formed County Home Demonstration Councils in
the early to mid 1920s. These racially segregated councils proved vital to the
perpetuation of women's extension work, because they represented an organized structure for the lobbying, coordination, and support of home demonstration and rural club activities. Federal support for home demonstration was cut dramatically at the end of World War I, when food conservation
and preservation no longer was vital to national interests, and the councils
stepped into the gap to try to minimize the shrinkage of services to rural families. Council members provided a valuable service as liaisons between the rural poor and bureaucratic institutions, helping to direct resources to areas of
greatest need. They advised home demonstration agents on developing a plan
of work for their communities, pressured county officials to provide funding,
and raised money for girls' scholarships and for the improvement of rural
schools. The councils helped to bring rural and urban club women together
in a common cause, but participants could not seem to bridge the distance
between the races. Thus the distribution of resources that disproportionately
benefited whites went unchallenged.[38]

37. Mrs. Newton C. Wing, "Report of the 'Made in Georgia' Campaign," *GFWC Yearbook,
1922–1923*, 150–153; records of the Waynesboro Woman's Club, Zillah Lee Bostick Redd Agerton
Papers, box 4, Georgia Department of Archives and History; Mrs. Z. I. Fitzpatrick, "Report of
the President," *GFWC Yearbook, 1916–1917*, 22.

38. Leila R. Mize (state home demonstration agent), "County Home Demonstration
Councils," LRM, box 1, folder 2; "Excerpts from State and County Reports, 1924, Home Dem-

The segregation of rural reform work and continued discrimination in the funding and staffing of services for African Americans left black Georgians mostly reliant upon their own resources and outside philanthropic assistance. Northern philanthropic foundations worked to maximize blacks' access to state resources and funded programs of assistance that helped to nurture an ethos of self-help and cooperation in rural communities. One of the most important of these programs was created in 1907, when Philadelphia Quaker Anna T. Jeanes established the Negro Rural School Fund to support educational improvements in the South. The Jeanes Fund, as it was more commonly known, focused primarily on using industrial education to improve the standard of living of rural blacks, although its goals included the general improvement of black elementary education and the establishment of black high schools. Jeanes teachers worked on a countywide basis, supervising industrial education in schools (hence the term *Jeanes supervisors*) and providing additional teacher training. Because they were authorized to engage in any community work they deemed necessary, the teachers were able to develop a broad program of rural uplift that included the organization of home, school, and community improvement clubs for women and children. The work began in Georgia in 1908, when five counties hired Jeanes supervisors. Initially, the Jeanes Fund and several other philanthropic groups assumed full financial responsibility for the program, but states gradually began contributing money as public support for the work grew. In the South as a whole, public funds did not pay a majority of the expenses until 1921, and in Georgia not until 1927.[39]

---

onstration Council Activities," LRM, box 1, folder 1; *A Monthly Statement of Negro Extension Work,* March 1925, May 1925, and January 1926.

39. Josie B. Sessoms, Ella A. Tackwood, Rebecca E. Davis, Maenelle D. Dempsey, Ethel W. Kight, Madie A. Kincy, and Susie W. Wheeler, *Jeanes Supervision in Georgia Schools: A Guiding Light in Education: A History of the Program from 1908–1975* (Athens: Georgia Association of Jeanes Curriculum Directors and Southern Education Foundation, 1975); Mildred M. Williams, Kara Vaughn Jackson, Madie A. Kincy, Susie W. Wheeler, Ethel Bell, Rebecca Davis, Rebecca A. Crawford, and Maggie Forte, *The Jeanes Story: A Chapter in the History of American Education, 1908–1968* (Jackson, MS: Jackson State University, 1979); Arthur D. Wright and Edward E. Redcay, *The Negro Rural School Fund, Inc., 1907–1933* (Washington, DC: Negro Rural School Fund, 1933). Unpublished works on Jeanes teachers include Lily Farley Ross Dale, "The Jeanes Supervisors in Alabama, 1909–1963" (Ph.D. diss., Auburn University, 1998); Bernadine Sharpe Chapman, "Northern Philanthropy and African-American Adult Education in the Rural South: He-

The black women employed by the Jeanes Fund played a crucial role in providing home demonstration services to blacks, since establishing the respectability of black homes was an integral part of their larger goal of race uplift. They knew that the continued denial of black domesticity and feminine respectability not only underpinned labor exploitation but historically had been used to justify sexual exploitation as well. Jeanes teachers encouraged rural women to adopt middle-class standards of housewifery as a strategy for combating negative racial stereotypes. As part of their community work, they personally visited rural homes to provide individual instruction and demonstrations in hygiene, sanitation, household cleaning, cooking, and sewing. Jeanes Fund employees often used group demonstrations to train other women so that they could further the work in their respective communities. Much of the home demonstration work that should have been part of the state Extension Division was shoved onto Jeanes teachers, who laboriously knitted together disparate sources of aid to create a comprehensive program of assistance. In 1913, when the U.S. Department of Agriculture asked southern states to organize homemaking clubs among black children to teach corn and tomato culture, gardening, and canning, the Jeanes teachers immediately acquiesced to state requests for assistance. Within two years they had enrolled almost sixteen hundred children in projects that brought improved nutrition to many rural homes. The teachers also acted as temporary extension division workers during World War I, when they were hired during the summer months to assist in food conservation and preservation drives.[40]

---

gemony and Resistance in the Jeanes Movement" (Ed.D. diss., Northern Illinois University, 1990); Donna Tyler Hollie, "'I Consecrate Myself to the Service of Teaching': The Jeanes Teachers, a Case Study in Faurquier County, Virginia" (Ph.D. diss., Morgan State University, 2000); and Courtney S. Woodfaulk, "The Jeanes Teachers of South Carolina: The Emergence, Existence, and Significance of Their Work" (Ed.D. diss., University of South Carolina, 1992). Jeanes teachers also played an important role in the implementation of the Rosenwald Fund (established by philanthropist Julius Rosenwald in 1912 for the purpose of constructing rural black schools in the South), by training Rosenwald schoolteachers, to compensate for the lack of black teacher training facilities, and by organizing the necessary community support for the schools; by 1929 more than 16 percent of Georgia's black students attended Rosenwald schools. Benjamin Brawley, *Doctor Dillard of the Jeanes Fund* (New York: Fleming H. Revell, 1930), 55–63; and Carter Godwin Woodson, *The Rural Negro* (Washington, DC: Association for the Study of Negro Life and History, 1930), 191–202.

40. The state agent for Negro schools, a position created within the Georgia Department of Education with GEB funds in 1913, summarized the work of Jeanes teachers in his annual re-

The resourcefulness of Jeanes teachers and rural black communities enabled them to maximize the benefits of farm and home demonstration services to a remarkable degree. Even though African Americans received little more than 6 percent of the state expenditures for extension services in 1925, a study published the following year found that in four representative counties across the state, 53 percent of all black farms reported contact with a home demonstration agent (compared to 66 percent of white farms). This remarkable statistic can be explained in part by the fact that Jeanes teachers, although usually not official employees of the Extension Division, helped to organize, supervise, and coordinate extension programs among blacks. Equally important, however, were the efforts of black communities to offset the negative impact of state neglect by developing broad networks of support. Some activities paralleled those in white communities, such as the demonstrations and lectures presented at local teachers' meetings and farmers' conferences, but other activities were more unique. Both public and private black colleges provided extensive support for home extension services, helping county agents to reach rural families in isolated communities even when that help came at the expense of their own operations. Spelman Seminary helped to pay the salaries of industrial teachers who organized homemaking clubs in Bartow County, and Spelman students assisted in rural community work in the summer. Black churches also lent a helping hand. The black extension report for 1922 noted that at meetings of "Baptist Associations, Methodist Conferences, [and] Sunday School Conventions, the agents are given places on the program and in several instances, a day of demonstrations has been given." These cooperative efforts at adult education could not negate the effects of discrimination, but they did make a difference in exposing more rural blacks to basic demonstration services.[41]

---

port, in Sessoms et al., *Jeanes Supervision in Georgia Schools,* 24–25; Georgia Department of Education, *Forty-Second Annual Report, 1913* (Atlanta: GDE, 1914), 56–58; GSCA, Extension Division, *Annual Report, 1918–1919,* 27–28.

41. "The Effectiveness of Extension in Reaching Rural People," Georgia State College of Agriculture *Bulletin* 15 (July 1926); GSCA, Extension Division, *Annual Report, 1922–23,* 52–53. Spelman was typical of black colleges in its attempts to inculcate in students their responsibility for race uplift, and it supported industrial education in urban as well as rural black households. Cynthia Neverdon-Morton, *Afro-American Women of the South and the Advancement of the Race, 1895–1925* (Knoxville: University of Tennessee Press, 1989), 2–6, 93–94. Christian missionary influence in black colleges also contributed to their focus on community service. For ex-

The forced self-reliance of rural blacks and the segregation of rural institutions hindered the effectiveness of female interracial cooperation by channeling black women into alliances with black men rather than white women. It would seem that the marginalization of women and children in black extension work, which was particularly marked in the early years, would have accentuated the subordination of female and domestic needs in black communities, but this was not necessarily the case. Black male agents showed a greater willingness than white male agents to cross over gender boundaries and instruct women and children in both agricultural and domestic activities. Male extension workers (who initially compiled the official reports for women's work as well as their own) said what they thought whites wanted to hear, stressing that their main concern was increasing cash crop production among farmers. However, because there were so few black home demonstration agents, in actuality the educational and organizational activities ostensibly aimed at men often included the entire community of families. Just as the dearth of funding for black higher education necessitated coeducational colleges, extension workers faced with scarce resources had to instruct rural African Americans en masse. The sense of camaraderie that developed can be read between the lines of black agents' reports. Black farmers' conferences were well attended by adults and children of both sexes, and extension agents reported that in Newton County "forty women and girls met with the farmers in their meetings and helped them buy their soy beans for planting." Most likely, these women and girls had raised their financial contributions through gardening and canning club sales.[42]

White women also were thrown upon their own resources, but by persistent discrimination based on gender rather than race. World War I proved a boon for home demonstration work, as federal funding for extension services increased and women no longer had to rely on the largesse of private philanthropy and county officials. In 1917–1918, the division of money between

---

ample, see Stephanie Shaw, *What a Woman Ought to Be and to Do: Black Professional Women Workers during the Jim Crow Era* (Chicago: University of Chicago Press, 1996), 68–103.

42. Tuskegee Institute encouraged just such a cooperative approach as a way to foster self-sufficiency in black communities. Max Bennett Thrasher, *Tuskegee: Its Story and Its Work* (Boston: Small Maynard, 1901). GSCA, *A Monthly Statement of Negro Extension Work,* quote from March 1925, p. 4; also see January 1926; for a similar discussion regarding southern extension services as a whole, see Hilton, "Both in the Field, Each with a Plow."

men's and women's extension services was as follows: federal funds, $236 for men and $30,175 for women; state funds, $45,014 for men and $6,594 for women. Club women and home demonstration agents greatly expanded their work in 1917–1919 to take advantage of federal assistance, only to find themselves stripped of most of their financial support at war's end. They had proved the public value of private domestic labor, but the proof did not translate into a fairer division of state resources. The agricultural depression that ensued did nothing to encourage white lawmakers to share funds with women. In 1921 Georgia legislators refused to match federal funds for home demonstration work as provided for under the Smith-Lever Act, and as a result the state lost most of its federal appropriations for this purpose. White club women had to retrench, seeking other sources of federal support and in many cases paying a portion or all of the salaries of female county agents to keep the work going. Such an unfavorable climate may have discouraged white women from integrating rural reform efforts, since their claim to a common race privilege was the only leverage they had in prying funds from the hands of white male political leaders.[43]

The politics of race that separated southern white women and blacks served to obscure the common sources of their subordination in agricultural institutions. One of these common sources was the historical definition of farmer as white and male. The exclusivity of the definition stemmed in part from its origins in the patriarchal concept of citizenship as a political identity conferred by (male) property ownership and head-of-household status. As the federal government backed away from a commitment to political and civil equality for blacks after Reconstruction, African American men increasingly were denied the private and public identities that constructed the basis of manhood and citizenship. Women, long denied the full rights of citizenship, further suffered from an agrarian ideology that defined the farm as a male enterprise in which women's labor fulfilled a supportive but subordinate role. Subordinate groups continually contested these assumptions, which none-

---

43. GSCA, Extension Division, *Annual Report of Extension Service, 1917–1918*, vol. 7, bulletin 157 (July 1918); Georgia Federation resolution in support of the Fess Bill, *GFWC Yearbook, 1920–1921*, 21; report of the "Home Demonstration Agent in Every County" committee, *GFWC Yearbook, 1921–1922*, 116–117; and *GFWC Yearbook, 1922–1923*, 124–125; club women paid for both the education and the salaries of some home demonstration agents. Report of the Student Aid Foundation, *GFWC Yearbook, 1924–1925* (Atlanta: GFWC, 1925), 133.

theless were incorporated into the structure of USDA services. The USDA embodied a federal version of white male political culture, focusing its resources on bolstering white male independence and encouraging economic development through the promotion of scientific agriculture. It was not until the 1890s, with the emergence of home economics and the growing demands of rural and urban women, that government services began to address household needs. Even then, women's educational services were designed to create a strict sexual division of labor that rendered much of women's productive labor invisible by recognizing only some tasks as appropriately female.[44]

The bias against women and blacks in federal agricultural services is particularly evident in the role allotted them within the USDA as compared to other federal departments. The federal Bureau of Education and the Department of Labor employed staffs of black researchers to conduct studies, collect data, and advise them on policies concerning African Americans. Similarly, the Bureau of Education spent considerable resources studying the status of female and public education, and the Department of Labor contained both a Women's Bureau and a Children's Bureau that were dominated by female employees. Yet the Department of Agriculture made no such provisions for addressing the problems of blacks and women. It employed no special workers and created no separate division to study the dimensions of need among African Americans, and although USDA officials did finally create a Bureau of Home Economics in 1923, its legitimacy was constantly under attack and the agency was dismantled after thirty years. Female employment within the department as a whole began to decline after World War II, and none of its agencies were headed by women after the Bureau of Home Economics was abolished.[45]

The bias of the USDA was obvious to both white and black Georgians. One white Georgia educator complained in 1920 that while all problems of

44. Deborah Fink, *Agrarian Women: Wives and Mothers in Rural Nebraska, 1880–1940* (Chapel Hill: University of North Carolina Press, 1992), 11–24; Jane Knowles, "Science and Farm Women's Work: The Agrarian Origins of Home Economic Extension," *Agriculture and Human Values* 2 (Winter 1985): 52–55.

45. Gladys L. Baker, "Women in the U.S. Department of Agriculture," *Agricultural History* 50 (January 1976): 190–201; Doxey A. Wilkerson, *Agricultural Extension Services among Negroes in the South* (n.p.: Conference of Presidents of Negro Land Grant Colleges, 1942).

southern agriculture "are vitally concerned with the Negro, there is nowhere, in the vast organization of the Department of Agriculture in Washington, a colored specialist who can concentrate on the problems of the 3,000,000 Negro farmers." The Conference of Presidents of Negro Land Grant Colleges repeatedly complained to the USDA of heavy discrimination against blacks by the Cooperative Extension Service, asking that the department increase funding for the work and allow black land-grant colleges to administer their own funds. Other black educational leaders also complained of the inadequacy of black extension services, but their efforts met with little response, because the USDA was complicit in the efforts of the directors of southern extension work to obfuscate the inequitable nature of funding. Club women's own difficulties in securing adequate funding for home demonstration work led the Georgia Federation of Women's Clubs to call for gender reform within the USDA. At their annual meeting in 1914, delegates endorsed a resolution presented by the International Congress of Farm Women that called for the establishment of a Bureau of Farm Women headed by a "practical woman farmer." The Federation argued that the creation of a bureau run by and for women was only logical and fair, since men and women were "co-equals" on the farm and the federal government had "always shown a willingness and desire . . . to increase the happiness and comfort of the man on the farm." Delegates sent a copy of this resolution to Senator Hoke Smith with the request that he present it to the appropriate authorities, knowing full well the gesture was largely symbolic.[46]

Many of women's reform goals in the campaign for home extension services were frustrated and their results were mixed at best, but female reformers did achieve important victories. Ultimately, they, like black farmers, were unable to overcome the discriminatory structure and function of state and federal agricultural institutions. The politics of race worked to obscure not only the class-based character of rural economic problems, but also the full dimensions of gender inequality in state agencies. Although a handful of urban reformers made tremendous strides in interracial cooperation, many (if not

---

46. First quote from Woofter, *Negro Migration*, 173–175; Robert R. Moton, "Economic Justice," in *Cooperation in Southern Communities: Suggested Activities for County and City Interracial Committees,* ed. T. J. Woofter Jr. and Isaac Fisher (Atlanta: Commission on Inter-racial Cooperation, 1921), 33–40; Wilkerson, *Agricultural Extension Services,* 2–3; *GFWC Yearbook, 1914–1915* (Atlanta: GFWC, 1915), 10–11.

most) white women remained either unable or unwilling to accept black women on equal ground as wives and mothers. The machinations of white rural elites encouraged the persistence of racial and gender discrimination in federal programs of assistance, with dire results for the rate of rural poverty in the South. However, the grassroots efforts of black and white club women, home economists, extension workers, and industrial teachers made a tremendous difference in the lives of individual women, their families, and their communities. The homemaking clubs, canning clubs, and Go-to-College Funds improved the standard of living in rural households while enabling many girls to realize greater educational and occupational opportunities in spite of formidable barriers of gender, class, and race. And even though it segregated female students into separate courses of study, the admission of women into the home economics department of the College of Agriculture was important step in the uphill battle for equality; it signaled the beginning of the end of women's exclusion from the state's premier institutions of higher education.

4

REFORMING THE MOUNTAINEERS
Education and the Politics of Gender, Race, and Reproduction

Although the volatility of southern race relations usually influenced white women to downplay the significance of race in their reform efforts, the campaign to uplift the mountaineers was a notable exception. Organized women's attempts to improve economic self-sufficiency and educational opportunities in highland communities coincided (both geographically and chronologically) with a movement of national reconciliation based on race, ensuring that concerns for racial purity and white supremacy would become linked to female reform goals. It was not that gender and class concerns were any less central to club women's highland campaign—if anything, the subordination of mountain women seemed to them more egregious and acute than that of rural women elsewhere—but rather that public ambivalence regarding the worthiness of this particular group of white southerners made appeals to race especially useful. Female reformers were able to use conservative means to progressive ends, drawing upon popular concepts of eugenics and race suicide to push forward educational reform and gender equality. Combining appeals to racial solidarity and motherhood, they used the politics of race, gender, and reproduction to pressure politicians and voters into addressing the needs of impoverished mountain schools. In contrast, at the local level they subverted the apparent gender conservatism of their appeals to racial purity by creating and funding boarding schools as alternative homes in which mountain youth could receive from women new definitions of domesticity.

Mountaineers first came to the attention of postbellum reformers when long-term social and economic trends culminated in the displacement of families. One reason for out-migration was the combination of high birthrates and partible inheritance practices. Because of an increase in the southern Appalachian birthrate that began in the 1830s, mountain couples were having children on the average of one every two years when other Americans were beginning to limit the size of their families. And because most highlanders followed the practice of dividing property equally among male heirs, farm sizes steadily shrank until they no longer were adequate sources of support.

This increased pressure on the land is reflected in tenure arrangements as early as 1860, when almost 40 percent of southern Appalachian farmers tilled land they did not own. In the Appalachian counties of North Georgia the proportion was slightly greater, around 43 percent, and a majority of these farmers were sharecroppers rather than cash renters. Mountaineers who no longer could support themselves in agriculture migrated to mill and factory towns or other urban areas to find new ways to make a living. In many cases husbands became itinerant workers, leaving home for days or even months at a time in search of wage labor, while women and children stayed on the land to tend the fields.[1]

The postbellum expansion of railroads exacerbated highland woes, since the economic development it brought to the southern Appalachians had negative consequences for the mountaineers. As the nineteenth century came to a close, three railroad companies had lines across the North Georgia mountains. The Southern Railway, centered in Atlanta, had one line to the coalfields in the far northwestern counties of Dade, Walker, and Chatooga and another running northeast to gold-mining operations in Lumpkin County. The Western and Atlantic line also ran through the northwestern portion of the state, connecting Atlanta with Chattanooga, Tennessee. The north central mountain counties were served by the Atlanta, Knoxville, and Northern, which operated between Marietta and the Tennessee line. The railroads and numerous highland rivers and tributaries attracted entrepreneurs from inside and outside the region who sought to take advantage of waterpower and natural resources. At the opening of the twentieth century, Georgia's mountain counties contained 9 cotton mills, 10 woolen mills, 33 sawmills, 4 tanneries, and 2 furniture factories, in addition to the mineral and coal mines. While industrial development did produce jobs for poor mountaineers, entrepreneurial business methods were not always honest or responsible. By the time educational reformers turned their eyes to the north, the property of many mountain families had been bought, swindled, or destroyed through destructive logging and mining practices.[2]

---

1. Wilma A. Dunaway, *The First American Frontier: Transition to Capitalism in Southern Appalachia, 1700–1860* (Chapel Hill: University of North Carolina Press, 1996), 87–98; Crandall A. Shifflett, *Coal Towns: Life, Work, and Culture in Company Towns of Southern Appalachia, 1880–1960* (Knoxville: University of Tennessee Press, 1991), 13–15.

2. *Georgia: Historical and Industrial* (Atlanta: State of Georgia, 1901), 74–123, 177–178.

The predicament of mountain whites presented a challenge to urban reformers who sought to address the causes and results of their impoverishment. Cotton mill employment represented at least one way to alleviate extreme poverty, but southerners were torn over the issues of millwork and child labor as solutions to the problem of displaced rural whites. While some southern reformers attacked child labor as unconscionable, others recognized the dire need of poor mountaineers and lowland whites for a way to make a living, especially those in female-headed households with limited means of support. The conditions of life in a mill town may have been difficult, but in many instances they were no worse than the living standards left behind. Some mountain families actually bettered their conditions by taking up millwork, or believed that they had bettered them, if for no other reason than that they had gained new options. Nonetheless, the presence of extremely rural mountaineers in towns created new problems for urban whites. Their unruliness, poor health, and susceptibility to political manipulation were all concerns that worried urban club women and Progressives. Educational reformers who recognized the economic necessity of migration suggested that the best solution would be to reform mountain education so that it enabled highland whites to earn a living and remain self-sufficient in their native environment.[3]

Southern economic interests also played a part in the movement to keep mountaineers in the mountains. Many New South and Progressive leaders hoped that an improved education would better enable highlanders to act as guardians of the region's natural resources. Historians have argued that the postbellum South—and especially the southern Appalachians—had colonial status within the national economy, and many southerners certainly perceived this to be true in the early twentieth century. Southern educational leaders may have sought northern assistance in funding and executing reform cam-

---

3. One reformer who argued that mountaineers were better off in the mills was Thomas R. Dawley Jr., "Our Southern Mountaineers," *World's Work* 19 (March 1910): 12704–12714, and *The Child That Toileth Not* (New York: Gracie Publishing, 1912); also see Shifflett, *Coal Towns,* 6–8. Felton regarded millwork as an honorable way for single and widowed women to earn a living, as discussed in LeeAnn Whites, "The De Graffenried Controversy: Class, Race, and Gender in the New South," *Journal of Southern History* 54 (August 1988): 449–478. On the problems mountaineers caused for towns, see Sallie Barker Hill, "The Case of the Southern Mountaineers," Walter B. Hill Papers, Sallie Barker Hill Division (hereafter SBH), box 54, folder 2, Hargrett Rare Book and Manuscript Collection, typescript.

paigns, but one of their primary goals in improving education was to enable the South to more effectively compete with the North economically. They were particularly concerned about retaining control of the vast natural resources contained in the highlands. When New South boosters looked to the untapped resources of the mountains, they saw the basis for a revival and expansion of southern industry. Progressive reformers were concerned about conservation and wanted to ensure that economic development would benefit the people of the region. Reformers had every reason to believe that if southerners failed to cooperate in protecting the forest and mineral wealth of the highlands, northern investors would completely strip the area of its value just as they had laid waste the longleaf pine forests of the southeastern piedmont after Reconstruction.[4]

Sectional competitiveness stemming from regional economic insecurities was an important motivating factor for women involved in mountain reform. The Southern Mountain Educational Association (SMEA), which was founded in Atlanta in 1909 by journalist Helen Gray, was one of several organizations established and run by women for the sole purpose of improving educational opportunities for mountaineers. As in similar groups, the leadership of the SMEA often portrayed highland children as an important but endangered human resource. In making an impassioned plea for funds, President Jennie LaZarus alluded to the fact that northern states more generously funded public education and offered a wider array of industrial and technical branches of study. She warned Georgia Federation of Women's Clubs (GFWC) members, "Unless we adopt the right kind and a thorough educational and vocational training for our boys and girls, they will become underlings and puppets in the hands of more rapidly advancing brothers and sis-

4. Edward L. Ayers, *The Promise of the New South: Life after Reconstruction* (New York: Oxford University Press, 1992), 123–131; Ronald D. Eller, *Miners, Millhands, and Mountaineers: Industrialization of the Appalachian South, 1880–1930* (Knoxville: University of Tennessee Press, 1982), 44–48; and on the South as an internal colony, see C. Vann Woodward, *Origins of the New South, 1877–1913* (Baton Rouge: Louisiana State University Press, 1951); Gavin Wright, *Old South, New South: Revolutions in the Southern Economy since the Civil War* (New York: Basic Books, 1986); and Robert C. McMath Jr., "Community, Region, and Hegemony in the Nineteenth-Century South," in *Toward a New South? Studies in Post–Civil War Southern Communities,* ed. Orville Vernon Burton and Robert C. McMath Jr. (Westport, CT: Greenwood Press, 1982), 281–300.

ters." Other reformers often expressed similar fears, arguing that southern poor whites would remain poor if their education prepared them only for the lowest rung on the industrial ladder, and that the South would remain a colony so long as it lacked skilled indigenous labor. The SMEA leader asked club women to consider "how many of our best positions are being filled by men and women from north of Mason and Dixon's Line." They had to realize, she cautioned, that "the plums will fall to the efficient."[5]

In his annual report of 1900, the Georgia state superintendent of schools made a compelling case for the economic costs of illiteracy in the mountain counties. The southern Appalachians encompass twenty counties in North Georgia, stretching from Polk in the west to Habersham in the northeast. Superintendent M. L. Brittain viewed the mountains and their residents as resources that needed to be developed in tandem for the benefit of the state. In arguing for the need of a constitutional amendment to facilitate local taxation for schools, he dramatically observed that the highland youth "cannot come here to lift its white hand and fix its pleading eyes upon the General Assembly to beg for a way of escape." The superintendent described the mountain child as a prisoner of his own ignorance with little defense against the outsider who came to swindle mineral rights from the mountaineer. "The stranger has gone to its mountain retreat and found the seams of gold that thread the back yard of its cottage home," he explained, "and it has bartered its heritage for a mess of potatoes because it knew not the wealth of its native hills." Noting the rapid diminishment of the state's pine forests and North Georgia's gold supply, Brittain urged Georgians to assume stewardship of the remaining natural wealth contained in the highlands. The way to do this, he argued, was "to develop in the hands and brains of our children a power that can be applied to these reserved and undeveloped resources of our vast estate."[6]

5. SMEA report, *Georgia Federation of Women's Clubs* [hereafter GFWC] *Yearbook, 1913–1914* (Atlanta: GFWC, 1914), 64; E. B. Gresham, "Industrial and Agricultural Education," in *Proceedings and Addresses of the Fortieth Annual Meeting of the Georgia Educational Association, 1906* (Athens, GA: McGregor Press, 1906), 33–36.

6. Georgia Department of Education (hereafter GDE), *Twenty-Ninth Annual Report, 1900* (Atlanta: GDE, 1901), 19–21; Brittain may have been guilty of melodrama in his description of the swindling of mineral rights, but his basic point was accurate—outside investors often took advantage of the ignorance of isolated mountain property owners and had numerous schemes for

Educational reformer Sallie Barker Hill, in an essay penned for local publication, echoed Brittain's concerns for the mountaineers and outlined specific remedies. She portrayed highlanders as a people squeezed from all sides by exploitative forces. In their native surroundings they were assaulted by "lumber men and mining prospectors" and "smooth-tongued pioneers of trade," but migrating to cotton mills did not necessarily improve their lives. Their natural "spirit of independence" was broken by the endless toil of wage labor, and reliance upon child labor perpetuated illiteracy. Meanwhile, the land they left behind was devastated by environmentally unsound practices that caused severe erosion, flooding, and the pollution and blockage of streams. The solution to all these problems, Hill argued, was to give highlanders the knowledge and skills necessary to bring prosperity to themselves and the state while also preserving environmental integrity. Mountain communities needed a wide array of improvements, including schools that integrated industrial education into their curriculum, separate agricultural and vocational schools, adequate roads to get children to class and farmers to market, and a government-sponsored system of rural credit to provide small loans at low interest rates. Only through such an investment of state resources, Hill concluded, could mountaineers become productive assets rather than social liabilities.[7]

When organized women sought to build a base of support for mountain reform, they had to tackle the lowland bias that underlay public neglect of highland needs. Mountaineers became isolated politically in the last years of the Civil War, as they increasingly protested against conscription practices that left their families facing starvation and as the mountains became a notorious haven for draft-dodgers and deserters. Mountaineer political dissent continued into the post-Reconstruction era, when North Georgia challenged the power of the Bourbon regime by exhibiting strong support for Independent and Farmers' Alliance candidates. After Democrats defeated their opposition with bribery, coercion, and ballot-box stuffing, mountaineers found themselves caught between the two groups battling for control of the party.

---

cheating them out of the value of their land; for example, see Eller, *Miners, Millhands, and Mountaineers,* 54–57. Also, I use Eller's geographical boundaries for the southern Appalachians in Georgia, although some mountain workers considered the highlands to include counties in the upper piedmont, namely Cherokee, Forsyth, Hall, Banks, and Stephens counties.

7. Hill, "The Case of the Southern Mountaineers."

The New South/Progressive urban faction supported regional economic development and a more efficient and powerful state bureaucracy, while rural elites were intent upon maintaining control of local politics and protecting their own narrow financial interests. Mountain men distrusted state authority and were inclined to support rural political leaders, but they stood to benefit from greater government control of transportation, health, and education—all services sadly lacking in their region. The movement for black disfranchisement, in which highland representatives stood virtually alone against a measure that could disfranchise poor whites as well, further alienated mountain counties. As an Atlanta minister described the situation in 1912, highlanders had felt "a certain sense of estrangement, especially since the Civil War," and their political representatives "have been ordinarily considered as negligible factors in the State's policies."[8]

Added to the problem of political tensions were the cultural differences separating rural highlanders from the urban middle class. Many middle-class southerners regarded mountaineers as a people stubbornly and irrationally adhering to a preindustrial past. Critics complained that they were afflicted with a "simplicity of needs and wants" that thwarted the development of ambition and a strong work ethic; accustomed to surviving on wild game and the produce of their small farms, highlanders saw no reason to work for more. While the actions of those who left the mountains in search of work refuted

8. Quote from John E. White, "Our Southern Highlands," in *The Home Mission Task,* ed. Victor I. Masters (Atlanta: Home Mission Board of the Southern Baptist Convention, 1912), 215; Steven Wayne Wrigley, "The Triumph of Provincialism: Public Life in Georgia, 1898–1917" (Ph.D. diss., Northwestern University, 1986). On women's role in mountain resistance in North Carolina, see Victoria Bynum, *Unruly Women: The Politics of Social and Sexual Control in the Old South* (Chapel Hill: University of North Carolina Press, 1992), 130–150; E. Merton Coulter, *A Short History of Georgia* (Chapel Hill: University of North Carolina Press, 1933), 313–314, 365–366; Barton C. Shaw, *The Wool-Hat Boys: Georgia's Populist Party* (Baton Rouge: Louisiana State University Press, 1984), 116–117, 120. On mountaineers' history of political dissent, see Carl Degler, *The Other South: Southern Dissenters in the Nineteenth Century* (New York: Harper and Row, 1974); and Michael R. Hyman, *The Anti-Redeemers: Hill-Country Political Dissenters in the Lower South from Redemption to Populism* (Baton Rouge: Louisiana State University Press, 1990). While populism was strongest in the piedmont of Georgia, there was significant mountain support, indicating a similarity of economic and political complaints among small-scale farmers, as discussed in Steven Hahn, *The Roots of Southern Populism: Yeoman Farmers and the Transformation of the Georgia Upcountry, 1850–1890* (New York: Oxford University Press, 1983); and Shaw, *The Wool-Hat Boys.*

claims that they lacked initiative, migrants were a source of regional embarrassment. Those who took up factory labor became the subject of negative publicity when social reformers concerned about female and child labor wrote critical accounts of their working and living conditions for publication in the national press. One such account of Georgia mill operatives, published in *Century Magazine* in 1891, argued that factory labor had a deleterious effect on workers' morals, families, and home life. Articles of this sort contributed to the construction of a national stereotype of southern poor whites as an especially degraded class. John Fiske's 1897 history of Virginia and neighboring states was influential in reinforcing this unflattering image. Fiske claimed that the early colonists who migrated out of Virginia and eventually settled in the Appalachians were "mean whites" composed of the "less thrifty and enterprising" indentured servants and criminals who fled "to escape the hangman."[9]

Although female reformers continued to struggle with persistent cultural prejudices, they benefited from a more positive interpretation of mountaineer distinctiveness that emerged at the turn of the century when Americans developed a new fascination with the Appalachians. The postbellum expansion of railroads in the southern highlands encouraged the development of a tourist trade and an influx of northern travelers, exposing mountaineers to the national public eye for the first time. White Americans troubled by the social impact of industrialization and immigration found new meaning in the simplicity of mountain life and the relative homogeneity of highland communities. The region appealed to their sense of nostalgia for an imagined preindustrial past free of class conflict and racial and ethnic diversity. Northern travelers tended to romanticize mountaineers for their supposed racial purity and physical hardiness and because they were reported to have preserved Anglo-Saxon culture as it was originally transplanted from western Europe. Collecting mountain ballads of European origin for preservation and publi-

9. First quote from White, "Our Southern Highlands," 224; Clare de Graffenried, "The Georgia Cracker in the Cotton Mills," *Century Magazine* 41 (February 1891): 483–498; John Fiske, *Old Virginia and Her Neighbors* (Boston: Houghton, Mifflin, 1897), 2:311–321, as cited in John C. Campbell, *The Southern Highlander and His Homeland* (New York: Russell Sage Foundation, 1921), 349–351. Rural poor whites were commonly accused of lacking a work ethic. Nicole Hahn Rafter, ed., *White Trash: The Eugenic Family Studies, 1877–1919* (Boston: Northeastern University Press, 1988), 16–17. On the public reaction in Georgia to de Graffenried's article, see Lee-Ann Whites, "The De Graffenried Controversy."

cation became a popular pastime for middle-class travelers and settlement workers, and some folklorists claimed to have witnessed mountain families speaking Elizabethan English. Both northern and southern writers participated in the "local color" trend in popular fiction, recounting stories of the feuding mountaineers in quaint dialect. Nostalgia for preindustrial life was particularly evident in the handicraft revival, in which settlement schools attempted to preserve skills such as weaving, carving, and basket making by offering classes to local children and adults and providing markets for their products.[10]

Americans' obsession with the racial purity of mountaineers reflected the profound influence of social Darwinism and eugenics on popular thought. Eugenics, a scientific approach to human reproduction, incorporated a naturalistic view of society as a competitive struggle for survival in which natural selection and acquired characteristics (character determined by heredity) determined the winners and losers. Eugenicists presumed white supremacy but paradoxically asserted that natural selection had to be controlled to maintain that supremacy. They proposed to direct evolutionary development through both positive and negative means, by preventing the unfit from breeding and by ensuring optimal conditions for those most fit to reproduce. While scientific opinion as to the efficacy of these dual strategies changed over time, eugenic theory had an enduring appeal to white Americans reeling from the impact of rapid change. It spoke to their fears of race suicide, it offered a commonsense explanation for class and race strife, and it could be used to justify a multitude of solutions to social problems. When it came to the ills of industrial life, eugenics seemed to offer something for everyone, a rationale for those who wanted to absolve themselves of responsibility as well as justification for those who sought authority to intervene in behalf of the greater good.[11]

10. Nina Silber, *The Romance of Reunion: Northerners and the South, 1865–1900* (Chapel Hill: University of North Carolina Press, 1993), 143–152. On local color writing discussed in relation to one such southern writer, Mary N. Murfree (who published under the pseudonym Charles Egbert Craddock), see Richard Cary, *Mary N. Murfree* (New York: Twayne Publishers, 1967), esp. 18–12, 34–35; and for an intriguing account of mountain settlement work as the creation of culture, see David E. Whisnant, *All That Is Native and Fine: The Politics of Culture in an American Region* (Chapel Hill: University of North Carolina Press, 1983).

11. Donald K. Pickens, *Eugenics and the Progressives* (Nashville: Vanderbilt University Press, 1968), 5, 42–46; Rafter, *White Trash*, 7–15; Johanna Schoen, "'A Great Thing for Poor Folks':

By universalizing the fears and insecurities of white Americans and rooting them in supposedly objective science, eugenics played an important role in bringing the racial attitudes of northern and southern whites closer together. Eugenicists' claim that some races were less evolved than others provided an important common ground. Northerners exhibited a new sympathy for southern methods of political control, since the concept of a social order based on genetic differences made Jeffersonian democracy appear idealistic and unworkable. Franchise restrictions were less objectionable when viewed as simply a reflection of the fact that some groups were naturally more fit to rule than others. The evolutionary hierarchy also justified racial segregation and immigration restrictions as necessary methods of protecting the national genetic inheritance. Eugenicists warned that white women's isolation from men of genetically inferior groups was necessary to avoid contamination of the Anglo-Saxon racial inheritance and the physical and moral degeneration that would result. Such claims validated southerners' obsession with white supremacy, and especially its connections between race and sex. While southern men's traditional opposition to government interference produced resistance to more intrusive eugenic policies such as involuntary sterilization of the unfit, they welcomed scientific theories that presented black disfranchisement and racial segregation as patriotic necessities. Even southern Progressives could justify curtailment of individual liberty if the end result was the promotion of the greater good of society.[12]

The influence of eugenic theory is clearly evident in the educational reform movement, and its racial politics helped to generate the national reconciliation based on race that took place in the early years of the Conference for Education in the South. At the first two conferences in 1898 and 1899, southern educators expressed white resentment regarding northern attempts to provide quality education for blacks. They argued that "sectional lines are fast disappearing, if not already obliterated," and it was time that northern phi-

Birth Control, Sterilization, and Abortion in Public Health and Welfare in the Twentieth Century" (Ph.D. diss., University of North Carolina–Chapel Hill, 1995), 20–44.

12. For the most thorough account of the origins of a national reconciliation based on race, see Silber, *The Romance of Reunion;* Edward J. Larson, *Sex, Race, and Science: Eugenics in the Deep South* (Baltimore: Johns Hopkins University Press, 1995); Pickens, *Eugenics and the Progressives,* 65–67, 171; William H. Tucker, *The Science and Politics of Racial Research* (Urbana: University of Illinois Press, 1994), 69–79, 85–86.

lanthropists conceded the right of white southerners to control the direction of black education in their own region. Southern members of the conference asserted that white education was their most "pressing and imperative need," and to meet this need they wanted to lay claim to a liberal portion of the private funds that were going to educational improvements in other areas of the nation. For their part, northern philanthropists and educators were willing to admit that their initial emphasis on the reconstruction of southern society through black education had been misguided, a mistake for which they hoped to compensate by relinquishing control of educational reform according to southern demands. The growing challenges to northern white men's political power from immigrant, black, and working-class men led some northern conference participants to express great admiration for the Old South social order, in their words a "democratic aristocracy" in which propertied white men held the reins of political power.[13]

When a member of the New York delegation spoke before conference participants at the 1905 meeting in Columbia, South Carolina, he directly addressed the racial basis of interregional cooperation. In a speech entitled "Sectional Misapprehension," Earnest Hamlin Abbott declared that the northern white men attending the conference represented a "New North." They accepted the southern version of the causes of the Civil War and the mistakes of Reconstruction and were in agreement with southerners on the issue of twentieth-century race relations as well. White men of the New North believed "with reference to the present and future" that "race integrity is to be assumed in any discussion of the problems affecting our country" and that the "division of mankind into certain great distinct races will continue in America . . . for all time." In accordance with southern wishes that white ed-

13. Charles F. Meserve, "Differences of Methods, If Any, in Work among Whites and Blacks," 17–20, first quote 19–20, and the Executive Committee's "Message and Appeal," 30–32 (second quote), both in *Proceedings of the First Capon Springs Conference for Christian Education in the South* [hereafter CES], *1898* (Raleigh, NC: Capital Printing, n.d.); "Resolutions of the Second Capon Springs Conference," in *Proceedings of the Second Capon Springs CES, 1899* (Raleigh, NC: Edwards and Broughton, 1899), 7–9; Robert C. Ogden, "A Few Suggestions upon the Objects of the Capon Springs Educational Conference, as Seen by a Northern Business Man," in *Proceedings of the Third Capon Springs CES, 1900* (Raleigh, NC: St. Augustine's School, n.d.), 33–34; third quote from Felix Adler, "Democracy, the American Ideal," in *Proceedings of the Fifth CES, held at Athens, Georgia, April 24, 25, and 26, 1902* (Knoxville, TN: Southern Education Board, 1902), 78.

ucation be the foremost concern of the conference, Abbott granted that "race justice means justice not only to the minority races, but also justice to the majority race; fairness to the Negro and the Mongol, and also to the white." He and other men of the New North agreed that the "right to administer the instruments of government is not a part of civil liberty," and so they recognized the validity of southern efforts to determine "what condition and limitations shall be put upon the exercise of the franchise." Abbott firmly concluded that sectional differences would cease to exist when northern and southern men recognized, among other things, that the need for "scrupulous preservation of racial integrity" was a given.[14]

It was within this larger context of national reconciliation that the Appalachians and its inhabitants came to represent a middle ground between North and South, a meeting place for the racial fears of both sections. The lower Appalachians extend from the southern border of Pennsylvania through the northern counties of Georgia and Alabama, a sort of geographical middle ground comprising almost 102,000 square miles. Andrew Richie, a native of the Georgia mountains who returned there to open a settlement school in 1903, described the area as "an intermediate territory of national integration" between the "two sections recently divided by Civil War." His further comments show that this national integration was based on a distinctly racial concept of American citizenship. Influenced by evolutionary and eugenic theories, educational reformers regarded the relatively homogeneous mountain population as a national reservoir of Anglo-Saxon Protestantism. Like most mountain workers, Richie made a point of noting the Scots-Irish ancestry of mountain folk, "preserved in the isolated mountain districts of the South as the purest and most distinct remnant of original American blood on the Continent." Richie suggested that mountaineers were worthy of assistance because they carried in themselves the genetic and cultural inheritance of the early colonial settlers, and it was from this "body of original American stock" that the "purest American blood is to be transmitted to future generations."[15]

14. Ernest Hamlin Abbott, "Sectional Misapprehension," in *Proceedings of the Eighth CES, Columbia, S.C., April 26–28, 1905* (New York: Committee on Publication, 1905), 130–137, quotes 134–135, except last quote 136.

15. Andrew J. Richie, *The Rabun Industrial School and Mountain School Extension Work among the Mountain Whites* (n.p., ca. 1904), 7–10; Samuel Tyndale Wilson, *The Southern Mountaineers* (New York: Presbyterian Board of Home Missions, 1906), 4–5, 8–11.

Coupled with the northern retreat from racial justice, heightened interest in mountaineers as the most racially pure of white Americans facilitated increased funding of highland reform. Northern philanthropic groups were discouraged by the slow pace of progress in their efforts to uplift southern blacks, and they found it more and more difficult to effectively continue their work as the racial climate worsened in the 1890s. Groups such as the American Missionary Association (AMA) turned to Appalachian whites as a less controversial group worthy of assistance, and one that had been largely neglected by earlier campaigns for moral and social uplift. In 1884 the AMA began a campaign to raise funds to educate mountain whites just as it previously had done for emancipated slaves. Similarly, northern Protestant churches involved in southern home mission work found mountain whites attractive recipients of assistance as programs for freed people became more problematic. In the 1880s and 1890s, northern Presbyterian and Methodist churches sent evangelists into the southern Appalachians and funded the establishment of churches and schools in mountain communities. The northern Presbyterian Church alone organized thirty-one schools for mountain whites between 1885 and 1895 and over the next ten years opened another thirty-four. Women's denominational auxiliaries also became active in the campaign, sponsoring and directing work in schools and settlements.[16]

The newly forged agreement to focus on the educational needs of whites and Americans' infatuation with mountain folk as "contemporary ancestors" were developments favorable to women's highland reform campaign. Educational improvements were expensive and mountaineers were cash-poor, and the overwhelmingly white highland counties lacked the lowland option of co-opting state funds based on the African American population. Northern reformers' repudiation of their commitment to black education promised to funnel more philanthropic funds into programs for rural whites. Ultimately, however, the success of mountain reform hinged on Georgians' willingness to accept collective responsibility for the needs of their most rural citizens.

16. James C. Klotter, "The Black South and White Appalachia," *Journal of American History* 66 (March 1980): 832–849; Henry D. Shapiro, *Appalachia on Our Mind: The Southern Mountains and Mountaineers in the American Consciousness, 1870–1920* (Chapel Hill: University of North Carolina Press, 1978), 41–57; also see Olive D. Campbell, *Southern Highland Schools Maintained by Denominational and Independent Agencies* (New York: Russell Sage Foundation, 1921).

Southern bias against the mountaineers had to be overcome if the general public was to be convinced to part with the large sums of money necessary for the construction and expansion of highland schools. It was here that emphasis on the racial purity of mountain residents could have the greatest impact, overcoming political and cultural differences and rehabilitating the image of the mountaineer in the minds of southerners. Eugenics could effect an internal reconciliation enabled by the national one, using race as a common ground for disparate groups and building white solidarity on the basis of a white racial patriotism.

Female educational reformers recognized the power of appeals to racial purity and racial solidarity and usually characterized their mountain work as a program of white race uplift when campaigning for public support. In explaining how she came to support the creation of a school for mountain whites, GFWC leader Mary Ann Lipscomb claimed to have been inspired by the racial integrity and worthiness of children in the North Georgia community of Tallulah Falls. While summering in the area, she discovered that the only school available to more than two hundred families was a small room above a dilapidated jail where the county held classes for three months each year. Lipscomb recounted that when she thought of the mountain children's "fine American heritage; that they were of the purest Anglo-Saxon blood in America," she became determined "to open a door of opportunity" to them. In August of 1903 she invited area residents, visitors, and friends from other summer homes to visit her cottage to discuss the establishment of a new school. She persuaded GFWC leaders to adopt the project as their own in 1905 and three years later received a donation of five acres of land. After the Georgia Federation raised two thousand dollars for construction costs, the school was able to open in June of 1909 with one building and twenty-one students. One of the first pamphlets issued by the GFWC to publicize the new institution described it as a "home school where boys and girls of our own blood and breed are given a chance in life." As late as 1950, the organization continued to advertise its mountain school (of which it still retains ownership) as an institution for the advancement of "worthy boys and girls of purest Anglo-Saxon strain." [17]

17. Educational Committee report, *GFWC Yearbook, 1907–1908* (Atlanta: GFWC, 1908), 17–18; Tallulah Falls School report, *GFWC Yearbook, 1908–1909* (Atlanta: GFWC, 1909), 104–106; quotes from Tennie DeJarnette, *A Pattern for Education in Living* (Tallulah Falls, GA: GFWC,

Women's groups dedicated exclusively to highland educational reform often described their motives in similar terms, referring to the racial purity of mountaineers as evidence that they deserved assistance. When members of the Southern Mountain Educational Association opened the Mineral Bluff Industrial School for Mountain Girls in Fannin County, their president assured supporters that "money for educational purposes cannot be appropriated to a more worthy cause than to the education of typical mountain girls." Students were "bright, but unawakened girls, with the purest Anglo-Saxon blood coursing through their veins." According to the SMEA president, the hills surrounding the school were full of such "worthy, neglected girls" whose future depended upon scholarship donations. Members of the Southern Association for the Education of Georgia Mountaineers (SAEGM), a similar group founded by Savannah club women in 1907, also made pointed racial appeals when trying to solicit financial support. The organization's literature noted that Georgia mountaineers had "coursing through their veins the purest Anglo-Saxon blood on this Continent" and were greatly admired for their "resolute, almost defiant independence." Claiming that an excessive focus on black education was responsible for the neglect of this "original sturdy stock," the SAEGM urged the public to join in "so righteous a cause" through generous donations.[18]

Of all the women's organizations involved in mountain reform, the Georgia Division of the United Daughters of the Confederacy (UDC) was by far the most vocal on the issue of racial motivations. The nature of national mountain reform as a backward-looking movement had special meaning for Daughters of the Confederacy. The main impetus behind UDC programs for educational reform was the desire to promulgate a regional patriotism that glorified the Lost Cause. The national organization and its state and local chapters pursued this goal by monitoring public school textbooks to ensure that they contained historical accounts sympathetic to the Confederacy, by

---

ca. 1950), 5, 10–11, 18; see also Sandra Lee Barney, *Authorized to Heal: Gender, Class, and the Transformation of Medicine in Appalachia, 1880–1930* (Chapel Hill: University of North Carolina Press, 2000), 89–90.

18. SMEA reports, *GFWC Yearbook, 1910–1911* (Atlanta: GFWC, 1911), 90–91; *GFWC Yearbook, 1912–1913* (Atlanta: GFWC, 1913), 74–75; and *GFWC Yearbook, 1913–1914,* 63–64; *The State Association for the Education of Georgia Mountaineers* (n.p., n.d.), Georgia Room, University of Georgia Libraries, Athens, pamphlet.

holding essay contests for school children on pro-Confederate topics, and by providing scholarships to descendants of Confederate veterans. Georgia women associated with other groups sometimes became frustrated with UDC chapters that restricted their philanthropic aid to Confederate descendants. A reformer who was trying to organize local club women for school improvement work complained to Sallie Hill that uncooperative UDC members were "much more interested . . . in the dead heroes than in the living ones of tomorrow." This was not exactly true, at least according to the Georgia Division, which argued that their scholarship fund was building "living monuments to our cause." Educating Confederate descendants was monument-building in the sense that it honored the fathers—dead Confederate soldiers who no longer could protect the interests of their families—by uplifting the children.[19]

As southern white women's participation in the educational reform movement increased, the UDC's restricted focus on educational aid for children of the Confederacy became a source of conflict within the national organization. In the case of mountain reform, some Daughters of the Confederacy believed that the racial purity of the children and the larger goal of maintaining white supremacy justified, and even demanded, their assistance. Alabama UDC member Martha Gielow became a prominent supporter of highland reform after founding the Southern Industrial Education Association (SIEA) in 1905 to promote educational opportunities for southern white children. Gielow was especially concerned about illiteracy among the "splendid girls and boys" of the Appalachians, "descendants of the best blood of America" who were being neglected by reformers. She appealed to UDC divisions and chapters across the nation to join in her cause, stressing that monuments to the dead would mean little if whites fell behind blacks in literacy and education. Although some chapters joined the SIEA, most did not, and Gielow's work provoked the criticism of the UDC president-general, who had not overcome her own political bias against the mountaineers. The national leader, Lizzie George Henderson, did not think it was appropriate for the UDC to expand

19. First quote from Mary Stone to Sallie B. Hill, April 8, 1910, SBH, box 54, folder 4; second quote from Report of Committee on Education, *Minutes of the Nineteenth Annual Convention, Georgia Division, UDC*, 1913, 61–62; Rebecca Latimer Felton, "Importance of the Education of the Poor Girls of the South," *Minutes of the Fourth Annual Meeting of the UDC*, 1897, 34–37.

its educational work beyond the descendants of veterans, and she particularly objected to helping the "children of the mountain whites who fought against the South." [20]

Georgia's UDC members apparently did not share Henderson's animosity toward the descendants of Unionists and deserters, but rather agreed with Gielow that a wider program of race uplift appropriately memorialized the Lost Cause by maintaining white supremacy. The Georgia Division decided to make an exception to UDC rules limiting assistance to Confederate descendants in the case of Andrew Richie's Rabun Gap School, which met the educational needs of poor white mountain children regardless of their parentage. A leading state officer argued that "education is essential supremacy" and hence that the educational reform of southern whites was a crucial aspect of race uplift. Daughters of the Confederacy contributed five hundred dollars annually to the Rabun Gap School and purchased a ten-thousand-dollar tract of land that they allowed the school to use for its own benefit. In addition, the division funded the construction of a girls' dormitory and established a library in the name of former state officer Emily Hendree Park. In 1908 a Georgia leader described the school as a "monument in the mountains . . . where the ignorant children of the purest Anglo-Saxon blood are to be educated into splendid men and women." The UDC state constitution was revised to reflect this new broader emphasis on white educational reform, with the insertion of a clause that proclaimed the organization's intent "to advance the educational interests of our state." [21]

Even though the Georgia Division was willing to overlook highland resis-

20. First quotes from Martha Gielow speech, in *Proceedings of the Tenth CES, with an Appendix in Review of Five Years; Pinhurst, N.C., April 9, 1907* (Richmond, VA: Executive Committee of the Conference, n.d.), 157; Martha Gielow, "Southern Industrial Education," *Confederate Veteran* 14 (March 1906): 113–114; also see Karen L. Cox, "Women, the Lost Cause, and the New South: The United Daughters of the Confederacy and the Transmission of Confederate Culture, 1894–1919" (Ph.D. diss., University of Southern Mississippi, 1997), 130–132; last quote as cited on 131; and Karen L. Cox, *Dixie's Daughters: The United Daughters of the Confederacy and the Preservation of Confederate Culture* (Gainesville: University Press of Florida, 2003).

21. First quote from Dorothy Blount Lamar, Georgia Division Report, *Minutes of the Fifteenth Annual Convention of the UDC*, 1908, 299; second quote from C. Helen Plane speech, *Minutes of the Fifteenth Annual Convention of the UDC*, 1908, 11; last quote from Dorothy Blount Lamar, Georgia Division Report, *Minutes of the Eighteenth Annual Meeting of the UDC*, 1911, 326.

tance to the Confederacy in the interest of white supremacy, reform leaders could not ignore the political tensions inherent in the UDC national controversy. Educational reformers found ingenious ways to defend the loyalty of mountaineers through appeals to both national and regional patriotism. On the one hand, they often expressed pride in highland support for the Revolutionary War, referring to the battle of King's Mountain as a battle "mainly of mountaineers" that proved the "turning point of the American Revolution." In her report on mountain work at the UDC national convention, the Georgia Division president boasted that in the veins of the region's mountain whites "flowed the blood of men who fought at Cowpens, Camden, King's Mountain, and triumphed with Washington at Yorktown." On the other hand, it was exactly because the mountain population had few slaves and strong Unionist sympathies during the sectional crisis that other reformers could perceive them as representing a heroism unsullied by connections to slavery. Rebecca Latimer Felton rejected the accusation that mountaineers had betrayed the South during the Civil War, arguing instead that they had exhibited a support for the Confederacy that was all the more patriotic because it was not based on self-interest, but on loyalty to "birthplace and home ties." Such arguments contributed to a blurring of the lines between racial and national identity, supporting a view of mountaineers as Americans exhibiting a pure patriotism that was all the more nationally representative because it was impeccably white.[22]

Women's focus on white race uplift was not just a strategy for building public support; it also reflected their genuine concern for the national reputation of the South and its poor whites. Their sense of regional pride was offended by exaggerated accounts of the primitive nature of highland life. Local-color writers often treated mountaineers as a cultural oddity, focusing on the more melodramatic aspects of mountain life—such as the notorious feuds and whiskey stills—that made highland society appear backward and barbaric. To make matters worse, northern ministers and philanthropists so-

22. Shapiro, *Appalachia on Our Mind*, x, 133–134; first quote from White, "Our Southern Highlands," 217; report of Lamar, *Minutes of the Eighteenth Annual Convention of the United Daughters of the Confederacy*, 1911, 325–326; Rebecca Latimer Felton, "Wards of the State," Rebecca Latimer Felton Collection (hereafter RLF), box 11, Hargrett Rare Book and Manuscript Collection, Special Collections, University of Georgia Libraries, Athens.

liciting donations for home mission work were prone to publicize the most dramatic cases of deprivation as proof of desperate need. The "typical mountaineer" stereotype was based on the most isolated of highlanders, those living in crude one-room cabins high up in the folds of ridges or on mountaintops. The soil was not well suited for agricultural use and there were few opportunities for wage labor, so families had to make do with the barest essentials in the way of food, clothing, and shelter. Home mission supporters argued that extreme poverty and isolation produced a moral degeneracy that cried out for intervention. In reality, only a portion of the highland population faced such harsh conditions. Those who lived in the lower hills and valleys and tilled more fertile lands had an existence virtually identical to that of small-scale farmers elsewhere in the region. Furthermore, the lawlessness, individualism, and resistance to change attributed to mountaineers represented only a more extreme version of the localism that characterized rural culture throughout the South.[23]

Perhaps most offensive to southern reformers were claims that the moral degeneracy of their region's poor whites was due to defective genes. Charles B. Davenport, a Harvard-trained biologist and one of America's leading eugenicists, fully accepted Fiske's account of the ancestral origins of highlanders and used eugenic organizations to push forward the theory that southern poor whites were an inferior class of Americans. He argued that even though white "germ plasm" was generally superior to that of blacks and Europeans of Mediterranean descent, there always had been undesirable genetic subgroups among persons of English, Scottish, and German origin. This neatly explained how mountaineers could be descendants of, in Davenport's words, the "original American stocks" without inheriting the noble character of colonists and revolutionaries. Davenport used his position as director of the Eugenics Records Office (ERO) (which became part of the Carnegie Institute's Department of Genetics in 1921) to suppress evidence that pellagra was caused by nutritional insufficiencies rather than the inferior genes of the southern poor. The legitimacy of Davenport's theories was threatened again in 1914, when the campaign to eradicate hookworm disease proved that many physical and mental problems afflicting poor whites had an environmental rather than hereditary cause. Nonetheless, the ERO maintained throughout the

23. *Georgia: Historical and Industrial,* 148–154.

1920s that southern poor whites were a "shiftless, ignorant, worthless class of anti-social whites" whose reproduction threatened national health.[24]

Northern attacks on the hereditary integrity of mountaineers and other poor whites violated southerners' view of their Anglo-Saxon cultural inheritance as the most white and most American. Rebecca Latimer Felton, one of Georgia's fiercest defenders of poor whites and probably the best-educated layperson on the subject of eugenics, interpreted critical accounts of mountaineers and mountain life as an assault on white supremacy and regional pride. After becoming outraged by the *Century* essay, she launched a prolonged writing campaign in defense of the character, honor, and genetic worth of mill workers and mountaineers. In one response she claimed that writers who portrayed southern poor whites as "ignorant, debased, inimical to refinement and inferior to the Negro in their lives and habits" were trying to support racial equality by disproving white supremacy. They were creating gross caricatures of poor whites "to prove the absurdity of resistance to social equality, and to substantiate the claims of the colored people to full and free association and equality with the white people of the late seceding states." Felton lambasted local-color writers for presenting "extremely rough but rare specimens" as typical mountaineers and sarcastically suggested that Charles Darwin "had missed the opportunity of a lifetime" in failing to study such a group of whites who started out with the "best blood of the Caucasian race" and quickly descended below the level of blacks.[25]

Felton's defensive tone was echoed in the words of countless other reformers, who usually turned to environmental influences to explain the backward state of highland life. Drawing upon the popular image of highlanders as Revolutionary era relics, mountain workers argued that isolation from outside influences had prevented their social progress even as it had preserved racial integrity. Club women emphasized lack of education as the single most important environmental cause of social ills troubling mountain families.

24. Fiske, *Old Virginia and Her Neighbors,* 311–321; first two Davenport quotes as cited by Tucker, *The Science and Politics of Racial Research,* 68; Allan Chase, *The Legacy of Malthus: The Social Costs of the New Scientific Racism* (New York: Alfred A. Knopf, 1977), 193–200, 208, 221–222, last quote as cited by Chase, 193.

25. De Graffenried, "The Georgia Cracker in the Cotton Mills"; newspaper clippings, September 24, 1891, and July 17, 1892, and quotes from Felton's handwritten draft of her published response to the de Graffenried article, RLF, box 11.

Lucy Lester Willet, director of Tallulah Falls School from 1913 to 1922, described for Georgia Federation members the "wretched homes" of mountain families in which overworked women eked out a thankless subsistence. She hastened to add that their impoverishment was "heroic, not debasing," because mountain women met it with "stoicism and Christian fortitude." It was "ignorance," Willet claimed, which caused the poverty that pressed like a weight on the shoulders of women and children—mountain people simply did not know better ways to live. SAEGM president Sara B. C. Morgan similarly argued that mountain whites had been "left in ignorance of the joys and duties and laws of the higher civilization" and needed to be "shown the avenues which lead to that development of mind and body that would give them a fair chance."[26]

Southern reformers' defensiveness on the issue of poor whites stemmed in part from the fact that there was little to distinguish poor mountaineers from poor blacks. The postbellum emergence of an industrial economy based on free labor had certain racial leveling effects. Ordinary whites no longer had slavery to lift them above the lowest level of servitude, to insulate them from economic competition with those below and above them in the social order. Lacking substantial access to financial resources and formal education, rural blacks and white mountaineers occupied similar positions in the economy. Their ability to survive on a combination of subsistence production and poorly paid wage labor fueled profits for landowners and employers who at once exploited and perpetuated their poverty. Even educational reformers sometimes described mountain whites in terms remarkably similar to those used to describe African Americans. Their statements expressed disapproval of both groups for lacking work habits appropriate to a capitalist industrial economy. One educator described the mountain man as a person who lived "altogether in the present," who "cannot look to the future, to remote ends, any more than can a child." He had to be taught the value of labor, to be inspired and enlightened by teachers who could "direct the energy now expended in hunt and dance and frolic toward more remote but far more useful ends."[27]

26. Tallulah Falls Industrial School report and SAEGM report, *GFWC Yearbook, 1921–1922* (Atlanta: GFWC, 1922), 66–67, 87–88.

27. On the relationship between industrialization and highland self-sufficiency, see Paul Salstrom, *Appalachia's Path to Dependency: Rethinking a Region's Economic History, 1730–1940* (Lex-

In defiance of the implications of their own words, educational reformers resisted collapsing the white and black poor into a single category and instead used Darwinist and eugenic theory to maintain an artificial distinction between the two groups. Educators who described mountain men as childlike were careful to note that their superior blood would prevail if only the negative aspects of their environment were remedied. Unlike blacks, whose origins in a barbaric people would forever retard their advancement, mountaineers needed only be exposed to uplifting influences to assume the superior position that their genetic inheritance guaranteed them. Most remarkable were the female reformers who praised mountaineers' fierce independence as evidence of their genetic worth even as they sought to transform male individualism into a more cooperative model of behavior. According to the evolutionary view of society, submission in the face of adversity was indicative of hereditary weakness, and charitable assistance could only further depress the spirit of self-reliance. Highlanders' love of autonomy was presented as additional proof of their Anglo-Saxon credentials, an acquired characteristic passed down from Revolutionary War ancestors who created a new nation because they could not abide the yoke of English oppression. Praising mountain families for their stubborn pride, especially their refusal to accept charity, served to set them apart from less worthy groups, such as blacks, who seemed ever in need of assistance.[28]

The claim that mountaineers' genetic inheritance distinguished them from blacks worked only if isolation truly had maintained their racial purity, but it is far from clear that this was the case. In 1910 UDC state president Dorothy Blount Lamar asserted that mountain whites had not even *seen* black people, much less had personal dealings with them. She related how mountaineers in

---

ington: University Press of Kentucky, 1994); quotes from J. T. Noe, "The Education of the Mountain Child," in *Southern Educational Association, Journal of Proceedings and Addresses of the Twenty-Second Annual Meeting Held at Houston, Texas, November 30, December 1, 2, 1911* (Nashville, TN: SEA, n.d.), 211–212; Andrew Richie made similar comments, although he believed that the most isolated of mountain adults were beyond help and that the "only hope is to be found in the children," *Rabun Industrial School*, 15.

28. Regarding the tension between dependence and independence in establishing the worthiness of recipients of aid, see Linda Gordon, *Heroes of Their Own Lives: The Politics and History of Family Violence, Boston, 1880–1960* (New York: Viking Penguin, 1988); and Michael B. Katz, *In the Shadow of the Poorhouse: A Social History of Welfare in America* (New York: Basic Books, 1986).

Rabun County had been so amazed to see a black servant accompanying a hunting party that "they asked to be allowed to rub his black hands to see if it would come off." Such claims are contradicted by 1910 census data, which shows that an extraordinary percentage of blacks in the mountain counties were categorized as mulattos. Statewide, little more than 17 percent of all blacks fell into this category. More than half of the mountain counties exceeded this proportion, and six had 30 percent or more blacks with some white ancestry. The counties with the highest proportion—Catoosa, Fannin, Gilmer, Habersham, Rabun, and Whitfield—were in the most remote northern section of the state bordering Tennessee. In the Rabun County of Lamar's tale, almost 65 percent of blacks were classified as mulatto! Granted, blacks made up a very small percentage of the mountain population, and in none of the above six counties did they comprise more than 11 percent of the population. Because the highland homes were sparsely scattered in the northern border region and there were few towns, it is possible that some mountain whites could have lived their lives without seeing an African American. However, mountaineers were not as isolated as reformers often depicted them, and the mixed-race population belied claims of complete racial separation.[29]

Since club women made frequent and extensive use of census data in their reform campaigns, it is likely that they were familiar with the evidence of miscegenation and were worried about its implications for the future of mountain whites. Southern proponents of eugenics often depicted miscegenation as the inevitable result of ignorance and poverty among white women, and mountaineers who were isolated from outside influences were free to estab-

---

29. Dorothy Blount Lamar quote from Georgia Division Report, *Minutes of the Eighteenth Annual Meeting of the UDC,* 1911, 326; U.S. Bureau of the Census, *Thirteenth Census of the U.S. Taken in the Year 1910: Abstracts of the Census, Statistics of Population, Agriculture, Manufactures, and Mining for the United States, the States, and Principal Cities, with Supplement for Georgia Containing Statistics for the State, Counties, Cities, and Other Divisions* (Washington, DC: Government Printing Office, 1913), 604–633; Gene Wilhelm Jr., "Appalachian Isolation: Fact or Fiction?" in *An Appalachian Symposium: Essays Written in Honor of Cratis D. Williams* (Boone, NC: Appalachian State University Press, 1977), 77–91; Eller, *Miners, Millhands, and Mountaineers,* 12–16. While there were persons in Tennessee of Mediterranean descent (sometimes called Melungeons) who were categorized as black, there is no evidence of such groups in North Georgia, so it is likely that Georgians categorized as mulatto were in fact, as the census states, persons with a mixture of Negro and white ancestry.

lish their own values and standards governing interracial relations. An apparent prevalence of miscegenation made the need for intervention more critical than ever, since it threatened white supremacy and further blurred the lines between the white and black poor. It seemed to confirm another unflattering stereotype of poor whites as having loose morals, and in fact some mountain workers claimed that more isolated mountaineers placed no stigma on illegitimacy and cohabitation outside the bonds of marriage. As part of their campaign of race uplift, middle-class club women were vitally concerned with impressing acceptable standards of behavior on mountain girls and women. They were especially preoccupied with children's early exposure to the "facts of life." Female reformers delicately mentioned the lack of privacy in one-room cabins as an unwholesome influence on young girls, presumably because the crowded quarters exposed them to nudity and sexual acts. Women needed to exert moral influence to secure for female mountaineers the social respectability that was the rightful inheritance of all white women, while using education to preserve racial integrity by raising poor whites above the level of blacks.[30]

The central way in which female reformers were to exert this critical influence was through the creation of their own educational institutions in North Georgia. The success of the mountain campaign, more so than in any other female reform effort, rested upon women's direct involvement in establishing, funding, and staffing schools. Impoverished mountain families whose mobility was limited by poor roads, rugged terrain, and harsh weather had few resources to contribute to the cause, necessitating a more intense level of engagement on the part of organized women. One potential source of assistance, the southern church, was slow to begin home mission work in the Appalachians. Northern Presbyterians had been operating mountain schools for twenty years when the Southern Baptists first entered the field in 1898 (although Georgia Baptists went on to establish four mountain schools over the next two decades). Georgia Federation members were among the southern

---

30. Organized women were among the most prominent supporters of southern eugenic legislation intended to "protect" the less capable of their sex, and in 1918 the Georgia Federation endorsed the findings of a eugenics institute whose survey of Georgia prisons included the recommendation that morally degenerate women such as prostitutes be confined to sexually segregated work farms. Larson, *Sex, Race, and Science*, 61–62, 68–76; Campbell, *The Southern Highlander*, 132–133.

pioneers in highland reform when they founded two model schools in the mountain counties of Floyd (1901) and Rabun (1908) and another in the foothills of Bartow County (1905). More importantly, women began opening their own privately owned boarding schools, beginning with Martha Berry's industrial school for mountain boys (1902); it was followed by the Georgia Federation's own Tallulah Falls School (1909) and the Southern Mountain Educational Association's industrial school for mountain girls (1912).[31]

Martha Berry's early attempts to establish day schools illustrate the myriad of problems that made organized women turn to boarding schools as the answer to their reform needs. Berry became concerned about the scarcity of highland schools while a young woman in her early twenties, and she responded by opening free day schools for children who lived in the hills surrounding her family's Floyd County home. It was not long before Berry became frustrated with the problems caused by irregular attendance. Students missed weeks and months of school at a time, either because bad weather made travel difficult or because good weather induced parents to keep them at work on the farm. Along with the annual six-month vacation, the numerous absences meant that Berry could not maintain a continuous influence on students' attitudes toward school and work. She felt that her efforts were futile; children who learned "new facts, new habits" for one half of the year promptly "forgot the facts and relapsed into old, careless ways" during the other half. Determined to provide an atmosphere in which to effect permanent change, Berry used a small farm that was part of her inheritance to found the Boys' Industrial School. The campus was to be a self-contained environment where students lived, worked, played, and worshipped, removed from the "influence of old associations" and "old customs."[32]

The Tallulah Falls School had similar beginnings. The GFWC institution

31. Campbell, *Southern Highland Schools;* White, "Our Southern Highlands," 229–235; GFWC report to the Women's Session, in *Proceedings of CES, 1907,* 147–150; Wilma Dykeman notes that state neglect (such as inadequate funding of roads and schools) functioned to maintain the stereotype of mountaineers as backward primitives, conveniently reinforcing regional prejudices that marginalized them politically. "Appalachia in Context," in *An Appalachian Symposium,* ed. Joel W. Williamson (Boone, NC: Appalachian State University Press, 1977), 28–42.

32. Martha Berry, "The Planting and Care of an Industrial School," in *Proceedings of the Ninth CES, Lexington, Kentucky, May 2–4, 1906* (Richmond, VA: Executive Committee of the Conference, 1906), 83–84; quotes from Harnett T. Kane and Inez Henry, *Miracle in the Mountains* (New York: Doubleday, 1956), 48–49.

opened as a day school in 1909, but a desire to widen their scope of influence quickly convinced club women of the need to expand their facilities. In 1912 the newly constructed Lipscomb cottage became a "model home" for seven pupils and three teachers, one of whom was the school principal. Six years later, when the number of boarders had doubled, principal Anne Carrington Davis informed the Federation that absenteeism had become a serious problem among day students who had to travel by foot or horse during the winter months. She also argued that it had become "obvious" that boarders "living under the direct influence of the teachers were undoubtedly getting greater advantages, more lasting benefits, and superior life training." School supporters responded by funding the expansion of the Lipscomb cottage so that it could accommodate an additional ten students. The Georgia Federation continued to add buildings to the Tallulah Fall campus over the next ten years, and by the 1926–1927 school year the institution was providing housing for half of its two hundred students.[33]

In addition to maintaining continuity in students' training, boarding schools had the benefit of maximizing reformers' influence by recasting them as surrogate parents. School administrators were fully aware of this benefit and deliberately tried to create a sense of family among teachers and students. Wren King, a member of the first group of students to attend Tallulah Falls, later recalled that the schoolhouse "was more like a home than a school" and contained on one side of its hallway a "room furnished like a living room with a piano, rug, and chairs." Mountain schools further simulated the home environment by providing dormitories where children lived under the direct supervision of their teachers. Club women justified this arrangement to parents on the grounds of necessity, since many families lived hours away, but they valued the opportunity to establish an intimate rapport with the children. Living together facilitated the development of reciprocal emotional ties between teachers and students, helping to overcome cultural differences and encouraging an awareness of common purpose. Resident student labor limited operating expenses for the schools, which were always strapped for cash, and enhanced the homelike atmosphere by having children share responsibility for chores just as they would have done on their parents' farms. As a descrip-

33. Carol Stevens Hancock, *The Light in the Mountains: A History of Tallulah Falls School* (Toccoa, GA: Tallulah Falls School, 1975), 24–57, quote 45.

tion of children's duties at Tallulah Falls explained it, "students are expected to assume the responsibility of family members, but they are richly rewarded with the feeling of 'belonging,' that is a rich and satisfying part of *family* and of *home*."[34]

Teachers and administrators in club women's nonsectarian schools were truly settlement workers, even though many considered themselves engaged in home mission work. Similar to the urban settlement houses that used education to "Americanize" immigrants, mountain schools served as mediators between highlanders and the wider culture outside of the hills. Leaders of the Southern Industrial Education Association made a direct analogy between mountain reform and programs for immigrant education, arguing that the "true and primitive Americans" of the highlands were in need of Americanization because they had been isolated from the rest of the nation for generations. In Georgia, the approach to highland reform differed from missionary work as it usually was defined, in that women did not attempt to further the influence of any particular denomination. Urban club women considered their work at once a patriotic and a Christian calling that far transcended any artificial institutional boundaries. Just as Georgia Division members could consider the Rabun Gap school to fulfill UDC goals in spirit even if it violated their technical rules, so too could Georgia Federation members interpret their moral instruction as spreading the spirit of the gospel even if it did not further the influence of any particular church. The GFWC dedicated its Tallulah Falls School to "the service of God through education" while strictly avoiding any denominational affiliation. Similarly, Martha Berry emphasized that her school was "non-sectarian, but distinctly Christian in character." Students were required to attend the church of their choice, while Berry and most of her faculty attended only the nondenominational services on campus to avoid the appearance of endorsing any particular sect.[35]

---

34. First quote from Hancock, *Light in the Mountains*, 19; second quote from DeJarnette, *A Pattern for Education in Living*, 16, emphasis in original; Tallulah Falls School report, *GFWC Yearbook, 1921–1922*, 64–65.

35. First quote from "Educational Association Makes Stirring Appeal," *Atlanta Constitution*, October 3, 1909; second quote from *Information Quiz*, Tallulah Falls School pamphlet, in author's file; third quote from Martha Berry, "The Boys' Industrial School, Rome, Georgia," *GDE Thirty-Second Annual Report, 1903*, 203; Kane and Henry, *Miracle in the Mountains*, 130. Although he does not deal with mountain reform, John P. McDowell addresses motivations for

In accordance with Sallie Hill's plan for a revival of the highland economy, all of the schools founded by female reformers emphasized the use of industrial and agricultural training. Club women had an abiding faith in both the moral and the economic value of a practical education. If mountaineers truly were a cultural artifact of an earlier time, then their way of life had to expire in the developing economy of the industrial South and they needed to learn new ways to survive. Women reformers wanted to provide these survival skills and believed that physical labor and strict work and study regimens would instill in children habits of behavior more appropriate to industrial society. GFWC leaders announced that a central purpose of the Tallulah Falls School was to teach the "dignity of labor and habits of industry" that would help students "to build up their own homes as well as to improve the school in which they are being trained." Martha Berry kept her boys busy for more than twelve hours per day and was quite open about her intent to impress upon them the importance of "time and system." As she explained in a report to the state Department of Education, "boys who have known nothing but the happy-go-lucky life of the farm are generally greatly lacking in anything like system and promptness, and possess but a vague idea of the value of time." [36]

The goal of the agricultural component of mountain schools necessarily differed from that of the movement for greater self-sufficiency among lowland whites. The mountain counties had never been a big cotton-growing area, outside of a few river valleys, so highland farms were more oriented toward subsistence agriculture than those of poor whites in the Black Belt. Consequently, mountaineers did not have to be convinced to plant something other than cotton, but they did have to be persuaded that new crops and farming techniques were necessary. The staples of mountain diet were corn and pork, usually supplemented by beans, potatoes, and wild apples and berries. These did not provide a nutritionally balanced diet for families, especially during

southern home mission work in *Social Gospel in the South: The Woman's Home Mission Movement in the Methodist Episcopal Church, South, 1886–1939* (Baton Rouge: Louisiana State University Press, 1982), 68–71, 144–145. For a comparison of settlement and mission work, see Mina Carson, *Settlement Folk: Social Thought and the American Settlement Movement, 1885–1930* (Chicago: University of Chicago Press, 1990), 56–57, 67–68.

36. First quote from report of Executive Board, *GFWC Yearbook, 1906–1907* (Atlanta: GFWC, 1907), 13–15; second quote from Berry, "The Boys' Industrial School," 203; last quote from Berry, "The Planting and Care of an Industrial School," 87.

winter months when stores of preserved foods ran low. Crops grown for the local market generally were of poor quality and did not take advantage of new methods (such as the use of fertilizers) that could increase yield. Most families had very little cash income from their small cotton or corn patches and still relied on barter for necessities that they could not produce themselves.[37]

Women reformers focused on providing their students with the means to improve agricultural production, increase household income, and generally enhance the quality of home life. The Tallulah Falls School offered a combination of elementary and vocational courses, with the focus on "usable knowledge" that could "train children for the life and the duties about them." The curriculum offered study in cooking, sewing, and basket making for girls and instruction in farming and carpentry for boys. School administrators later added girls' canning and poultry clubs and boys' corn and pig clubs in cooperation with the Georgia College of Agriculture extension services. At Martha Berry's Boys' Industrial School, the campus included a barn, a workshop, a woodshed, a laundry, and a dairy. Students provided all the labor necessary for everyday operations and participated in the clearing of land and construction of new buildings. Berry wanted to teach local boys the "many things which they would very probably find necessary to be done when they left the school and went out in the battles of everyday life." All students had to work on the school farm for two hours every day, during which time they received instruction in scientific agriculture. Ultimately, women reformers intended for the students to become ambassadors of progress, returning home imbued with enthusiasm for new ways of doing things and inspiring a similar enthusiasm in their parents.[38]

The women who ran highland schools wanted to reform more than just morals and farming methods; their concerns for the inadequacies of mountain life extended to gender relations as well. Martha Berry's incongruous de-

---

37. Campbell, *The Southern Highlander*, 198–200; Wayne Flynt, *Poor but Proud: Alabama's Poor Whites* (Tuscaloosa: University of Alabama Press, 1989), 162.

38. First quote from Emily Hendree Park, "The Educational Work of the Club Women of Georgia," in *Proceedings of the Twelfth CES Atlanta, Georgia, April 14–16, 1909* (Nashville, TN: Executive Committee of the Conference, n.d.), 145; Sallie Hill, report of GFWC School Improvement Section, in GDE, *Thirty-Eighth Annual Report, 1909* (Atlanta: GDE, 1910), 314; Tallulah Falls School report, *GFWC Yearbook, 1914–1915* (Atlanta: GFWC, 1915), 26; last quote from Berry, "The Boys' Industrial School," 197.

scription of her student's life on the family farm as "happy-go-lucky" obscures an underlying disapproval of highland men's behavior. Her comments reflected a common belief among reformers that mountain men worked only four or five months of the year. One typical description of the highland husband declared that "he toils hard in the field for long hours during the crop season but he does little work during the rest of the year"; instead of helping his wife during the off-season, "he sits around the country store or goes fishing a great deal of the time." This criticism arose from the cultural gulf separating reformers and mountaineers. Urban middle-class whites simply could not see hunting and fishing as labor that helped to support the household, and they were too much a part of industrial society to regard a seasonal work routine as appropriate. Mountain women's equal participation in outdoor agricultural labor provoked further disapproval among reformers who believed such work was best left to men and blacks. Ironically, the gendered division of labor that bothered middle-class whites the most was a strategy that mountain families deliberately pursued to remain on the land. In most instances, the woman toiling alone in the fields was there so that her husband could engage in wage labor, preventing the necessity of the entire family migrating to enter millwork.[39]

Highlander gender relations were of great interest to early-twentieth-century writers and reformers, who often commented on the unmitigated patriarchy of the mountain household. They described mountain men as the absolute rulers of their households, men who would brook no challenge to their authority inside or outside the home. Men roamed freely about the countryside and acted as the family's main contact with the outside world, while women were tied to the home by their extensive domestic duties and rarely even saw relatives. According to one survey of southern highland culture, women played no part in political or religious affairs and lacked all but the most rudimentary education. Mountaineers commonly believed that there

39. See Nora Miller's chapter "The Mountain Farm Family" in *The Girl in the Rural Family* (Chapel Hill: University of North Carolina Press, 1935), 15–26, quotes 21; Shifflett, *Coal Towns,* 15–16; John C. Campbell, who was more familiar with mountain culture than most reformers, noted that there was no stigma attached to female field work among mountaineers and that mountain women, like rural women elsewhere, often expressed a preference for outdoor work as opposed to indoor household chores. *The Southern Highlander,* 134.

was no need to educate girls because there was no future for them outside the home. Therefore, while intellectually gifted boys might leave to pursue further education or a career outside the highlands, promising girls had nothing to look forward to but marriage. A woman who did not marry was considered a failure by her family and had almost no possibilities for self-support— subsistence duties left little time for production for the market, and teaching was a part-time job that paid too poorly to allow financial independence. These conditions led observers to characterize mountain women as "drudges" who were considered by their husbands to be "little more than a sort of superior domestic animal."[40]

Club women had special reason to disapprove of the structure of the mountain household. The kinship-dominated culture of the highlands was very similar to that of the antebellum rural South, in that social institutions reinforced patriarchal authority and provided little space for a gender-identified public female culture. Even if some Daughters of the Confederacy were nostalgic for the old order, less conservative club women regarded pre-industrial society (and life in the Old South more generally) as a mixed blessing for women. In their view, the independent frontier household represented a life of isolation, deprivation, and above all, dependency. This was a past to which middle-class women did not wish to return. Emancipation, industrialization, and urbanization had offered them unprecedented opportunity—to organize, to realize their intellectual potential, to renegotiate their relationships with men, and to more fully acquire civil rights and legal protections. Mountaineers, as the most rural southerners and the whites with the least in common culturally with their reformers, represented a unique challenge to women engaged in the process of redefining regional concepts of citizenship and community in more gender-equal terms. Urban women could not help but see the patriarchy of the highland home as a central problem and the creation of a more egalitarian family relationship as its solution.[41]

40. Campbell, *The Southern Highlander,* 124–129; quote from Horace Kephart, *Our Southern Highlanders* (New York: Outing, 1913), 257–258.

41. Superintendent's report for Gilmer County, in GDE, *Annual Report, 1909,* 107–108; C. S. Parrish, Supervisor's report for North Georgia, in GDE, *Forty-First Annual Report, 1912* (Atlanta: GDE, 1913), 45–46; Jeanette Keith, *Country People in the New South: Tennessee's Upper Cumberland* (Chapel Hill: University of North Carolina Press, 1995), 31. On kinship and the sta-

Even though club women praised the independent spirit of highlanders as a group, they criticized the behavior of mountain men. They were disturbed by feuds and lawlessness, and many believed that corn liquor was at the bottom of all this male unruliness. Women mountain workers had some reason to believe this other than their own sympathies for temperance reform, given the extent of moonshine production in North Georgia. The topic gained extensive public exposure in the 1880s and 1890s, when the federal government stepped up its enforcement of the liquor tax and began scouring the southern Appalachians for stills. Dawson, Lumpkin, Gilmer, and Pickens counties were famous for whiskey production, and output only increased after the state prohibition law passed in 1907. Once federal prohibition took effect in the 1920s, almost half of the more than two thousand prisoners held in Atlanta's federal penitentiary were men arrested for running stills. Locals who informed Internal Revenue agents of the location of illegal whiskey operations were subject to retaliatory violence. A group of Pickens County moonshiners who called themselves the "The Honest Man's Friend and Protector" rode the countryside at night to intimidate locals into silence. They dressed in black hoods and robes much like the white garb of the Ku Klux Klan and burned the houses of several suspected informants before they were arrested. Andrew Richie complained of whiskey-related violence in Rabun County as well, arguing that "its trail of blood can be traced on every page of mountain criminal history." He was convinced that Rabun was a "banner county for the manufacture of this 'moonshine' product" and that it was "fairly swamped with whiskey and whiskey sentiment." [42]

Many club women agreed with Richie that "there is no greater source of moral or social deterioration" than moonshine, and they regarded it as a serious threat to the welfare of the highland household. Mountaineers devel-

tus of women in the Old South, see Jean E. Friedman, *The Enclosed Garden: Women and Community in the Evangelical South, 1830–1900* (Chapel Hill: University of North Carolina Press, 1985). Home mission workers in the American West also regarded patriarchy as a central problem and were concerned with improving the status of women in the frontier and immigrant households they wanted to reform. Peggy Pascoe, *Relations of Rescue: The Search for Female Moral Authority in the American West, 1874–1939* (New York: Oxford University Press, 1990), 36–46.

42. Joseph Earl Dabney, *Mountain Spirits: A Chronicle of Corn Whiskey from King James' Ulster Plantation to America's Appalachians and the Moonshine Life* (New York: Charles Scribner's Sons, 1974), 77, 111, 131–133; Richie, *Rabun Industrial School*, 12.

oped the manufacture of alcohol from corn as an economic necessity, because they were removed from major markets and transportation of crops across the hills was difficult. Eight gallons of corn could be condensed into one gallon of whiskey and then sold for five or six times the value of the product in its original form. For the most part, women reformers did not appreciate this ingenious adaptation to environment. Martha Berry was taken aback when a family used receipts from moonshine sales to send a son and a daughter to her school, but she was more understanding than most mountain workers in recognizing their limited options. Other women could not get past their conviction that making and drinking moonshine degraded home life. Like other directors of Tallulah Falls School, Lucy Lester Willet sometimes traveled the hills to visit the homes of students. In 1921 she reported to GFWC members that corn whiskey was "brutalizing" mountain men, and she cited one example in which the "husband is a tyrant and rules his family by fear." "He has not worked for years," she exclaimed, "and peddles freely himself of the fiery stuff." Meanwhile, his wife "labored like a slave in the fields with her children," with no assistance or even "one kind word" from her mate. Willet confessed that although she greatly admired the "strength and character" of the woman, "the repression of those eyes . . . haunt me still."[43]

Club women who used the word *slave* to describe mountain women intended it to have several meanings. Southern Mountain Educational Association members described the female students of the Mineral Bluff School as "slaves to the baneful effect of [their] deplorable environments." Used in this context, the label of slave indicated that girls were not free to determine the course of their lives because nothing in their environment offered them an alternative path, and especially not the Progressive path that club women wished for them. Willet, however, used the concept of slave in a different sense when she lamented that a mountain wife "labored like a slave in the fields." Urban middle-class women could not understand mountain men's attitudes toward women and work. As a southern home extension worker de-

43. Tracy Byers, *Martha Berry: The Sunday Lady of Possum Trot* (New York: G. P. Putnam's Sons, 1932), 204–210; Leo Downing and Ray Rensi, "A Touch of Mountain Dew: Art and History of Whiskey-Making in North Georgia," in *The Many Faces of Appalachia: Exploring a Region's Diversity*, ed. Sam Gray (Boone, NC: Appalachian Consortium Press, 1985), 195–204; Flynt, *Poor but Proud*, 166–168; quotes from Tallulah Falls Industrial School report, in *GFWC Yearbook, 1921–1922*, 66–67.

scribed the situation, the male highlander "regards his wife neither as his equal nor as a weak being who needs protecting from the hardships of life." It appeared to women reformers that the mountain home was stuck in a cultural limbo between the yeoman and plantation households, containing only the worst elements of both. On the one hand, highland women were expected to engage in hard physical labor unceasingly and without complaint, while on the other they were accorded none of the chivalric courtesies to which lowland white women were accustomed. They were subordinated to patriarchal authority with no special recognition or respect for their contributions, and thus there was nothing to distinguish them from slaves, or perhaps more appropriately, from black women.[44]

Southern reformers were perplexed by these peculiarities in highland gender relations and often remarked upon the lack of chivalry among mountain men. Reportedly, male highlanders did not hold doors open for women, or remove hats in their presence, or help them with difficult chores such as hauling water or chopping wood. Martha Berry witnessed this aspect of highland gender relations when one of her young friends married a mountain man. The husband helped his new wife carry water to the house from a spring at the bottom of the hill for the first week of marriage, but stopped after neighbors ridiculed his unmanly behavior. His bride was left to struggle on alone, having "learned that mountain men were not supposed to wait on their women." No doubt such observations were partly a product of class difference, since middle-class women considered the domestic ideal to be companionate marriage and a home in which women were relieved of most physical labor. However, it is interesting that the complaint rarely was made against rural men in lowland Georgia. Reformers criticized lowland farmers for not lightening the burden of domestic chores by allocating more resources to household improvements, but they did not accuse the men of being unchivalrous. Perhaps highlanders' isolation from plantation culture meant not only that hard physical labor did not become stigmatized through connection to enslavement, but also that there was no medium in which the "Southern Belle" image of womanhood could take root. It was no more

44. SMEA Mineral Bluff School report, *GFWC Yearbook, 1912–1913,* 74–75; Tallulah Falls Industrial School report, *GFWC Yearbook, 1921–1922,* 66–67; third quote from Miller, *The Girl in the Rural Family,* 21.

disgraceful or "low-class" for a white woman to work hard for a living than it was for a white man, so there was no need for male courtesies designed to honor women by hinting at their privileged status as white women and as dependents.[45]

Women reformers acted on their disapproval of highland men by using their influence as surrogate parents to promote more egalitarian gender relations. The course of study that Martha Berry chose for her male students illustrates one way in which this could be accomplished. Berry was ever present in student activities from sunup to sundown, directing work inside and outside the classroom and having fireside conversations with students every evening before bedtime. The boys had to engage in every aspect of labor necessary to keep the "home" running, whether it was industrial or domestic. Berry ran into difficulty a few weeks after the school opened, when students refused to do their own laundry because it was "woman's work." Instead of trying to force them into compliance, she undertook the work herself and claimed that the sight of her toiling over their soiled clothes so shamed the boys (who knew from firsthand experience how hard she worked) that they changed their minds. Thereafter, male students were responsible for almost all of their own cooking, cleaning, and laundering, even after Berry opened an adjacent girls' school in 1908. She kept the campuses and their chores strictly separate; girls did not cook and clean for boys, but rather each school was responsible for performing its own household duties. Berry purposefully required this labor of male students because she wanted to inculcate in them different values for home life as well as industrial work habits. The products of her school would be mountain men who did not believe themselves above domestic work and who appreciated the difficulty and importance of their wives' household contributions.[46]

SMEA members also wanted to change the highland home from within with their Mineral Bluff Industrial School for Girls, although their approach was more conservative. Like most rural reformers, the school's supporters be-

45. Quote from Kane and Henry, *Miracle in the Mountains,* 26–27; Kephart, *Our Southern Highlanders,* 257–258; Miller, *The Girl in the Rural Family,* 21.
46. Berry widely cited this laundry incident in speeches, and it is included in all biographical sketches of her work, such as Kane and Henry, *Miracle in the Mountains,* 60–61; Byers, *Martha Berry,* 87–88; and Mildred Sandison Fenner and Eleanor C. Fishburn, *Pioneer American Educators* (Washington, DC: National Education Association, 1944), 145–152.

lieved that immediate improvements in quality of life could be produced through training women for greater efficiency and innovation within the home. In accordance with their concern for the Progressive ideal of educating children for their environment, the SMEA maintained that a narrowly defined vocational curriculum was more appropriate for mountain girls than a collegiate education. The school offered students courses in cooking, preserving, gardening, and nutrition and focused on "food stuffs best produced in the vicinity of their homes." Club women believed that the restricted course of study would avoid giving girls ambitions that could not be realized within their home environment. If the Mineral Bluff school was to have a significant impact on the surrounding population, it had to convince students "that they can render the best service among their own people, the field of their greatest opportunity, by becoming good bakers, mattress makers, and gardeners." Just as with the Tallulah Falls School, supporters of Mineral Bluff Industrial School hoped that their graduates would "go with ambition aroused to better home conditions," making their contribution through either formal teaching or "practical home missionary work."[47]

Because club women's attitudes toward gender roles and social reform were shaped by their own class background, they believed mountain girls had a special part to play in improving highland society. Their own social activism led them to regard the domestic sphere as a civilizing force with the power to shape public concepts of acceptable, ethical behavior. According to the SMEA, the "moonshine districts," where "obedience to social and civil authority has little or no significance," were in particular need of civilizing influence. Club women could open schools to teach mountaineers the technical skills that led to a better life, but "little progress can be made until their social habits are reformed and higher ideals incorporated." The frontier nature of rural society, in which low population density and white male individualism hampered the creation of community, could not be overcome in the mountains exactly as it was in the lowland countryside. Highland towns were too few and too small, and mountain families too distant from one another, for an effective campaign to organize club women, teachers, and

---

47. Mineral Bluff School report, *GFWC Yearbook, 1912–1913,* 74–75; first quote from Mineral Bluff School report, *GFWC Yearbook, 1917–1918* (Atlanta: GFWC, 1918), 54–55; remaining quotes from SMEA report, *GFWC Yearbook, 1916–1917* (Atlanta: GFWC, 1917), 51–52.

parents. Furthermore, schools were even scarcer and more poorly equipped than in the rural piedmont and the Black Belt owing to the greater poverty of the mountain counties. The SMEA president argued to Georgia Federation members that these obstacles could be overcome only through changes in the home, and therefore the "salvation of the typical mountaineer lies in the education and cultivation of the girls."[48]

Georgia Federation leaders agreed with the supporters of the Mineral Bluff School that the key to mountain reform was improving the status of women, but their own commitment to gender equality influenced them to take a more democratic approach to achieving this goal. They believed that exceptional girls had an important role to play *outside* the home. They envisioned Tallulah Falls School as an institution that would cultivate the talents of especially bright female students and then send them forth to widen the scope of organized women's influence. School workers encouraged their best pupils to go on to college, and many obtained loans through the same GFWC financial aid committee that funded the education of girls in other parts of the state. Because of the close relationship between teachers and boarding students, women reformers sometimes took a personal interest and paid for advanced training out of their own pockets. In the summer of 1918, Principal Anne Davis took one of her more promising students, Eliza Shirley, to Lynchburg and New York for further instruction in "weaving and other lines of domestic science and industrial arts." In 1922 Davis reported that Shirley and another Tallulah Falls graduate had been hired to teach at the school, while three other former students had graduated from college and found jobs as principals elsewhere. Club women regarded this as a mutually beneficial relationship. The individual female student had the opportunity to have "her life broadened and her latent talents discovered and developed," while those who returned to their communities as teachers had the potential to impact the lives of many more children than could the individual mother in her home.[49]

A desire to improve the status of mountain women was at least partly responsible for the emphasis on race uplift and racial purity that characterized

48. Report of Mineral Bluff School, *GFWC Yearbook, 1912–1913*, 74–75.

49. Open letter from Anne "Nannie" C. Carrington to the club women of Georgia, 1922, reprinted in Hancock, *Light in the Mountains*, 216, also see 46; second quote from Tallulah Falls School report, *GFWC Yearbook, 1921–22*, 67.

club women's public relations campaigns for mountain reform. Whatever their individual beliefs regarding eugenic theory, female supporters of mountain reform clearly regarded the white supremacist functions of women's reproductive role as a potential source of their empowerment. Racial integrity, in the eugenic sense of maintenance of racial purity and cultivation of superior characteristics, was dependent upon the quality of mothers and mothering. In turn, the quality of maternal nurture was greatly affected by exposure to Progressive, scientific information on the function of heredity and environment in childhood development. Women whose poverty or isolation deprived them of access to this information were more likely to reproduce negative traits generation after generation, increasing the social costs (the resulting crime, disease, and inefficiency) and contributing to racial degeneration. The emphasis of the Southern Mountain Educational Association and the Southern Association for the Education of Georgia Mountaineers on highland girls as "mothers of the race" played directly to these concerns, justifying greater funding of mountain education by portraying it as in the collective interests of all white Americans. It was a racial appeal with overtones of regional patriotism—defense of southern whiteness—that served to sidestep the social and political differences separating mountaineers from other Georgians.

Many of the race and gender concerns of women reformers found expression in the opinions of Rebecca Felton, a club woman and political activist who was profoundly influenced by eugenics. In a series of lectures and articles written between 1897 and 1902, Felton developed her view of the politics of gender and reproduction and its implications for public education. A major theme that emerged in speeches before the United Daughters of the Confederacy, the National Congress of Mothers, the Atlanta Woman's Club, and the Georgia Sociological Society was the centrality of white female education to the preservation of racial integrity and regional and national identity. "If the American nation retains the force of character, the prowess, the progressive qualities and energy of its ancestry," Felton vehemently declared, "it will be done by preserving the race characteristics of these United States." She maintained that motherhood was at the heart of the environmental and hereditary influences that worked to produce a healthy or defective child; hence, the "education of the coming mothers of the white race" was necessary to ensure a sound citizenry. Felton believed that once early childhood development was stunted by an ignorant and degraded mother, subsequent training and assistance could not undo the damage. If women were "only valuable to the human race as burden-bearers for the office of maternity," she argued, "the magnitude of responsibility toward the child-bearing class cannot be over-estimated nor can the dangers that attend illiteracy and degraded character be overdrawn."[50]

Rebecca Felton knew that the race status and the gender status of white women were interrelated, and in her skillful hands the politics of reproduction became a tool for white female advancement rather than oppression. In making a case for women's enfranchisement, she argued that every man "owes his social status to his mother." She referred to antebellum race laws to prove this point, noting that white mothers always conferred freedom upon their offspring regardless of paternity, whereas slave mothers could produce only enslaved children. Felton further developed her arguments for gender equality by expanding her definition of the factors that influenced childhood development: it was not just the education and morals of the individual mother, but also the social and political status of women that shaped the character of children. Through this wider concept of environment, Felton was able to justify woman suffrage, prohibition, a higher legal age-of-consent, elimination of the sexual double standard, and equal pay for equal work as reforms designed to allow women to exert greater control over the quality of marriage and mothering. What Felton had cleverly done was to expose the extent to which the concept of racial integrity was a burden weighing more heavily on women and to hold men responsible for that fact. The maintenance of racial purity depended upon women's purity; yet in limiting their autonomy, white men denied them the ability to protect it.[51]

Georgia women's use of reproductive politics to push forward educational

50. Quotes from Felton, "Wards of the State," RLF, box 11; Felton, "Some of the Influences Which Affect Life and Character," speech to Atlanta Woman's Club, April 24, 1901, as reprinted in Felton, *Country Life in Georgia in the Days of My Youth* (Atlanta: Index Printing, 1919; repr., New York: Arno Press, 1980), 141–157 (citations are to the 1980 edition); also see Felton, "On Heredity," speech to National Congress of Mothers, February 19, 1897, clipping from *Atlanta Constitution*, RLF, box 12.

51. Quotes from Felton, "Why I Am a Suffragist," as reprinted in Felton, *Country Life*, 257. Felton's most developed version of this argument is in her 1902 address before the Georgia Sociological Society, "The Problems That Interest Motherhood," in Felton, *Country Life*, 279–295.

reform represented a "racialized" version of the maternalist rhetoric employed by many women's organizations in the late nineteenth and early twentieth centuries. The Women's Christian Temperance Union, formed in the 1870s as a result of a female grassroots movement, used the protection of home and motherhood as justification for a wide-ranging program of social reform. Like Felton, herself a state WCTU leader, the national organization tackled issues of sexuality and reproduction as part of their campaign to empower women inside and outside of the home. Groups that advocated protective legislation for female wage workers, such as the General Federation of Women's Clubs and the National Consumers' League, argued that women's role in childbearing and child-rearing necessitated legally limiting employers' ability to exploit their labor. The National Congress of Mothers and Parent-Teacher Associations argued for legislative reforms to protect child health and welfare based on the nation's collective interest in successful mothering. Although there were many differences among groups regarding the extent of commitment to gender equality, in all cases organized women sought to remove social constrictions that allowed the outside world to intrude upon the home while limiting women's ability to compensate.[52]

Despite the social force of their arguments and the remarkable initiative shown in opening their own independent schools, Georgia club women were less than successful in instituting larger structural reform. Highlanders made less progress between 1915 and 1925 than did rural white Georgians to the south. Black Belt schools for whites showed evidence of a high rate of consolidation, and the proportion with libraries more than doubled during the period, reaching almost 57 percent. White mountain schools realized little gain in either area, and in 1925 only one in five had its own library. Some reasons for the discrepancy are obvious: Black Belt counties were able to co-opt state funds meant for their more numerous black students, their greater prosperity made them more inclined to approve county or district taxes, and there were fewer physical and cultural obstacles to overcome in eliminating the one-room schoolhouse. Furthermore, a tax equalization measure that could

52. Barbara Leslie Epstein, *The Politics of Domesticity: Women, Evangelism, and Temperance in Nineteenth-Century America* (Middletown, CT: Wesleyan University Press, 1981), chaps. 4 and 5; Molly Ladd-Taylor, *Mother-Work: Women, Child Welfare, and the State, 1890–1930* (Urbana: University of Illinois Press, 1994), 44–53; Theda Skocpol, *Protecting Soldiers and Mothers: The Political Origins of Social Policy in the United States* (Cambridge, MA: Harvard University Press, 1992), 326–340, 382–401.

have produced more state funds for poor districts was rendered ineffective when county officials, at the instruction of local property-owning elites, simply refused to cooperate with the state tax board.[53]

Perhaps more importantly, the structure of mountain society did not provide enough open doors through which club women could extend their influence. There was considerable opposition to educational reform in the rural lowland portions of the state, but women reformers were able to overcome it by mobilizing their network of club women, teachers, and extension agents to exert influence on mothers and draw rural parents into the schoolhouse. In the highlands, rural churches and schools worked to reinforce the status quo, and low population density made communication among scattered club women difficult. It was not until the 1920s that the Seventh and Ninth District Federated clubs reported any rural outreach efforts other than distributing used magazines to mountain families who lacked access to reading materials. Celeste Parrish made some progress when she was appointed to the newly created position of state supervisor of rural schools for North Georgia in 1911. She maximized her influence by inviting parents, students, county boards of education, and local ministers to attend her teachers' institutes. Parrish had the assistance of club women and was fairly successful in organizing mothers and improving teacher training, but structural improvements were not necessarily forthcoming. One persistent problem was her inability to persuade county officials to enforce the state law regarding minimum size for school districts. She complained that resistance to consolidation "crippled" schools by dispersing available funds too widely and argued that "in some cases the evil is so great as to nullify any good influence of the money appropriated by the state."[54]

Organized women faced their own internal difficulties in trying to find an effective strategy for mountain reform. Boarding schools were expensive to operate and, instead of spreading resources around like school improvement

53. Statistical reports of the mountain counties of Chatooga, Glimer, Gordon, Habersham, Murray, and Pickens, and the Black Belt counties of Butts, Baldwin, McDuffie, Spaulding, Talbot, and Wilkinson, in GDE, *Forty-Fourth Annual Report, 1915* (Atlanta: GDE, 1916); and GDE, *Fifty-Fourth and Fifty-Fifth Annual Reports, 1925–1926* (Atlanta: GDE, 1927); Wrigley, "Triumph of Provincialism," 211–218.

54. Ninth District report, *GFWC Yearbook, 1912–1913;* also see district reports in GFWC yearbooks for 1917–1918 and 1922–1923; Celeste Parrish reports, in GDE annual reports, esp. *Forty-First Annual Report, 1912,* 42–46, quote 46.

clubs, they served to concentrate tremendous sums of money in a few areas. This fact proved problematic for fund-raising efforts, as the state's women's clubs were busy promoting and financing improvements for the urban and rural schools in their own communities and balked at taking on additional burdens. GFWC leaders repeatedly admonished affiliated clubs to fulfill their duty to Tallulah Falls School but realized few results for their efforts. In 1914 only 80 of the 246 Federated clubs pledged support, and of those only 30 actually contributed funds. A plan for a "dollar-a-member" contribution proved to be an abysmal failure when only one club responded. Teachers and principals in mountain schools sometimes had to resort to working without pay or using their salaries to buy essential supplies and equipment. The club women of Savannah, where the State Association for the Education of Georgia Mountaineers was based, were the only Federation members to consistently offer support. School administrators had to look to wealthy Georgians to establish a sufficient endowment for their institution, because, as one donor told director Passie Fenton Ottley, it seemed that "everyone knows about Tallulah Falls but the club women!" Much as the failures of the school improvement movement revealed the limitations of localism, the failures of mountain reform revealed the limitations of volunteerism.[55]

The strength of women's mountain schools was their ability to meet the immediate needs of the mountain population. John C. Campbell argued that independent schools such as those of Martha Berry and the Georgia Federation were especially effective in providing social services to mountaineers because they were run by "strong individuals" who lived either in the schools or nearby. These school directors were familiar with local needs and wishes and could formulate policies in accordance with changing conditions. In contrast, schools in which the authority rested in a distant church mission or philanthropic board proved to be less flexible, because they had to conform to outside agendas that did not necessarily address the reality facing teachers in the field. The flexibility of Georgia women reformers was reflected in their willingness to widen the scope of their work in response to the demands of mountaineers. Mountain whites refused to be treated as passive charity cases and instead actively participated in molding schools into community institu-

55. Hancock, *Light in the Mountains*, 37–38, 43–44, quote 67; DeJarnette, *A Pattern for Education in Living*, 12; also see *Passie Fenton Ottley*, Hargrett Rare Book and Manuscript Collection, booklet.

tions. Poverty and migration had weakened the mountain family's ability to care for its most helpless members, and so highlanders sent their orphans and physically disabled children to Martha Berry regardless of their age or ability to perform the work for which all students were responsible. Berry sometimes expressed exasperation at having these volunteer students thrust upon her, but she always acquiesced in the end. The administrators and teachers at Tallulah Falls faced similar circumstances and often found themselves in the position of having to provide employment, housing, and orphan placement services for local families.[56]

Perhaps the extraordinary circumstances of mountain reform warrant assessing club women's success or failure on their own terms, rather than in comparison with educational reform efforts elsewhere. They were living dangerously in utilizing the politics of race and reproduction in support of their gender interests. Feminists in the women's movement often criticized maternalist justifications for reform because treating women differently could so easily slide into treating them unequally, and racial maternalism had the potential to produce this negative result in its most extreme form. Theodore Roosevelt, whose mother was from North Georgia, was intensely interested in Martha Berry's school because of his concern for race suicide and white racial purity. He was impressed with the large size of families in southern Appalachia, which fulfilled his ideal for white Americans. He frequently argued that bearing and raising children—preferably at least four—was white women's patriotic duty and that their willingness to remain in the home was a measure of their commitment to national progress. This eugenic practice of placing women's reproductive functions under the purview of state interest encouraged legal sanction of their subordination, and in the case of "unfit" poor black and white women it justified their incarceration and sterilization. The 1919 Georgia and Florida statutes mandating the institutionalization of the "feebleminded" emphasized the need to confine "women of childbearing age" even though scientists believed men were just as likely as women to pass on mental abnormalities to their offspring.[57]

56. John C. Campbell, *The Future of the Church and Independent Schools in Our Southern Highlands* (New York: Russell Sage Foundation, 1916), 4.

57. The tension between "difference" and "equality" produced controversy and division among women's organizations. Nancy Cott, *The Grounding of Modern Feminism* (New Haven, CT: Yale University Press, 1987), 18–21; Pickens, *Eugenics and the Progressives*, 86–96, 119–130; see Theodore Roosevelt's speeches, "The Woman and the Home," "The Conservation of Wom-

Despite the many drawbacks of racial reproductive politics, club women effectively subverted its negative gender implications by using it as a tool to promote a more egalitarian concept of domesticity. Club women and mountain educators used race concerns to create and support a new form of household in which women were the heads. At the Berry, Tallulah Falls, and Mineral Bluff schools, resident women held the ultimate positions of authority. This was true even at Berry's boys' school and at the coeducational Tallulah Falls institution, where a few male instructors were employed. And not only were the heads of household in mountain boarding schools women, but in most cases they also were single women. Although the typical Tallulah Falls director was a married club woman who spent at least part of each summer at the school, the principal who lived there year-round was single. Martha Berry and Tallulah Falls principal Anne Davis were both mothers and fathers, women who presided over households of children but who were not subordinated to men. In many instances, female teachers taught a wide array of subjects to boys and girls regardless of commonly held notions of the appropriate sexual division of labor. Historically, the argument that racial supremacy rested on the quality of white womanhood also posited that female purity was maintained through women's isolation from the public sphere. By creating institutions that were ambiguous—neither completely public nor completely private—female reformers were able to launch what was arguably their most radical challenge to restrictive notions of domesticity.

---

anhood and Childhood," and "Women's Rights; and the Duties of Both Men and Women," reprinted in *The Works of Theodore Roosevelt* (New York: Charles Scribner's Sons, 1908), 18:225–233, 244–289. Roosevelt invited Martha Berry to visit him at the White House, helped her solicit funds in Washington, and paid the Berry school a personal visit after leaving the presidency. Kane and Henry, *Miracle in the Mountains,* 103–105, 124–128; Larson, *Sex, Race, and Science,* 83.

5

REFORMING WORKING-CLASS EDUCATION
Kindergartens, Mill Schools, and the Struggle against Child Labor

Women's efforts to improve working-class education epitomize many of the important connections between gender, education, and female political culture that shaped their approach to rural reform. The blurring of lines between single educators, married club women, and working-class mothers evident in the early kindergarten movement illustrates the inclusive approach made possible by belated professionalization and women's location outside of state institutions. As the campaign for public kindergartens transformed into a more sweeping child welfare reform movement, the philosophical foundations of kindergartens and women's commitment to the basic right of self-realization contributed to the development of a democratic and cooperative approach to reform. To reconcile their own goals with the priorities of workers, female activists had to balance promoting the authority of the state to intervene in families for the greater social good with acknowledgment of the integrity of the working-class family as an institution that existed primarily for the benefit of its own members. Club women and female educators were the "reconcilers," attempting both to convince mill workers that what was good for the state was good for the individual and to persuade politicians and businessmen that what was good for the individual was also good for the state.[1]

The increased interest in early childhood development that underlay the child welfare movement was a response to the growth of the market economy and industrialization, although it also had foundations in earlier concerns for the education of young children in the home. Americans' notion of "republican motherhood" recognized the importance of domestic life in preparing citizens for democracy, while the "new education" movement in Europe persuasively argued that home influence was critical in shaping the emotional

---

1. Edward L. Ayers's description of southern Progressives as reformers who "saw themselves as mediators, educators, facilitators" hints at this function of social activism, although it lacks a consideration of gender. *The Promise of the New South: Life after Reconstruction* (New York: Oxford University Press, 1992), 417.

and intellectual faculties of children. As most productive labor left the household and the expansion of industrial capitalism produced class divisions and insecurities, public attention increasingly focused on the role of mothers in socializing children to fit into wider society. Middle-class women became the target audience of a new genre of advice literature intended to instruct them on the best approach to education and discipline. The literature idealized the mother-child bond, advising women to use love and persuasion to inculcate in their children qualities that would be socially and financially advantageous to them as adults. This romantic treatment of women's domestic labor privatized mothering and discouraged the development of institutions for child nurture outside of the family.[2]

Friedrich Froebel, who launched the German kindergarten movement in the 1830s, argued that external pressures on the family necessitated the education of young children outside the home. Froebel worried that industrial capitalism had caused a deterioration of the mother-child bond, by allowing upper-class mothers to leave child-rearing to servants while forcing lower-class mothers into the workplace. Trained teachers could compensate, he claimed, by serving as ideal maternal figures for pupils and educating mothers in good parenting. Froebel's theories inspired the establishment of kindergartens in the northeastern and midwestern United States in the 1860s and 1870s. They began as private kindergartens for children of the middle and upper classes, but concern about the social costs of industrialization soon created interest in public or charitable institutions for the poor. As the urban "free" kindergarten movement emerged in the 1880s, teachers (called kindergartners) in close contact with working-class children and their parents came

2. Barbara Beatty, *Preschool Education in America: The Culture of Young Children from the Colonial Era to the Present* (New Haven, CT: Yale University Press, 1995), 5–19; Jeanne Boydston, *Home and Work: Housework, Wages, and the Ideology of Labor in the Early Republic* (New York: Oxford University Press, 1990); Carl N. Degler, *At Odds: Women and the Family in America from the Revolution to the Present* (New York: Oxford University Press, 1980); Linda K. Kerber, *Women of the Republic: Intellect and Ideas in Revolutionary America* (Chapel Hill: University of North Carolina Press, 1980); Mary P. Ryan, *Cradle of the Middle Class: The Family in Oneida County, New York, 1790–1865* (Cambridge: Cambridge University Press, 1981), and *The Empire of the Mother: American Writing about Domesticity, 1830–1860* (New York: Institute for Research in History, 1982); Michael Steven Shapiro, *Child's Garden: The Kindergarten Movement from Froebel to Dewey* (University Park: Pennsylvania State University Press, 1983), 1–12.

to believe that Froebel's approach could not meet all the needs of the poor. They valued his insights regarding the importance of early childhood development but increasingly turned to the emerging social sciences for more scientific and systematic pedagogical methods. They were strongly influenced by Progressive theorists who criticized Froebel's exclusive emphasis on individual development, arguing that pedagogical methods should internalize in children the process of subordinating the self to the common will of the group.[3]

The same social and economic changes that produced the kindergarten movement in other parts of the nation were at work in the South, but it lagged well behind other regions in accepting the kindergarten as a necessary part of state school systems. The lower degree of industrial development, the scarcity of large cities, the lack of well-established public school systems, and the depressed postbellum economy were all factors that contributed to a lack of public support for preschool education. As late as the 1930s, none of the states in the Deep South had kindergartens as a mandatory part of their public schools and none allocated money specifically for preschool classes. Although a few had "permissive" laws allowing school systems to use part of their regular state funds for this purpose, only large cities such as New Orleans, Birmingham, and Atlanta had the resources to finance public kindergartens without depriving the primary grades. Even then financial support was sporadic, and when cities suffered economic downturns, preschools often were the first items to be struck from the budget. Southern advocates of the movement complained that inadequate funding was a self-perpetuating problem; those who needed kindergartens the worst could not access them, and parents who had no contact with them were less likely to understand and appreciate their purpose and, thus, to support them. Lack of state support made local activism and the charitable free kindergarten movement critical

3. Beatty, *Preschool Education in America*, 28–38, 48–55, 72–73; Elizabeth Dale Ross, *The Kindergarten Crusade: The Establishment of Preschool Education in the United States* (Athens: Ohio University Press, 1976); Dom Cavallo, "From Perfection to Habit: Moral Training in the American Kindergarten, 1860–1920," *History of Education Quarterly* 16 (Summer 1976): 147–161; Caroline Winterer, "Avoiding a 'Hothouse System of Education': Nineteenth-Century Early Childhood Education from the Infant Schools to the Kindergartens," *History of Education Quarterly* 32 (Fall 1992): 288–314.

in establishing and maintaining preschool and daycare facilities for working families.[4]

The emergence of the southern kindergarten movement was directly tied to the migration of trained preschool professionals from outside the region. In the 1880s Atlanta, like most large southern cities, had several private kindergartens with close connections to the national movement. The first of these opened as a direct result of the influence of northeastern kindergartners who traveled to Atlanta in 1880 to attend the meeting of the National Education Association. Two additional kindergartens opened in private schools in 1888. One was taught by a Philadelphia training school graduate and the other by Lily Reynolds, who attended the Chicago Kindergarten College of Elizabeth Harrison, one of the nation's foremost Froebelian educators. These women and others like them played a central role in organizing Atlanta's kindergarten movement. They helped to found new professional organizations, worked with women's clubs in lobbying for child welfare and educational reforms, and actively promoted a scientific rather than a noblesse oblige approach to social problems. Their contributions infused a new vitality into the volunteer efforts of club women, as their emphasis on scientific child study hastened the transformation of the private and charitable kindergarten movement into multiple campaigns for child welfare reform.[5]

Willette Allen provides one of the most outstanding examples of external influences in the Georgia movement. Allen was born in Ohio in the mid-1860s to educated, middle-class parents. Her father was a teacher, writer, and "leader in all community movements for betterment," and her mother, Sophia Ober Allen, was a graduate of a Massachusetts normal school for women that was the first of its kind in the United States. Sophia was well versed in the new pedagogy and reportedly raised her daughter according to Froebelian

---

4. *History of the Kindergarten Movement in the Southeastern States, and Delaware, District of Columbia, New Jersey, and Pennsylvania* (Washington, DC: Association for Childhood Education, 1939).

5. "History of the Kindergarten Movement in Georgia," typed manuscript, 1938, Atlanta Kindergarten Alumnae Club Collection (hereafter AKAC), box 2, folder 1, Atlanta History Center Archives; "Outline of Professional Training and Experience of Miss Willette A. Allen," AKAC, box 1, folder 1; Lily Reynolds, "Some Effort at Kindergartning in Atlanta Forty Years Ago," AKAC, box 1, folder 3; Beatty, *Preschool Education in America*, 84–90; Ross, *The Kindergarten Crusade*, 85–87.

theory. Perhaps influenced by her mother's educational background, Allen pursued similar training herself. She first graduated from Ohio Central Normal School and then completed a course of study at Hailmann Kindergarten Training School in La Porte, Indiana. William and Eudora Hailmann, the husband-and-wife team who ran the school, were nationally known Froebelian theorists and writers who promoted kindergartens in the Midwest and were active in the National Education Association. Allen worked for them briefly before moving to California to take charge of the kindergarten training department of the University of the Pacific. Two years later, in 1890, she moved with her parents to Douglasville, Georgia. In addition to assisting Lillie Reynolds with a kindergarten at the Piedmont Chautauqua Assembly in Lithia Springs, Allen opened a kindergarten department in Atlanta's Capital Female College and volunteered at a mission in one of the mill districts.[6]

Willette Allen greatly increased her influence in the fledging Georgia movement when she opened a private kindergarten and training school in 1896. The curriculum of the Atlanta Kindergarten Normal School combined Froebel's holistic approach to child development with the scientific method of child study. This combination of emphasis reflected the dual purpose of Allen's school, what she termed the "cultural" and "professional" aspects of training. The cultural purpose of her school was to expose students to the "most accurate knowledge attainable of the source and evolution of human power—physical, intellectual, moral and spiritual," so that they might learn "to direct and develop the earliest manifestation of this power in the little child." Because successful child-rearing was of personal as well as social importance, the acquisition of such skills was appropriate for all women as potential mothers. The professional aim of the school was to instruct women in the formal knowledge necessary to become kindergartners. To this end, students took courses in child study and applied psychology and had to prove their ability "to formulate aims and corresponding methods which shall be truly educative in result." Allen took these standards seriously, only awarding 104 diplomas during her twenty-three years of teaching.[7]

The dual purpose of the Atlanta Kindergarten Normal School illustrates

6. "Outline of Professional Training and Experience of Miss Willette A. Allen."

7. Ibid.; quotes from *Atlanta Kindergarten Normal and Elementary School, 1915–1916*, AKAC, box 1, folder 1, booklet.

the inclusive, democratic approach to formal education that characterized the early stages of the kindergarten movement. Even though some degree of specialization had developed with the establishment of kindergarten normal schools in the Northeast and the Midwest, mothers and brides continued to sit in classrooms alongside women (many of whom would remain single) who were receiving their professional training. Child-rearing advice literature stimulated widespread interest in Froebel among women who had no intention or need of working, and indeed many of Allen's students were middle-class mothers who wanted to improve their parenting skills. Their shared training produced a camaraderie among mothers and teachers that led to mutual support on issues concerning child welfare and the professions dedicated to promoting it. This relationship was perpetuated by contact between kindergartners and the parents (especially the mothers) of their pupils. Mothers were expected to visit the kindergartens and become familiar with Froebelian principles, and teachers made home visits to consult with parents on the progress of their children. The instructional after-school "mothers' clubs" eventually evolved into chapters of the National Congress of Mothers, later known as the Parent-Teacher Association (PTA).[8]

The close working relationship that developed between married club women and single kindergartners soon led to the establishment of the first free kindergarten association of Atlanta. In preparation for the Cotton States and International Exposition of 1895, the Exposition Women's Board sent two unmarried professionals from its Committee on Education, Willette Allen and Nettie Sargent (principal of Atlanta Girls' High School) "to study the famous kindergartens of Louisville and to persuade them to send an exhibit and a demonstration teacher to the exposition." This trip not only resulted in a kindergarten exhibit, but it also established a permanent link between Atlanta and the nationally renowned Louisville Training School of Patty Smith Hill, a staunch advocate of Progressive pedagogy. The Exposition demonstration conducted by Hill's sister, Mary, stimulated enough in-

8. *Atlanta Kindergarten Normal;* Mrs. Leonard F. Johnson, "A Memoir of an Atlanta Living Mother," AKAC, box 2, folder 14. Participants in the Georgia kindergarten movement were particularly proud of the many social and child welfare organizations that were formed as a direct result of their clubs for mothers and children. For example, see Madge A. Bigham, "Kindergarten Memories," AKAC, box 1, folder 3; and Martha G. Waring, "Sketch of the History of the Kindergarten Movement in Savannah, Georgia, Kate Baldwin Free Kindergarten Association," AKAC, Scrapbooks, box 1, folder 11.

terest that a group of local men and women met immediately afterward to establish the Atlanta Free Kindergarten Association. At the time of its founding, the top two positions of the organization were held by men: Progressive Georgia governor William Northen was president, and John F. Barclay (who with his wife ran the mill mission at which Allen volunteered) was treasurer. By the time the association affiliated with the Georgia Federation of Women's Clubs a year later, however, all of its officers were married club women.[9]

Just as in the female and rural educational reform campaigns, the partnership between club women and professional women proved mutually beneficial in the kindergarten movement. At the most practical level, the Atlanta Free Kindergarten Association (AFKA) was a boon to kindergartners in that it created employment opportunities. In the early stages of the movement, it was the benevolent work of married club women that provided the vast majority of jobs sought by young women with professional ambitions. Although some graduates of Allen's normal school went on to open private schools, private kindergartens required capital or a sponsor and were limited to the city's wealthiest neighborhoods. Most of Allen's students found positions in the city's free kindergartens established and funded by the AFKA, women's church auxiliaries, and Sheltering Arms, another female charitable organization. When financial support for charity kindergartens began to wane around the time of World War I, volunteer women's organizations and kindergartners' professional groups launched a fierce campaign to incorporate kindergartens into the city's public school system. After the Atlanta Board of Education finally acquiesced in 1923, the number of kindergartens, and hence the number of available jobs, rapidly increased. The number of free, or public,

9. A Boston woman who recently had moved to Atlanta is credited with the founding of the Atlanta Free Kindergarten Association, although Nellie Peters Black, a widowed club woman who became its second president in 1896, provided the leadership that was responsible for its success. Quote from "Free Kindergarten Association," AKAC, box 1, folder 11; Nita Black (Mrs. Lamar) Rucker, "History of the Free Kindergarten as Told by Mrs. Rucker," *Atlanta Constitution*, February 17, 1924; and especially see Nellie Peters Black, Free Kindergarten Scrapbook, Nellie Peters Black Papers (hereafter NPB), box 6, folder 2, Hargrett Rare Books and Manuscripts Collection, Special Collections, University of Georgia Libraries, Athens. On the role of the exposition and the fair in women's organizing, see Ann Firor Scott, *The Southern Lady: From Pedestal to Politics, 1830–1930* (Chicago: University of Chicago Press, 1970), 156–158; and for the Georgia context, see Darlene Rebecca Roth, *Matronage: Patterns in Women's Organizations, Atlanta, Georgia, 1890–1940* (Brooklyn, NY: Carlson Publishing, 1994), 33–42.

kindergartens grew from about 12 in 1919–1920 to 52 in 1925–1926, and then to 70 in 1927–1928.[10]

The social connections of married club women and their status as mothers also benefited kindergartners by providing a protective shield of respectability for single career women. As the prolonged controversy over coeducation illustrates, the emergence of the New Woman produced considerable tension in the turn-of-the-century South. Even though kindergartners had chosen an occupational field that neither competed with men economically nor challenged common notions of womanhood, their status as single professional women was threatening nonetheless. Their personal and economic independence challenged the interlocking construction of the racial and gender hierarchies on several levels. In choosing a career over marriage, they had turned their backs on the duty of motherhood incumbent upon all white women, favoring personal interests over the preservation of national racial integrity. Equally importantly, their rejection of dependency undermined a central justification for racial discrimination and violence by disproving the need for white male protection. Kindergartners' partnership with married club women was invaluable in obscuring the challenge they represented to the social order, because it created an aura of legitimacy by presenting them as apprentice or surrogate mothers. Their association with socially prominent club women in training schools and charitable institutions also provided them with a base of political power by linking them to some of the most influential women in Georgia.[11]

10. The 1927–1928 school year represented the peak in Atlanta public kindergartens; the number began to decline in 1928–1929 because of the depression. *Announcement: Atlanta Kindergarten Alumnae Club,* for 1919–1920, 1925–1926, 1927–1928, 1928–1929, AKAC, box 1, folder 7, pamphlets; "Miss Willette Allen: A Promoter of Teacher Training," AKAC, box 1, folder 1; "Free Kindergarten Association."

11. Speaking without consideration of regional differences, Barbara Beatty notes that kindergartners only minimally challenged concepts of women's appropriate place, because their low pay and the charitable basis of their work tended to cast it in terms of natural feminine interest in children and benevolence rather than as commitment to women's economic independence. "'A Vocation from on High': Kindergartning as an Occupation for American Women," in *Changing Education: Women as Radicals and Conservators,* ed. Joyce Antler and Sari Knopp Biklen (Albany: State University of New York Press, 1990), 35–50. The emergence of the New Woman was one development that concerned members of the Second Klan, as discussed by Nancy MacLean in *Behind the Mask of Chivalry: The Making of the Second Ku Klux Klan* (New York: Oxford University Press, 1994).

One of the most powerful champions of the Atlanta kindergarten movement, Nellie Peters Black, provides an excellent example of the legitimacy and protection that married club women could offer their single professional supporters. When Black first became involved in educational reform, she was a widow with three children and four stepchildren. She enjoyed all the benefits and privileges bestowed by marriage and motherhood and had sterling credentials as a southern blue blood and a Christian humanitarian. Residents of Atlanta were familiar with her long history of benevolent work, which started in her youth and became the focus of her energies after the death of her husband. In addition to her many other activities in church and community, Black helped to found the Atlanta Free Kindergarten Association and served as its president for more than twenty years. She simultaneously chaired the Georgia Federation's Kindergarten Committee. Photographs of Black reveal a matronly woman with an air of dignity and a determined expression, a prototype of the public mother who extends her maternal concern to all children. Her leadership in the volunteer branch of the kindergarten movement empowered kindergartners by putting opponents in the uncomfortable position of having to challenge the authority of one of the most respected and respectable women in the state.[12]

Kindergartners were able to reciprocate club women's support of their profession by contributing their scientific expertise to campaigns for reform. The Atlanta Kindergarten Alumnae Club (AKAC), formed around 1902 by a group of Allen's former students, played a central role in lobbying for a permissive kindergarten bill and stimulating further organizing activity among club women and teachers. Initially limited to graduates of Allen's school, within a few years the club's membership was open to the alumnae of any kindergarten normal school. Club members considered their purpose both vocational and social, to promote "high standards of achievements" within the profession and to advocate legislation and services for "the little children of the entire state." One of the most important activities of the club was the collection of data for use in lobbying efforts. The AKAC solicited information on kindergartens in other Georgia cities and compiled annual statistical reports on the status of kindergartens in Atlanta and the state. Members joined other kindergartners and club women in forming the Georgia Kindergarten Association (GKA) in 1923. GKA officers represented a powerful cadre

12. Biographical sketch of Nellie Peters Black, NPB, box 1, folder 1.

of female leaders from the Georgia Federation, the AKAC, the PTA, the League of Women Voters, and the Southern Association of Collegiate Women, all of whom were united in their resolve to make kindergartens a part of public school systems. Mary Dickinson, who held various offices in the Alumnae Club while also serving as chair of the GKA Publicity Committee, regularly forwarded reports to the city and state Federations of Women's Clubs, the National Kindergarten Association, the International Kindergarten Union, and the federal Bureau of Education.[13]

Kindergarten professionals' expertise in educational theory also aided club women by providing them with justifications for reform that transcended the immediate interests of parents and the financial considerations of municipalities. Nellie Peters Black called upon the authority of the "science given us by the great Froebel" when she publicly chastised a member of the Atlanta Board of Education for expressing opposition to free kindergartens. She patiently explained that the "best educators of our state" recognized the importance of taking the "plastic, pure mind of the child and implanting there noble thoughts and moral traits before the powers of evil can exert their influences." The Georgia Federation of Women's Clubs Kindergarten Committee made similar arguments in a petition to Georgia legislators requesting the passage of a permissive kindergarten bill to allow school systems to use state funds for preschools. Committee members asserted that kindergarten children were at "impressionistic ages" when they "began to form habits, good or bad." Their petition referred to the opinions of experienced educators (including one member of the committee) and the federal Bureau of Education in arguing that children who had the benefit of early mental and physical training were more observant, "self-reliant, helpful, unselfish, and apt to show a budding community spirit."[14]

13. "Historical Facts about the Kindergarten Club," AKAC, box 1, folder 6; quotes from Mary Dickenson to Harvey W. Cox, president of Emory University, April 27, 1923, AKAC, box 1, folder 2; clipping from *Atlanta Journal,* June 10, 1923, AKAC, box 2, folder 13; "Report of Mary Dickinson, Chairman of Publicity for the Georgia State Kindergarten Association, to Members," April 16, 1926, AKAC, box 2, folder 6; also see biographical sketch, "Miss Mary Dickinson, President of the Kindergarten Club," *Atlanta Constitution,* August 21, 1921.

14. Black quotes from clipping, 1897, "Mrs. Black's Comments on Mr. Pendleton's Remarks"; remaining quotes from Georgia Federation of Women's Clubs petition to the legislature, both in Nellie Peters Black, Free Kindergarten Scrapbook, NPB. The petition signatures show that the chair and all Kindergarten Committee members except for Black were single women educators,

Reformers' focus on character development has led some historians to regard the kindergarten movement as yet another branch of educational reform motivated by middle-class concerns for social control, but such an interpretation is too simplistic. Women's activism was deeply rooted in a female political culture that assumed the interdependence of classes and the necessity of collective responsibility for the needs of all homes and families. Although a desire for social order was a motivating factor in reform at all levels, club women had a distinctive approach to the issue of early childhood education that derived from their position as mothers and educated women. They believed that the relative deprivation of working-class children gave them a particular need for nurture and guidance, but they regarded early childhood education as appropriate for all classes. From their perspective, kindergartens and intelligent mothering were important ways in which they could ensure that their own children would become "well developed human being[s]," and they presumed that most women (and men) would want the same for their offspring. This presumption is apparent in club women's public appeals for support of preschool education in which they focused as much on the advantages it offered to the individual child as on its social benefits. In one press release, the chair of the legislative committee of the state PTA described the kindergarten as a "child garden providing for individuality," a "place for the little child to expand naturally, to express his own ideas in deeds, words, play and work." [15]

Single kindergartners also expressed a maternal concern for students, reflecting their conception of themselves as surrogate mothers who were fulfilling a nurturing and protective role. Madge Bigham, a graduate of the Atlanta Kindergarten Normal School, was fond of repeating a story that illustrated what she viewed as the greatest reward of her work. While serving as principal of an AFKA free kindergarten, she taught an Irish boy for three years, until his entrance into the first grade. He had been in primary school for only one month when she was surprised to find him once again knocking at the

including kindergartners Willette Allen, Carol Oppenheimer, and Edwina Wood and the superintendent of primary grades for Atlanta public schools, Laura Smith—one of the "experts" cited in the petition.

15. First quote from *AFKA Annual Meeting April 28th, 1908—Report of the President*, AKAC, box 2, folder 3, pamphlet; second quote from "Kindergarten Bill Is Important, P.T.A. Says," July 2, 1922, AKAC, box 2, folder 13, clipping.

kindergarten door. As an explanation for his presence, he told her through his tears that he had returned because "They do not love 'em at the big school—they jess LEARNS 'em!" Kindergartners regarded this aspect of their work—the loving nurture of children—as the most important element separating their professional activities from mere schooling. Although unmarried kindergartners did not contest the definition of mothering as inherently female, they did challenge the meaning of family by defying the notion that mothering was solely the province of birth mothers. They made child nurture a public rather than purely private concern and made its social importance more visible by removing it from the home.[16]

The peculiar position of kindergartners influenced them to view their work as a way to reconcile tensions inherent between private and public, home and school. The kindergarten was the first step in socialization outside the family and had the potential to give children a positive impression of the external world during their most formative years. It was closer to the home than the primary school, because parents were more protective of very young children and thus more likely to take an active interest in their activities. The teachers themselves were a hybrid of private and public: women who mothered but who were not mothers, who created homes that were public institutions, who were public educators but not part of the state school system. They were neither confined to the domestic sphere nor entrenched in official bureaucracies, and their separate location gave them a particular flexibility. They had close connections to the family, a child-centered pedagogy that could be adapted to individual circumstances, and a link to formal education—all of which worked together to enable them to ease the transition of young children from the individual care of the mother to the impersonal instruction of the classroom. Kindergartners worked to prepare their students for the demands that would be placed upon them in society while also trying to make that society more hospitable by serving as child advocates in the political arena.[17]

16. Bigham, "Kindergarten Memories," 4.

17. Carol P. Oppenheimer, "The Relationship of the Kindergarten to the Home," in *Southern Educational Association* [hereafter SEA] *Journal of Proceedings and Addresses of the Nineteenth Annual Session Held at Atlanta, Georgia, December 29–31, 1908* (Chattanooga, TN: SEA, n.d.), 695–700; Patty Smith Hill, "The Strategic Position of the Kindergarten in American Education," *Georgia Education Journal* (November 1929): 13–15.

Kindergartners' interpretation of their role as that of mediator was reinforced by their professional training and their particular interests as women. Froebel considered the kindergarten a medium for bringing domestic virtues into the public realm (through the teacher) and at the same time injecting social consciousness and the values of citizenship into the home (through the child). In addition, Hegelian kindergarten advocates regarded the socialization of children in a maternal institutional setting as a way to reconcile the tension between individual and social needs. Their concept of early childhood education reflected the socialist critique of the bourgeois family as excessively individualist, which in Germany firmly connected the kindergarten with class radicalism. Although this was not the case in the United States, American Progressives articulated a middle ground that acknowledged the need to subordinate individual interests to the greater social good. Kindergartners and club women in Georgia's movement tended to fuse aspects of Froebel with Progressivism. As activists fighting for women's right to self-realization, they were attracted to the individualist emphasis of Froebelian methods; as reformers who regarded male individualism as socially problematic, they were drawn to the Progressive focus on cultivation of mutuality. Because of these two concerns, female reformers were more likely than men to stress the potential of the kindergarten to further democratize education and ameliorate the exploitation of workers, rather than valuing it primarily as a tool to promote behaviors protective of private property and business interests.[18]

The kindergarten seemed to hold forth much democratic potential because its location between the home environment and formal, state-provided education facilitated grassroots activism. Savannah kindergartner Caroline Oppenheimer explained the significance of the kindergarten's location by saying it ensured that "one great educational reform, at least, will grow logically from the bottom upward, instead of in the customary manner, from the college down." Her statement is curious given the formal training of kindergartners, but there were several reasons why they would have regarded themselves as professionals who operated outside the boundaries of academe. First, they had (and have) the lowest pay and status of all teachers, and their field of study

18. Ann Taylor Allen, "'Let Us Live with Our Children': Kindergarten Movements in Germany and the United States, 1840–1914," *History of Education Quarterly* 28 (Spring 1988): 23–48; and for a discussion of Georg Hegel's influence in the St. Louis kindergarten movement, see Beatty, *Preschool Education in America*, 66–67.

had yet to gain complete acceptance within the field of education. Second, they did not see themselves as authorities who presided over parents, but rather as participants in a mutually beneficial partnership in which formal knowledge and practical experience were united for the child's best interests. Oppenheimer described the relationship between parents and kindergartners as one of "kindly cooperation" and "helpful give and take," one in which parental influence served to shape the role of the institution and "to advance the cause of the kindergarten in whatever direction the kindergarten most needs [to] advance." Here was the cooperative model of educational reform that urban club women later extended to their rural school improvement campaigns with such success.[19]

In Georgia as elsewhere, kindergartners' favorite methods for maintaining a close link between home and school were the home visit and the mothers' club. Between April of 1907 and April of 1908, teachers in the seven free kindergartens of the AFKA made more than twelve hundred visits and held about one hundred meetings for mothers. Kindergartners wanted to maximize the positive impact of the domestic environment by educating mothers on basic health and safety issues. They also wanted to ensure continuity of influence on children, which necessitated reaching an agreement with parents on the best approach to discipline and character development. Kindergartners expressed a desire to put the work of both surrogate and biological mothers on firm scientific footing. Advocates of child study believed that mothers' "instinctive" maternal "insight" and the many hours they spent with children gave them an important part to play in shaping early character. Some went so far as to claim that if mothers had training in scientific method, they could be valuable assistants in official research projects. The kindergarten movement's demand for educated motherhood quickly merged with the struggles for gender equality in education and civil law, since it provided a powerful argument for why women needed greater control of their environment.[20]

The concept of scientific mothering was particularly appealing to middle-class women who had the luxury of time to devote to the subject, and in many

19. Oppenheimer, "The Relationship of the Kindergarten to the Home," 697.

20. *AFKA Annual Meeting, 1908;* quotes from Celeste Parrish, "Child Study in the School and Home," in *SEA Journal of Proceedings and Addresses of the Tenth Annual Meeting, Held at Richmond, Virginia, December 27–29, 1900* (Richmond, VA: SEA, 1901), 260–273.

ways it represented the democratic uses to which formal knowledge could be put when not constrained within bureaucratic institutions. The Atlanta Woman's Club formed a "child study class" in 1898, only four years after the organization was founded. The purpose of the class was to analyze the work of the "best authorities in that science," but its leader made a point of noting that the study group also "encourages and practices visiting the schools." Club women believed that a scientific, informed maternal concern gave them the authority to inspect and evaluate the quality of education in public schools, a level of participation that was only one step removed from the formulation of policy. The kindergarten mothers' clubs had a similar impact on middle-class women, and one former member actually claimed that her family's participation had resulted in a legacy of social activism. She was a member of an educational mothers' group for years while each of her three children was of preschool age. Her two daughters later became officers in the PTA, and her son worked with Jane Addams at Hull House before returning south to become a "leader in civic activities" who was "particularly interested in child-welfare work." She directly attributed her children's adult interests to the quality of their preschool training and to the intelligent parenting classes given her by the kindergarten teacher.[21]

If working-class mothers' response to kindergartners and child study clubs is any indication, they also found personal satisfaction in the scientific study of mothering and childhood. In the 1920s and 1930s, when the Atlanta Kindergarten Alumnae Club began collecting autobiographical sketches from participants in the free kindergarten movement, the firsthand accounts frequently referred to working-class women's enthusiasm and to the quality of relationships formed between teachers and mothers. Eva Richardson, who began teaching in the Holy Innocents' Mission kindergarten in 1905, recalled that she "did much visiting in the homes and was always made so welcome." Writing in 1937, twenty years after the kindergarten closed, Richardson described the mothers' club members as "a group of such fine loyal women and among the very best friends I possess." Virginia Bryan Hendren claimed that the mothers of her Athens mill-district school were the most avid "friends and

<hr>

21. *More Light: Fourth Annual Announcement of the Atlanta Woman's Club, 1898–1899*, 10, Atlanta Woman's Club Collection (hereafter AWC), Atlanta History Center Archives; Johnson, "Memoir of an Atlanta Living Mother."

supporters of the kindergarten." They held monthly meetings and showed great interest in their children's work. The close ties of friendship binding teachers and mothers was evident in the recreational events that the clubs sponsored, such as the wedding shower that mothers at the Exposition Cotton Mills gave for kindergartner Susie Sandiford in 1919.[22]

The mothers' clubs were a learning experience for the kindergartners as well, and their exposure to working-class mothers and families contributed to the evolution of the free preschool movement into a more broadly conceived social welfare program. As club women and teachers became more familiar with the needs of working-class families, they increasingly worked to offer a wider array of services. In 1908 Nellie Peters Black informed AFKA members that their kindergartners, "without any request from us," had "undertaken additional measures for the good of the neighborhoods where the schools are located, and a settlement work quite similar to that of Miss Jane Addams . . . is being carried on here in connection with the seven schools." After-school clubs, precursors of the Boy Scouts and Camp Fire Girls, provided directed activity for primary students, and industrial education courses and night schools were available to older children. The teacher of the free kindergarten at Nixon Woolen Mill used her classroom for sewing classes and night school during the week and for Sunday school on the weekend. Free kindergartens also began to address the many health care needs of working-class communities by offering dispensaries, examinations, vaccinations, minor treatments, and help obtaining free medical and dental care from other sources. Kindergartners came to see their schools as all-purpose community centers or, as one put it, the "social center of the neighborhood." This concept represented yet another similarity between urban and rural reform, evidence of the dynamic interaction between the campaign for kindergartens and the push for rural school improvement.[23]

Free kindergartens sometimes built upon existing home mission work, acting as catalysts for the emergence of new settlements and other organiza-

22. Eva Richardson, "The Holy Innocents' Kindergarten," AKAC, Scrapbooks, box 1, folder 11; handwritten account of Virginia Bryan (Mrs. L. L.) Hendren, AKAC, box 2, folder 11; clipping, November 22, 1919, AKAC, box 1, folder 12.

23. First quotes from *AFKA Annual Meeting, 1908;* AKAC Scrapbooks; clipping, 1921, "Nellie Peters Black Free Kindergarten Opens," AKAC, box 1, folder 12; last quote from Bigham, "Kindergarten Memories," 3.

tions dedicated to improving living conditions in mill and factory districts. The Exposition Cotton Mills kindergarten had its beginnings in the Barclay Mission, which a group of Atlantans established in 1884 as a Sunday school for workers. The mission was surrounded by "factories, foundries, mills and railroad shops with their multitudes of laboring men, women, and children," in a neighborhood where the air was filled with the "sound of the ever going and coming trains, the clang of factory whistles, the gongs of electric cars, the rumble of wheels on rough stones." After seven years of ministry, the mission added a kindergarten when Willette Allen and May Close volunteered their labor and the Young Women's Christian Temperance Union agreed to pay operating expenses. The struggle to maintain this service led to the formation of Sheltering Arms, a women's charitable organization that eventually founded several other kindergartens in the city's poorer areas. Sheltering Arms sponsored the Barclay kindergarten from about 1900 to 1915, when mill authorities assumed responsibility for funding. Under the leadership of club women the mission grew into a community settlement that offered, in addition to preschool classes, a day nursery for infants of working parents, night schools for working children, a library and reading rooms, baths, "sleeping rooms," and a lunch counter.[24]

Although black club women followed roughly the same path of development from free kindergartens to settlement work evident in white women's activism, there were significant differences separating the two groups. Atlanta's black free kindergarten movement was a product of both national and local influences and reflected the reform emphasis on racial betterment necessitated by prejudice and discrimination. Throughout the 1890s and early 1900s, Mary Church Terrell (first president of the National Association of Colored Women), Martha Murray Washington (of Tuskegee), and other prominent female reformers preached that black club women's goal of race uplift could best be accomplished in two ways: through kindergartens that provided a wholesome environment for children, and through mothers' clubs that improved parenting skills and the quality of home life. Atlanta women did not have to look to the national arena for guidance, however, because the city's

24. Quotes from Belle Robinson Butler, "A Mission Born in a Railroad Car," *Christian Herald and Signs of Our Times,* August 14, 1901; history of Sheltering Arms and Barclay Mission from AKAC Scrapbooks; "Outline of Professional Training and Experience of Miss Willette A. Allen."

black colleges concentrated considerable resources at their doorstep. Atlanta University's Annual Conference for the Study of the Negro Problems and its associated women's meetings brought educated blacks together and provided a forum for female leadership. At the Second Annual Conference, in 1897, the Women's Section issued a resolution advocating "mothers' meetings, day nurseries, family support and kindergartens" as ways to improve the moral and physical health of African Americans.[25]

Middle-class women of both races were concerned with improving the quality of mothering, but the issue had special importance for African American activists who daily faced white stereotypes of the immoral black woman and the dysfunctional black home. Georgia women shared with Mary Church Terrell the belief that higher moral standards and better homes were the keys to racial progress. They hoped that mothers' clubs and home visits would improve perceptions of black womanhood by inculcating middle-class values in the working poor. Female participants in the 1897 Atlanta University conference expressed concern about "an apparent increase in immorality," and urged black club women to use community-based organizations to promote chastity, thrift, temperance, and cleanliness. Georgia Swift King of Atlanta asserted that since "the destiny of the Negro race is largely in the hands of its mothers," educational mothers' meetings could positively impact entire communities. Selena Sloan Butler, who later founded the Georgia Congress of Colored Parents and Teachers, urged the establishment of day nurseries for young children whose mothers and older siblings had to work outside the home. Like white kindergartners, black middle-class women came to see themselves as surrogate mothers, but their commitment to racial progress— and to instilling a sense of race pride and unity in the poor—imparted another dimension to their public mothering. Alleviating the negative effects of

25. Quote from *Social and Physical Condition of Negroes in Cities,* Atlanta University Press Publications, no. 2 (Atlanta: Atlanta University Press, 1897; repr., New York: Arno Press, 1968), 32–34 (citations are to the 1968 edition); Beverly W. Jones, "Mary Church Terrell and the National Association of Colored Women, 1896–1901," *Journal of Negro History* 67 (Spring 1982): 20–33; Anna J. Murray, "A New Key to the Situation," *Southern Workman* 29 (September 1900): 503–507; Edyth L. Ross, "Black Heritage in Social Welfare: A Case Study of Atlanta," *Phylon* 37 (Winter 1976): 297–307; Martha Murray Washington, "The Gain in the Life of Negro Women," *Outlook* 76 (January 1904): 271–274; Josephine Silone Yates, "Kindergartens and Mothers' Clubs as Related to the Work of the NACW," *Colored American Magazine* 8 (June 1905): 304–311.

poverty and ignorance combated racist stereotypes in addition to improving the quality of life for individuals and communities.[26]

The state's egregious neglect of black educational needs and the segregated nature of educational reform forced Atlanta's black club women to form a separate kindergarten movement. The immediate impetus for organization came from the Atlanta University conference of 1905. Gertrude Ware, the white supervisor of the university's Kindergarten Training School, addressed the Women's Section on the needs of young children in working families. A group of black women in attendance concurred that free kindergartens should be established to care for children who otherwise would be left alone at home or on the streets. At the urging of W. E. B. Du Bois, they formally organized into the Gate City Free Kindergarten Association (GCFKA), and within three years they had founded five kindergartens in the city's most needy black neighborhoods. The schools were maintained through the donations of churches and black philanthropists and the assistance of "working circles" of neighborhood volunteers. Kindergarten supporters contributed food and coal, organized sewing guilds to make clothing, collected used shoes for repair and distribution, and held fund-raising events. The work necessarily involved a broad array of services, since the extreme poverty of many black families required that kindergartens provide for the physical as well as emotional and intellectual needs of children. From the moment the association was formed, its first president, Lugenia Burns Hope, dreamed of transforming preschools into centers of community life that would serve as all-purpose social welfare institutions.[27]

Members of the Gate City Free Kindergarten Association resisted Hope's

26. *Social and Physical Condition of Negroes,* 37–68, quotes 33–34, 61. *Golden Anniversary History, Georgia Congress of Colored Parents and Teachers* (Atlanta: The Organization, 1970), 8–11; Jones, "Mary Church Terrell," 23–24, 26–27.

27. "The Gate City Free Kindergarten," Neighborhood Union Collection (hereafter NU), box 12, folder 24, Atlanta University Woodruff Library, Archives and Special Collections; "The Story of the Gate City Free Kindergarten Association," NU, box 12, folder 25; "Kindergartens," in *Efforts for Social Betterment among Negro Americans,* Atlanta University Press Publications, no. 14 (Atlanta: Atlanta University Press, 1909; repr., New York: Arno Press, 1968), 126–127 (citations are to the 1968 edition); Jacqueline Anne Rouse, *Lugenia Burns Hope: Black Southern Reformer* (Athens: University of Georgia Press, 1989), 28–30; Ross, "Black Heritage in Social Welfare," 304.

efforts to expand the group's work beyond kindergartens, most likely because they were struggling financially and wished to focus their resources in one area. It was difficult enough just to find the funds to consistently provide kindergarten pupils with nutritional food and adequate clothing. Association members realized from the beginning that poor families needed day care as well as preschools, since children who were responsible for their younger siblings would bring their wards with them to kindergarten. Being aware of the need and being able to address it were two different things, however, and it was more than a decade before the Gate City group was financially able to establish nurseries. When the first one opened in 1918, members officially changed their organization's name to the Gate City Day Nursery Association. The nurseries initially accepted children ages two through twelve, but by the 1920s they had expanded the age range to six months through sixteen years. The association continued the practice of providing for basic physical needs, such as baths, food, and clothing, while also tutoring preschool and school children. One account of the organization proudly asserted that it had "aided in producing future citizens for the race" by providing "a mother and home life for the underprivileged children whose mothers were away earning a support for them." [28]

Although GCFKA members wanted to keep the organization focused on the needs of children, their growing familiarity with the problems of the wider community led to the formation of a separate group with a more broadly based program of social services. Community activists were concerned that Atlanta had no agencies to provide health, educational, and recreational services for the city's approximately ninety thousand black residents, many of whom were in desperate need of assistance. In July of 1908, founding members of the GCFKA moved to remedy state and municipal neglect by establishing the Neighborhood Union (NU). With Lugenia Burns Hope once again at the helm, the women quickly mapped out a strategy for determining community needs. The West End neighborhood surrounding Atlanta Uni-

---

28. Quote from "The Story of the Gate City Free Kindergarten Association"; "Board Manual, Gate City Day Nursery Association," GCFKA unprocessed collection, Atlanta University Center Woodruff Library, Archives and Special Collections, Atlanta, typed manuscript; "One Year Ago and NOW: A Contrast," NU, box 10, folder 11, pamphlet; Rouse, *Lugenia Burns Hope,* 29–30.

versity and Spelman and Morehouse Colleges was divided into sections, each with a director who supervised the workers assigned to each block. After conducting a door-to-door survey of the neighborhood, NU members began lobbying for improved municipal services while also launching multiple programs designed to educate and uplift poor blacks. Although the women were not formally trained in social work, they received expert advice from professors of sociology and social work at Morehouse College, where Hope's husband was president. Their methods, later extended to other black neighborhoods around the city, became widely regarded as a model of professionalism and efficiency in public welfare and settlement work.[29]

The close association between NU members and Morehouse professors illustrates how racial ties further blurred the lines between volunteer and professional. Black club women's collaboration with kindergartners and other female educators was similar to that of white women, in that they created jobs for college graduates and helped uphold educational standards. The Gate City group, for example, hired only kindergartners who had attended Atlanta University's Training School. However, segregation further broke down institutional boundaries by concentrating black club women in communities with professionals—male and female—who shared their commitment to racial progress. Like Lugenia Burns Hope, most members of the GCFKA and NU were married to professors and administrators and lived in the neighborhoods surrounding the black colleges. The close proximity of slums meant that the problems of the poor were their problems, and club women nurtured a sense of common cause. Morehouse College enabled the Neighborhood Union to establish the city's first playground for black children by donating part of the campus to be used for that purpose. Students and teachers from Spelman and Morehouse actively supported the NU work by teaching classes and holding meetings for children and parents and assisting in free health clinics. Male faculty from all three colleges worked closely with club women

---

29. Neighborhood Union Constitution of 1908, NU, box 2, folder 5; "The Neighborhood Union: Pioneer Social Organization of Atlanta," NU, box 2, folder 9; "History of the Neighborhood Union," NU, box 2, folder 12. For a more detailed account of the NU, see Gerda Lerner, "Early Community Work of Black Club Women," *Journal of Negro History* 59 (April 1974): 158–167; and Rouse, "The Legacy of Community Organizing: Lugenia Burns Hope and the Neighborhood Union," *Journal of Negro History* 69 (Summer-Autumn 1984): 114–133.

in their child welfare and social service programs, lending their expertise in educational institutes and lobbying campaigns.[30]

The commitment to formal study and scientific method that characterized the child welfare work of both black and white club women was essential in promoting and politicizing the field of child study. Their contributions were recognized in 1907 by Mary Jones, a professor at Peabody College in Nashville, Tennessee, who argued that female activism was an important remedy to the inadequacies of southern academic institutions. Jones, who was a member of the Southern Educational Association's Department of Child Study, conducted a survey of colleges, public schools, and women's organizations to discern the extent to which research and instruction in child study had permeated the South. She found that while institutions of higher education were doing "comparatively little" in the field, the practical work of kindergartners had encouraged a social science approach to the subject of child development. "Much of what was based on the speculative philosophy of Froebel has been subjected to the light of modern science," she explained, "and modifications of theory and practice have followed." One significant outcome was a new understanding of the importance of physical development that led not only to medical examinations and educational programs for mothers, but also to child labor reform and compulsory education laws. Jones concluded that club women's demands for child welfare reforms were the "result not of a sentimental fad, not merely of a wave of pity and sympathy, but of a well defined knowledge of the physical and mental needs of the growing child."[31]

Jones showed great insight in concluding that the "spirit" of child study, rather than the institutionalized academic field itself, motivated southern women to embark on public campaigns for child welfare reform. According to one recent analysis of women's role in the creation of the welfare state, the repression of academic activism in the late nineteenth century helped to make a space for female leadership while also rendering that leadership critical. Po-

30. "The Neighborhood Union, A Survey," NU, box 2, folder 8; clippings from the *Spelman Messenger,* NU, box 5, folders 7 and 8.

31. Mary P. Jones, "Some Results of Child Study in the South," in *SEA Journal of Proceedings and Addresses of the Eighteenth Annual Session held at Lexington, Kentucky, December 26–28, 1907* (Chattanooga, TN: SEA, n.d.), 266–273, quotes 267, 270–271.

litical conservatives intent upon maintaining the American tradition of limited government made it clear to male social scientists that "radicalism" in higher education would not be tolerated, thereby stunting the development of a source of social leadership that played a key role in reform in other nations. The relatively greater conservatism of southern institutions, their backwardness in social science research more generally, and the looming threat of reactionary racism placed further limitations on Progressive men within academia. Kindergartners, teachers, and club women who were educated and informed on the latest research in pedagogy and developmental psychology operated largely outside these constraints. Female volunteer organizations became the most prominent leaders of the campaigns for child labor reform and compulsory education legislation, and women gained considerable confidence from the scientific evidence that backed up their demands. A leader in the Georgia Federation's child labor reform campaign noted in 1908 that "it was a frequent thing in the beginning for women to hear themselves spoken of as 'silly' or 'meddlesome' or worse still, 'sentimental,' but the testimony of fact to the need of their work soon took away the sting of such epithets."[32]

Georgia women's involvement with free kindergartens and urban charitable organizations gave them firsthand experience with the problems of child labor, producing concerns that were reinforced by the priorities of national women's organizations. In the 1890s, their participation in the reform movement was locally motivated, a consequence of organized labor's request for their assistance and their own increasing alarm at the social problems caused by the growth of the textile industry. By the early 1900s, however, the National Consumers' League's reform campaign had become an integral part of the Federated club movement. The president of the General Federation of Women's Clubs between 1894 and 1900, Ellen Henrotin, was a Chicago ac-

32. Kathryn Kish Sklar, "The Historical Foundations of Women's Power in the Creation of the American Welfare State, 1830–1930," in *Mothers of a New World: Maternalist Politics and the Origins of Welfare States,* ed. Seth Koven and Sonya Michel (New York: Routledge and Kegan Paul, 1993), 54–55, 58–59; Joseph M. Stetar, "In Search of Direction: Southern Higher Education after the Civil War," *History of Education Quarterly* 25 (Fall 1985): 341–367; quote from Caroline Granger National Child Labor Committee speech as printed in the *Atlanta Constitution,* April 5, 1908.

tivist with close ties to Hull House who urged state Federations to tackle social justice issues. At the biennial meeting of the General Federation in 1900, representatives of the Consumers' League educated club women on the problems of sweatshop and tenement work. Two years later, at the Federation's meeting in Los Angeles, delegates considered the problems of child labor in the southern cotton industry and adopted a resolution "to work for the lessening of child labor all over the country." Caroline Granger, a Georgia woman who chaired the child labor committees for both the state and General Federations, provided an avenue through which the national campaign could shape the direction of reform within the state. She took over the chair of the national committee from Jane Addams, who, along with Florence Kelley, continued to strongly influence Federated clubs' involvement in child welfare reform.[33]

The National Consumers' League played an important role in convincing Georgia women that it was their responsibility as consumers to ensure favorable working conditions for producers. The Atlanta Woman's Club, which provided most of the state's female leadership in child labor and educational reform, established an Industrial Committee in 1900 to "inquire into the number and conditions of women [and children] in Atlanta in industrial occupations, compiling statistics for reference." A few years later, the committee chair reported that "individual responsibility for existing labor conditions will be urged by the presentation of the principles of the Consumers' League." Shortly thereafter, Atlanta club women formed their own Consumers' League, which the Woman's Club urged its members to join. The Industrial Committee continued to lobby for child labor reform bills, and several club women also served on a committee created by the Atlanta City Council to inspect all workplaces employing women and girls. By the time Florence Kelley addressed child welfare activists at the Atlanta meeting of the National Child Labor Committee (NCLC) in 1908, she was preaching to the choir. As general secretary of the National Consumers' League, she urged club women to boycott the services and products of businesses that employed young chil-

33. *Atlanta Constitution*, November 4, 1899; April 5, 1908 (quote from this issue); Elizabeth H. Davidson, *Child Labor Legislation in the Southern Textile States* (Chapel Hill: University of North Carolina Press, 1939), 79–80; Kathryn Kish Sklar, *Florence Kelley and the Nation's Work: The Rise of Women's Political Culture, 1830–1900* (New Haven, CT: Yale University Press, 1995), 307–308.

dren and to form committees to investigate the working environments of local employers.[34]

The president of the Atlanta Federation of Women's Clubs also addressed the 1908 NCLC conference on the subject of consumer activism. Corinne Douglas, who previously had chaired the Industrial Committee, informed her audience that women's interest in the production of goods for the household was in no way diminished because that production had become a part of the public sphere. "Just as the wise woman took care of her household when that household was in her sight," she argued, "so the ideal woman of today must take care of those who are doing her work for her, wherever they may be." Douglas maintained that women and children who produced goods for her home were an extended part of her household, and it was her responsibility to see that they got fair treatment and recompense for their labor no less than if they lived under her roof and ate at her table. And the "ideal woman's club," she claimed, "is the club that helps women to see that far-off worker, that far-off member of the household, and just so far as any woman's club fails to help in that way, it fails of its highest ideal and is not fit to survive." Hamilton's insightful comments were designed to break down the artificial barriers between public and private. She sought to tear down the factory walls that obscured the relationships between labor and product, worker and consumer, and industry and home, in order to assert collective responsibility and culpability for the quality of those relationships.[35]

Club women and other child welfare activists were convinced that the degradation of work was necessarily connected to the degradation of worker character, which is why the issues of public kindergartens, compulsory education, and child labor reform became so intertwined. Jane Addams, who shared the platform with Caroline Granger at the NCLC annual meeting in New York City in 1905, depicted the employment of young children in mills and factories as a denial of childhood. She regarded this as an alarming and

34. First quote from *More Light: Fifth Annual Announcement of the Atlanta Woman's Club*, 1899–1900, 10–11, AWC; second quote from *More Light*, 1902–1903, 11–12, AWC; *More Light*, 1903–1904, 11–12, AWC; *More Light*, 1905–1906, 12, AWC; Florence Kelley, "The Responsibility of the Consumer," in *Child Labor and Social Progress: Proceedings of the Fourth Annual Meeting of the National Child Labor Committee*, supplement to *Annals* 25 (July 1908): 108–112; address of Atlanta Mayor W. R. Joyner, in *Child Labor and Social Progress*, 159.

35. Address of Corinne (Mrs. Hamilton) Douglas, *Child Labor and Social Progress*, 162–163.

destructive extension of the industrial work process, with its repression of individual agency, creative choice, and artistic expression. Addams described the new pedagogy that underlay the field of child study and the kindergarten movement as a corrective for the degrading influence of industry on the individual: "In proportion as the child in later life is to be subjected to a mechanical and one-sided activity and as a highly-subdivided labor is to be demanded from him, it is therefore most important that he should have his full period of childhood and youth for this play expression, that he may cultivate within himself the root of that culture which can alone give his later activity a meaning." Addams further argued that eliminating this period of "child play" was harmful to society as well as to the worker. It constituted eliminating a step in the socialization of the individual to the group—a step, she believed, that was necessary for the development of a cooperative spirit and for the successful integration of workers into crowded communities and factories.[36]

Georgia kindergartners were in full accord with Addams's explanation of the importance of their work, and eventually they were compelled to acknowledge the demands for activism it placed upon them. They were directly confronted with the implications of an inactive state and growing class differences and consequently were forced to think about the individual needs of children in the context of larger social problems and solutions. This process of political enlightenment could begin in small ways. Eva Richardson, who was from New York, was "much surprised" to see how many older children were enrolled in the Holy Innocents' kindergarten, but she quickly realized that the lack of a compulsory attendance law was to blame. Grace Graybill McDowell was shocked at the contrast between the free kindergartens in which she had assisted as a student and Willette Allen's exclusive private "model" school, where she was hired to work after graduation. The free kindergartens were always short of funds, and McDowell was accustomed to scrimping on supplies. Shortly after beginning her new job, she was made acutely aware of the huge social gulf separating her new pupils from her old ones when a small boy handed her his engraved calling card with a hand that

36. Jane Addams, "Child Labor Legislation—A Requisite for Industrial Efficiency," in *Addresses from [the First] Annual Meeting of the NCLC*, 1905, supplement to *Annals* 25 (May 1905): 542–550, quotes 547–548.

sported "polished nails and gold linked cuff buttons." McDowell felt silly re-membering that she had divided a piece of fruit into thirteen pieces at lunch. She later recalled being intimidated by the realization that "these children were going out into the world with money, education, and influence," and she was so uncomfortable that she counted the days until the end of the school year.[37]

The development of a political consciousness among kindergartners often was complicated by their ties to mills and mill owners. Mills in Atlanta, Athens, Columbus, and West Point paid part or all of the salaries of women who conducted kindergartens for their workers, and mill owners frequently advertised their philanthropy as a way to discredit the campaign for child labor reform. In 1905 the Eagle and Phenix Mills of Columbus built two schools for the children of employees who lived across the Chattahoochee River in Alabama. Mill management printed a pamphlet, with pictures and a description of the new facilities, that they sent out to groups such as the National Association for the Promotion of Kindergarten Education. The publication proclaimed that mill officials were motivated by the noble sentiment that it was "incumbent upon the artificial person known as the corporation, just as it is on the natural person, to devote a certain portion of time, thought and work to making this world a better place." In Atlanta, the Gate City and Exposition Cotton Mills were fond of printing pictures of their kindergartens in the local press, accompanied by such captions as, "This is an example of the work which cotton mill manufacturers of Georgia generally are doing to make life brighter for their operatives and the operatives' families." These public relations efforts were designed to assure Georgians that there was no need for state intervention to defend the integrity of the working-class family against unchecked exploitation.[38]

37. Richardson, "The Holy Innocents' Kindergarten"; Grace Graybill McDowell, "A Tribute to the Kindergartens," AKAC, box 1, folder 3.

38. *The Manufactory and the Kindergarten,* Eagle and Phenix Mills pamphlet, Free Kindergarten Scrapbook, NPB. An arrangement similar to that in Columbus existed in West Point, Georgia, where the West Point Manufacturing Company provided several kindergartens for employees who lived in the Alabama mill villages of Lanett, Shawmut, Langdale, Fairfax, and Riverview. *History of the Kindergarten Movement in the Southeastern States,* 6–7. One national public relations campaign conducted by southern cotton mill owners consisted of a series of illustrated articles published in the *Washington Post* entitled "Life in the Southern Cotton Mills,"

Some social workers in mill communities harbored idealistic hopes that teachers, operatives, and management could become one big happy family, but that did not necessarily prevent them from endorsing an extension of state authority. Katherine Dozier, who directed the school and settlement work at New Holland Mill in northeast Georgia, tried to create such a community spirit by getting mill officials and teachers to attend Bible school with the workers. After almost a decade of activism, she continued to have faith in the ability of personal interaction to cultivate mutual understanding and respect and thereby to "promote the common welfare." She also came to realize, however, that educational leaders had an obligation to inform the public of social conditions and then to "spur on the awakened citizen to constructive, corrective building of equalization of opportunity." Dozier decided that the needs of mill children were the needs of *all* children, and she decried the tendency to put them into a separate category calling for special treatment. She was convinced that social and economic problems would be resolved only when the state guaranteed the right of self-development to children from all backgrounds—mill, farm, village, and city—through legislative reform and the creation of new agencies.[39]

As Dozier's assessment suggests, even women who initially were sympathetic to the interests of owners and management came to believe that the individual and social costs of child labor necessitated state intervention. In 1902 Georgia's ninety cotton mills employed between 35,000 and 40,000 operatives, and according to the State Federation of Labor, about 10 percent of them were children under twelve years of age who worked an average of twelve hours per day. Although the youthfulness of the workers may have been an exaggeration, it was true that roughly a quarter of all mill operatives in the state were children younger than sixteen years of age who lacked any legal protections against the sixty-six-hour week typical for mill workers. Children represented the same proportion of mill workers between 1890 and 1900, but the absolute number of child workers rose from about 2,500 to al-

---

as discussed in an editorial, "Life in Southern Mill Towns," *American Child* 2 (August 1920): 108–110. Second quote from Clippings, AKAC, box 1, folder 12.

39. Katherine Dozier, "Our School at New Holland," in *Fifty-First Annual Meeting of the Georgia Educational Association, 1917* (Macon, GA: GEA, n.d.), 47–53; Dozier, "What the Supervision of Mill Schools Has Taught Me," *High School Quarterly* 14 (October 1925): 21–25, quotes 22–23.

most 4,500 during that decade. There was ample evidence of the ill effects of mill employment on children. The four southern cotton-manufacturing states contained 40 percent of the nation's children between the ages of ten and fourteen who could not read or write. The 1900 census revealed that the percentage of illiteracy among mill children in Georgia and the Carolinas was three to four times greater than that of the general population of white children in those states. Equally alarming to reformers were the health risks associated with child labor. Young workers had lower body weights and higher mortality rates than did other children, and they were more likely than older employees to have work accidents resulting in serious injury.[40]

Mounting evidence of the destructive impact of child labor persuaded club women and teachers of the need for serious legislative reforms. A. J. McKelway, the southern director of the National Child Labor Committee, called Alabama, Georgia, and the Carolinas the "sore spot of the nation" because of their intransigence on the issue of child labor reform. In Georgia, labor unions, religious groups, and the state Federation of Women's Clubs lobbied for reform legislation almost every year beginning in 1896, but they suffered repeated defeat due to the vigorous opposition of cotton manufacturing interests. In 1900 mill owners formed the Georgia Industrial Association and made an informal "gentleman's agreement" not to employ children younger than twelve, but it was only a thinly disguised ruse to stave off reform, and violations were notoriously widespread. While traveling on a train, two club women from the Georgia Federation reportedly overheard one "mill man" say to another that the agreement was a formality "that was only for the legislature." In 1903 Virginia, Alabama, and the Carolinas approved bills establishing twelve as the minimum age of employment, leaving Georgia as the only state in the nation allowing children as young as ten to work in mills and factories. Persistent work by organized women and the Georgia Child Labor Committee helped to push through reform bills in 1906 and 1914 that even-

40. A. J. McKelway, "The Cotton Mill: The Herod among Industries," *Annals* 38 (July 1911): 45; Rev. J. E. Wray, *The Herod of the South; or, the Child Labor Iniquity,* introduction by the Central Federation of Labor (Columbus, GA: Central Federation of Labor, n.d.), pamphlet; Davidson, *Child Labor Legislation in the Southern Textile States,* 5–6; *Some Interesting Information concerning Child Labor in Georgia* (Atlanta: Georgia Federation of Labor, ca. 1902), pamphlet; Anna Rochester and Florence Taylor, "What the Government Says about Cotton Mills," *Child Labor Bulletin* 3 (February 1915): 20–24.

tually raised the legal minimum age to twelve, but manufacturing interests managed to water down other aspects of state regulations and to ensure there was almost no provision for enforcement.[41]

Women associated with mill schools were all too familiar with the inadequacies of manufacturers' laissez-faire philosophy, because they could see for themselves the hypocrisy of "industrial welfare" (later called "welfare capitalism"). Employers loudly proclaimed that they were providing kindergartens and schools for operative families out of concern for their well being, while at the same time they engaged in practices that pressured parents to put children to work. One example was the use of young children as "dinner toters." Workers preferred a warm meal for their midday break, and it was the responsibility of their youngest children to carry lunch pails from home to mill at eleven o'clock each day. In cotton manufacturing centers such as Augusta and Columbus, it was common to see throngs of little boys and girls crowding down the streets and into the mills at mealtime. A school official whose students carried meals to parents in the Eagle and Phenix Mill complained to NCLC investigators that mill management "encouraged dinner toting because in that way they trained the children to work." Dinner toters tended the machines while their parents ate, which meant not only that management was training future employees without having to pay them, but also that the mills were able to maintain production during mealtimes. This practice presented a problem for teachers because dinner toters had a poor record of attendance, and those who did come to school in the morning usually did not return in the afternoon. These students were getting only a few hours of schooling per day and had no reason to take their education seriously.[42]

41. First quote from A. J. McKelway, "Ten Years of Child Labor Reform in the South," *Child Labor Bulletin* 2 (February 1914): 35–39, quote 36. For a description of the cotton mill industry's use of child labor, see Howell Cheney, "Practical Restrictions on Child Labor in Textiles Industries: Higher Educational and Physical Qualifications," *Annals of the American Academy* 33 (March 1909): supplement, 86–99; and Idus A. Newby, *Plain Folk in the New South: Social Change and Cultural Persistence, 1880–1915* (Baton Rouge: Louisiana State University Press, 1989), 119–125; Davidson, *Child Labor Legislation in the Southern Textile States,* 71–88; remaining quotes from Caroline Dickson (Mrs. A. O.) Granger, "The Work of the General Federation of Women's Clubs against Child Labor," in *Addresses from Annual Meeting of the NCLC,* 1905, 520; A. J. McKelway, "Child Labor in Georgia: A Story for Grownups," *Child Labor Bulletin* 2 (August 1913): 59.

42. Mary H. Newell (secretary of Associated Charities, Columbus), "Shall Charitable Societies Relieve Family Distress by Finding Work for Children," *Child Labor Bulletin* 2 (May 1913):

Mill management had many ways to get the message across to parents that the entire family's labor was needed. This preference was expressed from the moment of recruitment. The Fulton Bag and Cotton Mill in Atlanta had a standing "help wanted" newspaper advertisement that informed readers, "can use complete families." Mills commonly sent agents into the countryside to look for potential employees among rural families, especially those containing widows and numerous children. One Columbus mill made child labor more attractive by charging less rent for families with more workers. The rent scale for company housing was $1.25 per room per month for "old and new houses, one hand at work," 80 cents per room for new houses with two hands at work, and 75 cents per room for new houses with three or more hands at work. In some cases, supervisors informed parents that they needed to bring their oldest children to work the next day, or they simply sent someone from the mill to get the children out of class. When the federal Bureau of Labor conducted an extensive survey of southern cotton mills in 1910, it found that the "school work of the child from 12 to 16 years of age is *frequently* interrupted by a hurry call from the mill superintendent." Such pressure tactics cast into serious doubt the frequent claims of mill owners and their representatives that they only employed minors as a favor to poor families.[43]

While child welfare activists recognized the duplicity of cotton manufacturers as a hindrance to reform, they also understood that the cooperation of parents and children was a significant part of the problem. NCLC investiga-

---

39–41; McKelway, "Child Labor in Georgia," 70, quote 73. The Fulton Mills of Atlanta greatly increased their welfare capitalism programs in response to the bitter strike of 1914–1915. Clifford Kuhn, *Contesting the New South Order: The 1914–1915 Strike at Atlanta's Fulton Mills* (Chapel Hill: University of North Carolina Press, 2001), 226.

43. First quote as cited in Gary M. Fink, *The Fulton Bag and Cotton Mills Strike of 1914–1915* (Ithaca, NY: ILR Press, 1993), 39; second quote from Mary Brown Sumner, "What the Government Found When It Broadened Out Its Interest in Boll-Weevils and Began to Study Children," *Survey* 27 (December 1911): 1375; McKelway, "Child Labor in Georgia," 73; *Some Interesting Information concerning Child Labor in Georgia*. Child labor reformers found much evidence to support their cause in the federal Bureau of Labor's *Report on the Conditions of Woman and Child Wage-Earners in the U.S.,* 61st Cong., 2nd sess., 1909–1910, S. Doc. 645, 19 volumes, esp. vol. 14, *The Cotton Textile Industry,* last quote from the latter as cited in E. N. Clopper, "The Education of Factory Children in the South," in *SEA, Journal of Proceedings and Addresses of the Twenty-Second Annual Meeting Held at Houston, Texas, November 30, December 1, 2, 1911* (Nashville, TN: SEA, n.d.), 192, emphasis in original.

tors documented numerous cases in the cotton manufacturing states in which parents deliberately violated the law by lying about children's ages or about the hardship circumstances that allowed legal exemptions. In 1913 Georgia was one of four states still without a birth registration law, so authorities had to rely on the parents' word that children were old enough to work. Orphans and children of widowed or dependent parents were allowed exceptions to the minimum age, and again, employers and local officials usually had to accept at face value adult explanations for the necessity of child labor. Many child welfare activists were outraged that parents, and especially fathers, would willingly send their young children into the mill in defiance of laws intended to protect them. While she was chair of the General Federation's Child Welfare Committee, Caroline Dickson Granger stridently condemned the "vampire father" who lived "upon the money earned by the sapping of the vital forces of his children." Other activists recognized that many mill workers were recently removed from the farm, where child labor was a way of life, and argued that such parents had to be educated as to the comparatively worse effects of factory work on young children.[44]

An even greater problem for reformers than the "vampire father" was the prevalence of children who preferred millwork to school. Child welfare workers conducted numerous studies to ascertain why most boys and girls from mill families dropped out of school as soon as they reached the minimum age of employment. In 1910 a study of 622 working children in five states (including Alabama, Georgia, and South Carolina) found that only 2.8 percent came from families with dependent fathers who were capable of working. Although poverty was a major reason for child employment, many young workers said they took jobs because they did not like school, and 60 percent of those respondents had no immediate financial need to work. Other studies conducted at the end of World War I showed similar results, with poverty and "dissatisfaction with school" being the most commonly cited reasons for child labor. Reformers who reported on these studies concluded that there must be something wrong with school. One writer noted that children who had access to schools with manual training were less likely to leave from lack

---

44. "An Address to the Citizens of Twelve States on the Child Labor Laws You Should Enact in 1914," *Child Labor Bulletin* 2 (November 1913): 34; Granger, "Work of the General Federation," 518; Neal L. Anderson, "Child Labor Legislation in the South," *Addresses from Annual Meeting of the NCLC,* 1905, 500–501.

of interest. Another critic went even further, arguing that the child labor problem was a "problem of stagnant school curriculum, of underpaid teachers, of minds overfed with indigestible material, and of souls undernourished in their craving for adventure and real preparation for the lives they are to live."[45]

Reformers were correct in assuming that there was an important connection between child labor and the characteristics of formal education, but their understanding of that connection was limited by the cultural differences separating them from mill families. Child labor was a way of life, but not necessarily just on the farm; by the 1890s Georgia had a substantial second generation of textile workers who had grown up in the mills. Children often started as "helpers" who assisted parents or older siblings before they became old enough and experienced enough to be entered on the payrolls in their own names. It was because millwork was a family affair and the source of most social interaction in the mill village that children who had to go to school felt they were "missing out." They did not want to be treated as children but rather wanted the opportunity to earn their own pay. Reports of social workers and interviews of operatives recount many instances in which children begged their parents for permission to leave school to become wage earners. In most cases parents eventually acquiesced. Adults who had contributed to family income when they were young saw nothing inherently wrong with children helping to earn their keep. Furthermore, mill operatives believed there was little value in obtaining a formal education beyond basic literacy. They had few expectations of upward mobility and tended to believe that decisions regarding length of schooling ultimately rested with the individual child. This parental flexibility on the issue of education was puzzling and frustrating to social workers, who often interpreted it as a sign of hopelessness or ignorance.[46]

Kindergartners, whose primary professional mission was to enhance the

---

45. Sumner, "What the Government Found," 1376; Theresa Wolfson, "Why, When, and How Children Leave School," *American Child* 1 (May 1919): 59–64, quote 64.

46. This discussion of mill-worker culture relies heavily on an extensive study of operatives' oral histories: Newby, *Plain Folk in the New South*, and in particular the chapters titled "Education" and "Child Labor"; also see Jennings J. Rhyne, *Some Southern Cotton Mill Workers and Their Villages* (Chapel Hill: University of North Carolina Press, 1930), 200–204; and Harriet L. Herring, *Welfare Work in Mill Villages: The Story of Extra-Mill Activities in North Carolina* (Chapel Hill, University of North Carolina Press, 1929), 42–43.

development of the individual child, believed that their approach to early childhood education could resolve some of the objections on the part of the working-class family. The expectation was that the nurturing, child-centered atmosphere of the preschool could give children a positive attitude toward teachers and school that would make them less likely to want to leave the classroom for the mill. If they were motivated to work by the sense of belonging derived from association with the mill "family," then perhaps creating a homelike classroom with a motherly teacher could form competing attachments to woo them away. Since efforts to pass a permissive kindergarten bill were repeatedly thwarted and the number of preschools in the state remained small, kindergartners advocated making primary school more like preschool as a way to increase its appeal to children. They were critical of the old disciplinarian classroom approach that distanced teacher from pupil and suggested that instructors in the primary grades adopt a more child-centered pedagogy. An Atlanta kindergartner boldly asserted that "every child has a right to be understood" and that teachers needed to be willing to adapt their methods to the needs of the individual student. Kindergartners were impatient with teachers who complained that preschool spoiled children by giving them too much individual attention, or that it produced discipline problems in the primary grades because its graduates were more outspoken and easily bored. One southern kindergartner dismissed these objections as coming from the unambitious teacher "who shuts out new methods" and "gives no work to little, restless hands, but directs all energies and efforts to the acquirement of printed and written words."[47]

As the above quote suggests, kindergartners believed that continuing the preschool manual work (essentially "arts and crafts" activities) in the primary grades could make school more attractive to mill children. Middle-class women engaged in social work in the mill community often remarked on the social stigma attached to being an operative, and mill children who attended public schools with students from other backgrounds had to contend with this prejudice daily. Their sense of isolation was compounded by their relatively lower levels of academic training, since it was not uncommon for chil-

47. First quote from Mary Taylor, "The Study of Children," *SEA Proceedings, 1903*, 246–247. Mrs. J. T. Stoddard, "The Relation of Kindergarten to Primary and Subsequent School Work," in *SEA Proceedings, 1908*, 721–732, second quote 722.

dren of ten or twelve to be in the first grade. An essay printed in Willette Allen's "Kindergarten and the Primary" section of the *Southern Educational Journal* argued that manual work could build self-esteem in "backward" students by setting them up to succeed rather than fail. The author of the article relayed the story of a child who had always been a discipline problem until he was put in a primary classroom where the teacher employed manual training. Although he was far behind in academic skills, he was accomplished at activities such as woodworking and clay modeling. By stressing his achievements in the latter, the teacher was able to build his self-confidence and improve his attitude toward school. According to the story, when he was placed in a classroom the following year that had no manual work, he quickly returned to fighting, swearing, and truancy.[48]

While kindergartners argued that manual training could combat illiteracy by improving students' attitudes toward themselves and learning, child labor reformers claimed that industrial education could counteract the lure of the workplace by offering marketable skills. Owen Lovejoy, general secretary of the NCLC, lamented that a high dropout rate after fourth grade persisted despite evidence that students who continued school until age sixteen advanced further and more quickly in terms of job position and salary. He argued that industrial education could hold potential dropouts for an additional two years by offering vocational training to help them enter skilled labor positions with superior pay and potential for advancement. Lovejoy acknowledged the dangers inherent in his proposal, namely the possibility that schools would just prepare students to go to work in nearby factories, thereby relieving employers of the cost of training workers themselves. However, he suggested that this problem could be avoided by introducing students to a variety of occupational categories, enabling them to make an informed decision for themselves and putting them in a better position to bargain with prospective employers.[49]

Progressive reformers were divided over the desirability of introducing

48. Louisa Parsons Hopkins, "Object Lessons in Moral Training," clipping from *Southern Educational Journal,* AKAC, box 2, folder 10.

49. Mary Flexner, "A Plea for Vocational Training," *Survey* 22 (August 1909): 1375–1377; Owen R. Lovejoy, "Will Trade Training Solve the Child Labor Problem?" *North American Review* 191 (June 1910): 773–784.

industrial education into public schools, for the reasons listed by Lovejoy as well as many others. John Dewey, Columbia University professor and national educational leader, published an essay in 1913 in which he warned child labor reformers that the "question of industrial education is fraught with consequences for the future of democracy." He agreed that industrial education had potential value to society, and he had no quarrel with integrating some manual and industrial training into the traditional academic curriculum. When employed in this manner, he argued, industrial training could produce better citizens by impressing children with the dignity and social worth of all vocations. The danger lay in dissociating it from general education, because doing so would serve to accentuate and reproduce class difference. Dewey condemned the practice of creating vocational schools that segregated the "laboring classes" into institutions separate from those attended by middle- and upper-class children. He argued that creating different curricula for different classes was undemocratic and would siphon money away from traditional schools that already suffered from a lack of funds. Wryly noting that "some employers of labor would doubtless rejoice to have schools, supported by public taxation, supply them with additional food for their mills," Dewey admonished "all others" to oppose the trend.[50]

At first glance, the public mill schools of Columbus appear to have suffered from most of the negative aspects of industrial education described by Lovejoy and Dewey. By the end of the nineteenth century, Columbus had a population of over 17,000, more than a dozen cotton and woolen mills, and around 1,000 children who were not attending school. In 1902 city officials created a "primary industrial school" in a mill district containing about 500 school-age children. The hours and curriculum of the school were structured especially for dinner toters, and it was commonly referred to as the "dinner toters' school." Classes met from eight until ten-thirty in the morning, broke so that students could carry dinner to the mills, and then resumed from one until four in the afternoon. Since the majority of students had little if any previous schooling, course work adhered closely to the fundamentals of the "three R's." The school was ungraded, meaning that the work was remedial and children did not progress from one grade to the next based on stan-

50. John Dewey, "Some Dangers in the Present Movement for Industrial Education," *Child Labor Bulletin* 1 (February 1913): 69–74, first quote 70, all others 73.

dardized evaluations. The last one and a half hours of every day were spent in "industrial work," including cleaning, gardening, sewing, and simple carpentry. This unconventional "school of handcrafts" embodied that class-based separation of educational services that Dewey so vehemently opposed.[51]

Although primary students were too young for true vocational education, Columbus's "secondary industrial school" oriented its curriculum toward producing trained workers, many of whom found employment in local mills. City officials opened the secondary school in 1906 for students who had graduated from the primary industrial or elementary schools. The city superintendent who presided over the school's opening proclaimed that its purpose was "to prepare the youth of Columbus and vicinity for intelligent and efficient service, and for good earning power in business life or in the more important industries." This high school for mill children combined an "abridged course in academic subjects" with instruction in trades. Mandatory studies included English, mathematics, history, and science, while elective vocational courses were available in mechanical arts, textile arts, and commercial business training. The textile department contained a "complete cotton mill"[52] that demonstrated every stage of factory production with the "most up-to-date machinery." Students in the textile arts spent the last three months of their three-year training course working in Columbus mills under managers who reported back to the school on their progress. The expanded curriculum necessitated that classes meet for five and a half days a week, year-round, with only a six-week vacation, a schedule that school officials bragged would prepare students for the demands of the real workplace.[53]

51. Selene Armstrong, "Magnificent Public School System and Industrial Advantages of Columbus, Georgia," in Georgia Department of Education, *Thirty-Fifth Annual Report, 1906* (Atlanta: GDE, 1907), 301–303; first quote from "History of Kindergartens in Columbus," AKAC Scrapbooks; remaining quotes from Roland B. Daniel, "Greater Efficiency in Education," in *SEA Journal of Proceedings and Addresses of the Twenty-First Annual Meeting Held at Chattanooga, Tenn., December 27–29, 1910* (Nashville, TN: SEA, n.d.), 115; Carleton B. Gibson, "Education through Handicraft," in *Proceedings of the Fifth Conference for Education in the South, held at Athens, Georgia, April 24, 25, and 26, 1902* (Knoxville, TN: Southern Education Board, 1902), 68–71.

52. Carleton B. Gibson, "A Brief Account of Industrial Education at Columbus, Georgia," in *SEA Proceedings, 1907*, 130–131.

53. Roland B. Daniel, "Greater Efficiency in Education, in *SEA Proceedings, 1910*, 116–117, quote 116.

While the Columbus mill schools appear to be blatant examples of how business interests could constrict educational opportunity, the city's female reformers were not captive to financial concerns but adopted a more holistic approach that reflected their distinctive political culture. In Columbus as in Atlanta, kindergartners and club women were active participants in the campaign for urban educational reform from its very beginnings. They established a Free Kindergarten Association in 1894 to serve the children of cotton mill workers. The association's two Louisville-trained kindergartners established a Free Kindergarten Training School, which produced teachers for all of the city's private and public preschools. The Free Kindergarten Association's influence was at least partly responsible for the introduction of manual training in the elementary school curriculum four years later. Women's educational philosophy was evident in the primary industrial school as well, which was located in an antebellum residence so that it would appear more as a home than as a school. Three teachers lived and worked in the schoolhouse and established further ties to the community through visiting. With the assistance of club women and city funds, they were able to turn the building into a community center with health care services, library and reading rooms, a day nursery, a kindergarten, a playground, and a swimming pool. Women were concerned with meeting the needs of the entire family, and children's industrial activities were designed to improve living conditions by producing food, furniture, and clothing for home use.[54]

Mary Newell, a teacher who lived in the primary industrial school, illustrates how women could use public institutions for egalitarian purposes not necessarily intended by city administrators and their financial backers. Newell's larger objective was to keep mill children in school as long as possible so that they could decide for themselves what they wanted to do with their lives. To achieve this end, she developed personal relationships with students and their parents, greeted each child as he or she came to class every morning, and tried to find financial relief for families who relied on children's labor to meet

---

54. Gibson, "A Brief Account of Industrial Education," 128–132; Roland B. Daniel, "Some Experiments in Vocational Education in a Mill Community," in *Proceedings of the Seventeenth Conference for Education in the South and the Twenty-Fifth Annual Meeting of the SEA, Joint Session, Louisville, Kentucky, April 7, 8, 9, and 10, 1914* (Washington, DC, and Birmingham, AL: Executive Committee of the Conference and the SEA, n.d.), 302–305.

subsistence needs. In answer to those who asked what she hoped to accomplish, Newell described two modest goals. First, she wanted to establish a new tradition of more lengthy schooling in working families. This was of particular concern for urban charities that tried to get relatives to help subsidize the education of their poor kin by making up part of the loss in child wages. When Newell, who worked for the city's main charitable society, approached extended family members to determine their ability to contribute, she often faced resistance. Relatives who themselves had started work at age nine or ten informed her that they were "not going to pay a cent into that family because they see no reason why every one of those children should not be working." Newell hoped that keeping children in school until age fourteen would produce a new generation of workers who accepted "that their children must not go to work until they are fourteen," that attitudes would gradually change.[55]

Newell's second goal more directly addressed the purposes of the secondary industrial school. Even though the Columbus city superintendent claimed in regard to mill operatives, "It is no desire of ours particularly to change them to other vocations," Newell made it clear that she hoped to channel children into more promising careers. She described millwork as a "dead-end occupation" that so stigmatized workers that once they became operatives they were able to do nothing else. She came to realize this fact when trying to obtain apprenticeships for several older boys who participated in evening clubs at the primary school settlement. She was able to find positions for them in an iron foundry, only to have them dismissed their first day on the job after their boss discovered that they had worked in the cotton mill for several years. According to Newell, employers commonly believed that boys from operative families were a "shiftless class," and they would not hire them. It was her belief that keeping students in class and out of the mills until they reached the typical working age for other occupations would allow them to "get into the iron foundries and machine shops," so that they would "not have to go into the cotton mills at all." This goal fitted closely with the intent of Progressive educational reformers and child welfare advocates who argued that industrial or vocational training should be used to widen, rather than narrow, the options of working-class children.[56]

55. Newell, "Shall Charitable Societies Relieve Family Distress," 39–41.
56. Ibid., 41.

Women activists and Progressive city officials had some success with using manual training and industrial education to keep children out of the mills. Despite the arduous schedule of the secondary industrial school, attendance doubled during the first four years of operation. The city superintendent claimed that, without exception, all graduates had either entered the trade for which they had prepared or pursued further study at the Georgia Institute of Technology or Alabama Polytechnic Institute. The enrollment at the primary industrial school increased as well, from about 75 to 350 students between 1902 and 1914. Daily attendance continued to fluctuate dramatically, suggesting that financial necessity was still forcing many parents to send their children to work some days. What was most remarkable was the number of students who requested transfers to traditional standard grammar schools. More than 100 mill children asked to be placed in regular city schools so that "they might be regularly graded and promoted from year to year." In response the city Board of Education constructed a modern grammar school in the mill district and announced plans to institute a graded, standardized curriculum with remedial classes for the remaining "backward" students. The improved academic skills of mill children were a credit not only to the reformers who provided a hospitable environment in which they could learn, but also to the students and their parents, who did not hesitate to demand equal access to a quality education when given a chance. Their initiative belied the generalizations of social workers who claimed that mill operatives were indifferent of the value of an education.[57]

Recognizing the family sacrifices involved in keeping children in school, organized women tried to provide compensation through mothers' pensions and other forms of child subsidies. In 1915, according to federal statistics, among southern mill families with children under fourteen years of age at work, child wages contributed more than 19 percent of annual household income; and among female-headed households, that figure was 26 percent. Even though three-quarters of child workers younger than fourteen had two able-bodied parents, their labor might be required to build up a financial

57. Daniel, "Greater Efficiency in Education," 116–117; quotes from Daniel, "Some Experiments in Vocational Education," 304–305; Daniel claimed that 25 percent of the industrial high school graduates went on to college. "Industrial Education in Columbus, Georgia," in *Proceedings of the SEA, 1914,* 196–197.

"buffer" that could prevent family destitution in the event of the illness, injury, or death of one or more wage earners. Some women's clubs took the advice of the General Federation and sponsored scholarships for mill children based on family need. They recognized that such private efforts were inadequate to address the larger problems of poverty and child labor, and they turned to the state to provide mothers' pensions for widows or abandoned wives. Although a study of reform in South Carolina claims that the concept of mothers' pensions "never went beyond the stage of idle talk," this was more true of politicians than of club women. Georgia legislators, like their counterparts in Mississippi, Alabama, and South Carolina, refused to establish mothers' pensions, but it was not for lack of commitment or effort on the part of female activists.[58]

While white women battled to remove children from factories and place them in schools, black club women struggled to ensure basic educational services for children already enrolled. Members of the Gate City Free Kindergarten Association provided day care and preschool for the youngest children of Atlanta's working-class families, but it was the responsibility of the municipal government to provide access to elementary and secondary education. In 1913 the Neighborhood Union aggressively tackled the failures of the city to fulfill this obligation. Members recruited prominent black women to join them in establishing a Social Improvement Committee, which over a period of six months painstakingly investigated and evaluated black schools. In addition to the usual problem of shabby facilities, the women found that there were more than six thousand children enrolled for little more than four thousand available seats. The city was dealing with the problem of overcrowding by dividing students into morning and afternoon sessions, giving children a half-day of class and teachers a double workload. Committee members sent a detailed letter of complaint on their findings to the city council, lobbied council members and the mayor individually, and repeatedly petitioned the city Board of Education to address the problems. They also made personal visits to white club women and ministers to enlist their support. The committee won small but important concessions from the city, including pay

58. Rochester and Taylor, "What the Government Says about Cotton Mills," 22–23; David L. Carlton, *Mill and Town in South Carolina, 1880–1920* (Baton Rouge: Louisiana State University Press, 1982), 204.

raises for black teachers and the establishment of an additional black school in South Atlanta.[59]

Female activists attempting to resolve long-standing inadequacies in Atlanta's black schools continually faced attempts to widen the gap of educational opportunity. Late in 1913, the city Board of Education began considering a proposal to substitute extended industrial education for the seventh and eighth grades in black schools. The Social Improvement Committee immediately launched a public relations campaign to oppose the changes, which were being sold as way to create more efficient workers. Committee members argued that they supported the expansion of manual and domestic science training for black youth, but not as a substitute for a liberal arts education. Their protest had mixed results, since city officials responded by eliminating the eighth grade in both black and white schools. Three years later, when a proposal surfaced to eliminate the seventh grade in black schools only, a newly established chapter of the NAACP helped to defeat the measure. It was not until 1921 that the city approved plans to construct more black schools, and only then because black voters threatened to continue defeating bond issues needed for white school improvements. By that time, the black population had grown so dramatically that the city had fallen far behind in meeting the educational needs of school children. The Neighborhood Union noted in 1923 that the discrepancy between enrollment and available seats had actually increased over the previous decade.[60]

Although the urban reform campaigns remained segregated, black club women received expressions of encouragement and support from Atlanta's white female leadership. Atlanta Free Kindergarten Association president Nellie Peters Black publicly praised the Gate City group for raising educational standards by using teachers trained in the Spelman and Atlanta University normal schools. She also corresponded with a national kindergarten association and assisted it in fund-raising campaigns for Gate City preschools.

59. NU annual report, 1913–1914, clipping from *Spelman Messenger,* NU, box 5, folder 7; Petition to the City Council, August 19, 1913, NU, box 2, folder 19; Petition to the Atlanta Board of Education, NU, box 2, folder 20.

60. Rosa Lowe to Lugenia Burns Hope, and enclosed school questionnaire, February 19, 1917, NU, box 2, folder 28; Petition to the Atlanta Mayor and City Council, September 29, 1923, NU, box 6, folder 9; Edgar A. Toppin, "Walter White and the Atlanta NAACP's Fight for Equal Schools, 1916–1917," *History of Education Quarterly* 7 (Spring 1967): 3–21.

Black reformers received assistance from white professionals in 1923, when members of the Atlanta Kindergarten Alumnae Club joined social workers in lobbying city officials to include blacks in the plan to incorporate free kindergartens into the municipal school system. Passie Fenton Ottley, another prominent educational reformer from Atlanta, went so far as to write Hampton Institute's *Southern Workman* in 1900 to advocate support for black kindergartens and mothers' clubs. She heaped praise on black educator Alice Cary, of Morris Brown Institute, for her work in child welfare. Describing Cary as "a woman of excellent scholarship and unimpeachable character" who had dedicated her life "to the effort to inspire the Negro mother," Ottley passionately urged readers to assist the expansion of such work throughout the South. Other white club women showed their support by helping to establish black kindergartens in Atlanta, Athens, Columbus, and Savannah.[61]

Interracial cooperation in child welfare reform was problematic for white women in that it was likely to provoke both class- and race-based opposition. Efforts to broaden the role of the state and redistribute wealth downward always faced stiff resistance, and the inclusion of black children increased the stakes by threatening to lessen white control of state resources and labor. This combination of concerns most likely underlay the stubborn refusal of the Georgia General Assembly to pass a permissive kindergarten bill. After financial support for free kindergartens began a sharp decline during World War I, the Atlanta Kindergarten Alumnae Club called for a revision of the state constitution so that the school fund could be used for the education of children younger than six. The state PTA and Georgia Kindergarten Association assumed primary responsibility for sponsoring annual legislative proposals, while club women issued press releases and sent letters to politicians requesting their support, addressed the education committees in House and Senate, and personally met with the leaders of the legislative opposition. After their proposed bill was defeated in 1921 and again in 1922, women lobbyists agreed to restrict funding to local tax moneys and to limit the instances in which

61. Although these clippings date near the time of Black's death, they describe community activism stretching back to the mid-1890s: *Atlanta Constitution*, April 13, August 31, 1919, NPB, box 1, folder 1; Geraldine O'Grady to Nellie Peters Black, November 29, 1910, Free Kindergarten Scrapbook, NPB, box 6, folder 2; Ada S. Woolfolk to Mrs. Ashby Jones, December 19, 1924, AKAC, box 1, folder 6; Passie Fenton Ottley to the editor, *Southern Workman* 29 (October 1900): 553; *History of the Kindergarten Movement in the Southeastern States*, 16–20; AKAC Scrapbooks.

kindergartens would be maintained by local boards of education. Opponents of the earlier bill proclaimed their satisfaction with the revisions, and the educational committees of both houses consistently approved the bill every year, but legislators repeatedly failed to pass it.[62]

Club women seemed bewildered at the rejection of their bill year after year, since opposition to it was not nearly so strident as that which faced the more successful child labor and compulsory attendance bills. After all, they had compromised on the important issue of state funds and retained the "permissive" aspect of the bill despite the belief of many women that kindergartens should be a mandatory part of public schools. Some rural political leaders opposed the reform because it stood to benefit cities more than the countryside, leading Georgia Federation of Women's Clubs leader Louise Frederick Hays to complain in a moment of exasperation that her senator belonged to the "Tom Watson, J. J. Brown faction" and was "hopeless." Only three years later, however, the women who guided the bill through the 1928 legislative session "found comparatively little opposition from the legislators themselves." The men expressed doubt that rural school districts would be able to support kindergartens but were not adamantly opposed to the concept "if money could be found." Nonetheless, the bill was tabled without a hearing several times, and in the 1929 legislature no politician would even agree to present it.[63]

One reason for male political leaders' stubborn refusal to act can be found in a clause of the bill that had the potential to empower white and black working families. The revised copy of the bill provided that the initiative for establishing kindergartens lay with parents. Section one stated that "upon the petition of the parents or guardians of twenty-five or more children between

62. "To President and Members of State Federation of Women's Clubs," letter, AKAC, box 2, folder 15; "Kindergarten Bill Should be Urged," AKAC, box 2, folder 13, clipping; McKelway, "Child Labor in Georgia," 74–75; "Present Status of Legislation Endorsed by Women's Organizations," and "Important Session of Legislative Council Held at Woman's Club," AKAC, box 2, folder 13, clippings; press releases, information sheets, copy of kindergarten bill, and PTA form letter to senators, AKAC, box 2, folder 12.

63. Mary Dickinson to Julia (Mrs. C. A.) Ver Nooy, August 7, 1925; Hays quote as cited in Ver Nooy to Dickinson, August 17, 1925; and Dickinson to Gay (Mrs. Lee) Worsham, April 10, 1929, all in AKAC, box 2, folder 12; "Early Historical Sketch of the Georgia State Kindergarten Association," AKAC, box 2, folder 6; PTA form letter to senators.

the ages of four and six years, the Board of Education of any city, town, or school district, may maintain kindergartens which shall be free to resident children as named." Even though boards of education were not compelled to act and could use the excuse of inadequate finances as an easy out, the clause established an avenue through which poor families could make demands of government. Once parents had signed petitions, the creation of kindergartens represented the will of the people and would be politically difficult to oppose. The class foundations of this struggle are illustrated by the state school superintendent's description of the constitutional ban on preschools as one of the laws "enacted to keep the carpet-baggers from ruining the state by wasteful expenditures." It was not the carpet-baggers they feared, of course, but the Reconstruction coalition of poor whites and blacks who redistributed wealth downward through state services. In encouraging the expansion of the kindergarten movement at the grassroots level, the permissive kindergarten bill would have redistributed power downward as well.[64]

What politicians had to fear in the latter half of the 1920s was a new coalition between white and black club women that further increased the democratic potential of the permissive bill. The resolutions of the 1920 interracial women's conference in Memphis included a section on child welfare that urged the establishment of day nurseries and kindergartens for the children of black working mothers. The subsequent activism of Carrie Parks Johnson and other women members of the Atlanta-based Commission on Interracial Cooperation signaled a new willingness among white female leaders to cross the color line in pursuit of social welfare reforms. Given the sophisticated level of organization among club women of both races, Georgia politicians had every reason to believe that the permissive bill would give women the opening they needed to incorporate free kindergartens into every city school system. Even if the poor lacked the initiative or political influence to make demands, female activists had proved their ability to garner support from workers and the middle class. They had connections to educational institutions, organized labor, and national child welfare groups and could be counted upon to lead skillful and spirited campaigns to sway public opinion. Moreover, local and state political leaders no longer could be certain that white

64. Kindergarten Bill, AKAC, box 2, folder 12; Superintendent Brittain quote from clipping, February 18, 1921, AKAC, box 2, folder 13.

women would stand by as educational improvements were implemented for the benefit of white children only; thus, as interracial cooperation increased the potential influence of club women, it also increased the opposition.[65]

Despite the difficulties of interracial cooperation and the failure of the permissive-bill campaign, child welfare reformers had accomplished much as the decade of the 1920s drew to a close. In fostering connections with educational innovators from outside the South and helping their students get established in Georgia, club women infused the state with female activists whose scientific approach to child welfare gave added weight to demands for reform. Club women's support enabled female professionals to expand their work, create their own associations, and provide expert assistance in legislative campaigns. Equally importantly, their activism advanced the field of child study at a time when southern institutions of higher education were inadequate to the task. Even though organized women had mixed success at institutionalizing kindergartens and forcing the removal of children from work to school, their persistent activism at the local level won small victories in improving the educational opportunities of working-class children. In these latter accomplishments, the influence of women's own struggle for the right to self-realization was clear. Unlike male reformers, who often seemed most concerned about delivering trained workers to local industry, female activists' awareness of the tensions between individualism and mutuality and their sensitivity to the injustice of limited options produced a more democratic approach to reform that provided Georgia's working families with new services and new choices.

65. *Southern Women and Race Cooperation: A Story of the Memphis Conference, October 6 and 7, 1920,* NU, box 10, folder 31, booklet. On the development of interracial cooperation among southern club women after World War I, see Jacquelyn Dowd Hall, *Revolt against Chivalry: Jessie Daniel Ames and the Women's Campaign against Lynching* (New York: Columbia University Press, 1974), 59–106.

CONCLUSION

As members of the Georgia Federation of Women's Clubs gathered at Macon for their annual meeting in May of 1930, they briefly took notice of the leadership role they had played in educational reform over the previous decades. The twenty-first anniversary of the Federation's Tallulah Falls School was an occasion for recalling the words of the state superintendent of education at the school's dedication in 1909. In addressing the county superintendents attending the ceremony, Jere Pound had noted that while club women's activism initially was "received with many raisings of the eyebrows and curlings of the lips," male educational leaders now found themselves "following at a distance and laboriously" the very plans female reformers had developed ten years earlier. What club women left unsaid in their proceedings was that state reforms still lagged behind the Federation's goals. Participants in the 1930 convention also reflected on the long-range impact of their support of female education. The Student Aid Fund, the Celeste Parrish Memorial Fund, and individual club scholarships continued to help hundreds of women attend educational institutions inside and outside the state, including—thanks to female activism—the University of Georgia. The chair of the Student Aid Foundation claimed that visible improvements in rural homes, schools, and villages could be attributed to the influence of college-educated women trained for both teaching and leadership who returned to their communities to pass on the legacy of service.[1]

When Federation members turned to the business at hand, they faced many of the same problems that plagued the state in the early years of their reform campaigns. The national economy was in the beginnings of the Great Depression and rural poverty was Georgia club women's primary concern. According to a Georgia Federation of Women's Clubs survey, only 33 of 161 counties had a population and tax base sufficient to support the school

1. *Georgia Federation of Women's Clubs* [hereafter GFWC] *Yearbook, 1929–1930* (Atlanta: GFWC, 1930), 133–134 (Pound quote from reprint of article in *Atlanta Constitution*, July 4, 1909), 150–151, 162.

improvements and social welfare services promoted by organized women. Loss of rural population was so great that Georgia's representation in Congress was reduced by two seats after the 1930 census results were tabulated. Women's disillusionment with the Georgia General Assembly and white male political culture was evident in the comment of one committee chair that "the organization of our farm women would do more to bring about economic justice and rural prosperity than all the legislatures can ever do." While her remark reflects reformers' abiding faith in women's ability to effect change for the common good, it also suggests that politicians' failure to pursue a just course of reform still required women to organize at the grassroots level, where they had to contend with rural-urban differences and a narrowed scope of influence. GFWC leaders urged club women to stay focused on the day-to-day needs of ordinary folk in their communities.[2]

The failures of white male political culture were fairly clear. The greater impoverishment of the South in relation to other regions made increased public spending a greater sacrifice, but it was male opposition to distributing the costs of government more equally that consistently stymied reform efforts into the 1930s. More often than not, Georgia governors showed little interest in social welfare reforms, especially when they required increasing costs to wealthy landowners and businessmen. Political leaders restricted spending during the Progressive Era by maintaining a single-rate ad valorem tax on all land (regardless of use) as the state's main source of revenue, leaving other forms of property largely untaxed. Support for increased spending virtually disappeared after 1923, when the governor's office was held by a series of politicians who exhibited a single-minded devotion to economy in government that only worsened with the onset of the depression. After Richard B. Russell took office in 1930, he reduced the number of executive agencies and committees from one hundred to nineteen, and his successor, Eugene Talmadge, pushed through reductions in state taxes that disproportionately benefited businesses and large-scale property owners.[3] Although organized

2. Ibid., 22–28, 172–176, quote 225–226; Mrs. Clyde F. Anderson Jr., *A Walk through History* (n.p.: Georgia Federation of Women's Clubs, 1986).

3. Numan V. Bartley, Kenneth Coleman, William F. Holmes, F. N. Boney, Phinizy Spalding, and Charles E. Wynes, *A History of Georgia*, 2nd ed., gen. ed. Kenneth Coleman (Athens: University of Georgia Press, 1991), 308, 310–312. The South as a whole had fewer resources upon which to draw in support of social services, since most southern states had higher debts and tax rates and lower revenues than other regions. George Tindall, *The Emergence of the New South,*

women hoped that local taxation would remedy the tightfisted policies of the state and distribute resources more equitably, they soon realized that rural poverty limited its scope of usefulness.

White male political leaders opposed reforms for more than financial reasons, since female activism frequently challenged their private and public authority as men as well as their economic interests. The marked reluctance of male officials to spend state funds on home extension services, the strong resistance to opening the University of Georgia and Georgia Institute of Technology to women, and even opposition to mothers' pensions show that many male leaders wanted women to continue receiving the benefits of state resources only indirectly, through men. Whether by denying assistance completely or by channeling funds through male farmers and professionals, they resisted establishing female citizens as equal and independent agents in relationship to male citizens and the state. In the case of extension services, providing assistance to the fields rather than the farmhouse also furthered men's goal of economic development. This combination of gender and financial concerns is equally evident in opposition to compulsory education and child labor reform. The defiant mill owners and landlords who spoke out against such legislation obviously resented attempts to limit their access to and control of cheap labor, but they built popular resistance by casting the issue in terms of fathers' authority over their children.[4]

Women faced other, related obstacles in their struggle to get the Georgia General Assembly to enact and enforce effective legislative reforms. Pervasive racial prejudice and the gender and sexual politics of white supremacy hindered the early formation of interracial alliances on the part of women that, like the Reconstruction coalitions of ordinary whites and blacks, could have

---

1913–1945 (Baton Rouge and Austin: Louisiana State University Press and the Littlefield Fund for Southern History, University of Texas, 1967), 232.

4. For a detailed analysis of how this indirect relationship between women and public resources became embedded in New Deal policy, see Alice Kessler-Harris, *In Pursuit of Equity: Women, Men, and the Quest for Economic Citizenship in 20th-Century America* (New York: Oxford University Press, 2001). Women repeatedly condemned the paternal-rights argument against compulsory education and child labor reform as a classic example of the selfish southern male individualism that hindered improvements for the common good. For example, see "School Attendance Bill Favorably Reported; a Very Important Measure," August 11, 1907; and "Mrs. Granger Makes Strong Address before the Child Labor Convention," April 5, 1908, both in *Atlanta Constitution*.

pushed through substantial structural reforms for the benefit of the politically marginalized. White female activists did not challenge the wisdom or justice of segregation, and by the time they publicly condemned racial discrimination and violence, the influence of the Second Klan was in ascendancy. Klansmen had one of their own serving as Atlanta's mayor in the mid-1920s, and they defeated the reelection bid of the last reformist governor in 1923 after he threatened to force them to unmask. Moreover, Klansmen's reactionary response to social change included an opposition to the New Woman that was almost as strong as their despisement of the New Negro. The fusion of gender and racial hierarchies ensured that southern white men would continue to oppose female political power and its goal of a more socially activist state. Legislators rushed to make Georgia the first state to reject ratification of the Nineteenth Amendment, and although women were enfranchised anyway, they still had to contend with the limitations of male-dominated electoral politics in the Solid South.[5]

Female activism changed significantly between 1890 and 1930, as organized women expanded their work in response to the shortcomings of male political culture. They continued the early campaigns for improving wages and conditions for working women and promoting child welfare, but their rural and interracial work grew by leaps and bounds. By 1930 Georgia Federation programs for alleviating the effects of rural poverty included the establishment of rural community centers, child welfare clinics, and municipal markets for rural handicrafts and produce. Federated clubs also provided financing for additional home extension agents and sponsored canning clubs, Farmers' Week events, and scholarships for rural women. Furthermore, many of the campaigns that initially focused on whites only had expanded to include entire communities. White club women now included blacks in their

5. Bartley et al., *A History of Georgia*, 310; Governor Thomas W. Hardwick's defeat was ironic considering that he was a Klan sympathizer who had criticized his predecessor, Hugh M. Dorsey, for publishing a statement condemning vigilante violence. Nancy MacLean, *Behind the Mask of Chivalry: The Making of the Second Ku Klux Klan* (New York: Oxford University Press, 1994), 125–126. Paula Baker argues that the link between white supremacy and suffrage prevented the merging of male and female political cultures in the South even though politics had become "domesticated" in most other parts of the country as Americans came to accept state responsibility for social problems too vast to be solved locally or through private aid. "The Domestication of Politics: Women and American Political Society, 1780–1920," *American Historical Review* 89 (June 1984): 620–647, esp. 642–647.

school improvement activities, such as the beautification of buildings and grounds, the establishment and upgrading of libraries, and the founding of Parent-Teacher Association chapters. They sponsored child welfare clinics so that black children could receive immunizations and dental exams, and they financed and taught adult literacy classes for black parents. They also addressed the needs of the black home with cooking schools, instruction in household sanitation, and even the organization of black women's clubs.[6]

Changes occurred within government as well as within Federated clubs, as three decades of female activism succeeded in making the state more responsive to the educational needs of its citizens. Organized women's sponsorship of agricultural clubs and home extension services was pivotal in establishing programs that began to bridge the gap between the College of Agriculture and the rural household. Opening that same college to female students was a landmark accomplishment that at once advanced the cause of gender equality and increased services to rural communities through the training of extension agents. Female reformers' advocacy of a more flexible and diverse curriculum also worked to check the historical tendency of public educational institutions to cater to the needs of elites. Although industrial and vocational education could be shaped by the class and gender biases of educators, women who endorsed a democratic interpretation of Progressive pedagogy opposed using it to restrict the options of students. They envisioned education as a reciprocal process in which private and public needs carried equal weight. Throughout their campaigns for higher standards, better funding, and increased services, female activists maintained that just as citizens had obligations to the state, so the state had obligations to its citizens.

Organized women were able to expand state obligations in areas other than education despite rigorous opposition to labor reforms. Social welfare reforms that did not overtly challenge power relations of class, race, and gender, and that served as positive publicity for the state, fared slightly better in the Georgia General Assembly. Even before they got the vote, female activists successfully lobbied legislators to create juvenile reformatories, a juvenile court system, and a state Board (later Department) of Public Welfare. Soon

---

6. See district reports, *GFWC Yearbook, 1929–1930*, 39–124, which also show the persistence of racial conservatism among many white club women, since the state Federation's War Veterans Committee lobbied for legislation to transfer blacks in one Atlanta veterans' hospital to an all-black hospital at Tuskegee, Alabama.

after the Nineteenth Amendment became law, Georgia club women created the Legislative League, made up of the legislative committees of all women's organizations, to coordinate the creation of a single legislative agenda for female voters. Within a year they had secured laws approving two items on that agenda—a juvenile training school and a Children's Code (a set of laws regulating treatment of "dependent, delinquent, neglected, and defective children"). In cooperation with the Georgia Association of Workers for the Blind, the Federation also worked to improve training and employment services in state institutions for the disabled. State Federation president Louise Hays had reason to boast in 1922 when she proudly proclaimed that since the club woman first organized, "there have been no laws enacted having to do with public welfare in which she has not been a part, no progressive step taken in which she has not figured."[7]

Hays's pride was justified, considering that organized women produced one of the most sustained movements for socially responsible government the South has ever seen. Their activism began as educational campaigns in behalf of women and children but quickly expanded to embrace a broad program of reforms that illustrated organized women's commitment to social and economic justice. Female reformers who were willing to step outside the protective boundaries of home and community to act as mediators between citizens and the state (even though they lacked the full rights of citizenship themselves) provide a powerful example of how ordinary Americans can change society through political activism. In the twenty-first century, women's organizations and social welfare agencies continue to cooperate in representing the needs of home and family in the halls of state and federal government, and female-founded groups such as the Parent-Teacher Association continue to use public schools to bridge the gap between private and public. Progressive organizations also continue to battle male-dominated political systems in which the obligations of citizen and state are interpreted in individualist terms. As national politics increasingly mirrors southern politics in its commitment to local control and restricted social welfare spending, the strategies and goals of female activists provide an alternative blueprint for all those who still harbor a vision of a more humane state and a more progressive South.

7. First quote from Anderson, *A Walk through History; GFWC Yearbook, 1920 –1921* (Atlanta: GFWC, 1921), 21; the Federation motto for women voters was "measures, not men; policies, not parties." *GFWC Yearbook, 1921–1922* (Atlanta: GFWC, 1922), 19–23, quote 19.

SELECTED BIBLIOGRAPHY

PRIMARY SOURCES

ARCHIVES

Atlanta History Center Archives
Atlanta Kindergarten Alumnae Club Collection
Atlanta Woman's Club Collection

Robert Woodruff Library, Archives and Special Collections, Atlanta University
Neighborhood Union Collection

Georgia Department of Archives and History, Morrow
Zillah Lee Bostick Redd Agerton Papers
American Association of University Women, Georgia Division Records
Georgia Home Economics Association Collection
Clara Nelms Scrapbook

Hargrett Rare Book and Manuscript Collection, Special Collections,
University of Georgia Libraries, Athens
Nellie Peters Black Papers
Katherine Lanier Clarke Papers
Rebecca Latimer Felton Collection
Walter B. Hill Papers, Sallie Barker Hill Division
Celeste Parrish Memorials

University Archives, University of Georgia, Athens
Mary E. Creswell Papers
Leila R. Mize Papers
Andrew M. Soule Collection
State Normal School Records

ORGANIZATION AND GOVERNMENT RECORDS

Atlanta University Publications, proceedings of the annual Conference for the Study
    of Negro Problems, 1896–1914.
Conference for Education in the South, proceedings of annual meetings, 1898–1914.
Georgia Department of Education, annual reports, 1900–1930.
Georgia Federation of Women's Clubs, yearbooks, 1902–1930.

Georgia State College of Agriculture, bulletins.

Georgia State College of Agriculture, Extension Division, annual reports, 1916–1927; service reports, 1928–1930; service bulletins (monthly reports of Negro extension work), 1923–1926.

Georgia Teachers Association (later Georgia Educational Association), proceedings and addresses of annual meetings, 1896–1920.

National Child Labor Committee, addresses from the annual meetings.

Southern Educational Association, proceedings and addresses of annual meetings, 1900–1914.

United Daughters of the Confederacy (national organization and Georgia Division), annual convention minutes.

PUBLISHED PRIMARY SOURCES

Atkinson, W. Y. *Speech of Hon. W. Y. Atkinson.* Atlanta: Constitution Publishing, 1889.

Baker, Ray Stannard. *Following the Color Line: American Negro Citizenship in the Progressive Era.* New York: Doubleday, Page, 1908. Reprint, New York: Harper and Row, 1964.

Barrett, Charles Simon. *The Mission, History, and Times of the Farmers' Union.* Nashville: Marshall and Bruce, 1909.

Branson, Eugene C. "The Real Southern Question." *World's Work* 3 (March 1902): 1888–1891.

Brawley, Benjamin. *Doctor Dillard of the Jeanes Fund.* New York: Fleming H. Revell, 1930.

Campbell, John C. *The Future of the Church and Independent Schools in Our Southern Highlands.* New York: Russell Sage Foundation, 1916.

———. *The Southern Highlander and His Homeland.* New York: Russell Sage Foundation, 1921.

Campbell, Olive D. *Southern Highland Schools Maintained by Denominational and Independent Agencies.* New York: Russell Sage Foundation, 1921.

Clark, J. O. A. *The Races and Their Future: A Plea for Their Education.* Macon, GA: J. W. Burke, 1889.

Coffman, Lotus Delta. *The Social Composition of the Teaching Population.* New York: Teachers College, Columbia University, 1911.

Coleman, Herbert T. "The Status of Education in the South Prior of the War between the States." *Confederate Veteran* 15 (October 1907): 441–447.

Colton, Elizabeth. "How Southern Colleges for Women Might More Effectively Fit Women for Their Life Work." *High School Quarterly* 4 (October 1915): 45–48.

———. "The Past and Future Work of the Southern Association of College Women." *High School Quarterly* 6 (July 1918): 224–225.

Davidson, Donald, John Gould Fletcher, H. B. Kline, Lyle H. Lanier, Andrew Nelson Lytle, H. C. Nixon, Frank Lawrence Owsley, John Crowe Ransom, Allen Tate, John Donald Wade, Robert Penn Warren, and Stark Young. *I'll Take My Stand: The South and the Agrarian Tradition*. New York: Harper and Brothers, 1930. Reprint, Baton Rouge: Louisiana State University Press, 1977.

De Graffenried, Clare. "The Georgia Cracker in the Cotton Mills." *Century Magazine* 41 (February 1891): 483–498.

DeJarnette, Tennie. *A Pattern for Education in Living*. Tallulah Falls: Georgia Federation of Women's Clubs, ca. 1950.

Du Bois, W. E. Burghardt. "Georgia: Invisible Empire State." *Nation*, January 21, 1925, 63–67.

Fanning, John William. *Negro Migration*. Phelps-Stokes Fellowship Studies no. 9, Bulletin of the University of Georgia, vol. 30 (June 1930).

Farmer, Mrs. Ira I. "The Woman and the Home in Rural Development." *Georgia Magazine* 2 (September 1926): 12.

Felton, Rebecca Latimer. *Country Life in Georgia in the Days of My Youth*. Atlanta: Index Printing, 1919. Reprint, New York: Arno Press, 1980.

Fitzhugh, George. *Sociology for the South, or the Failure of Free Society*. Richmond, VA: A. Morris, 1854.

Flisch, Julia A. "The Purposes and Results of Education." *Southern Woman*, March 25, 1901.

Georgia: Historical and Industrial. Atlanta: State of Georgia, 1901.

Harrison, Emily. *In Memoriam: Frances Liggett Wey, July 22, 1851–November 20, 1928*. Atlanta: Georgia Federation of Women's Clubs, ca. 1929.

Hawthorne, Dolly. "The Economic Surplus of Georgia: What It Is." *Educational Monthly* 1 (June 1915): 115–119.

Haygood, Atticus G. "The South and the School Problem." *Harper's New Monthly Magazine* 79 (July 1889): 225–231.

Hunt, H. A. "Negroes Leaving the South, and Why." *School and Home* 8 (December 1916): 8–9.

Kephart, Horace. *Our Southern Highlanders*. New York: Outing, 1913.

Mayo, A. D. *Southern Women in the Recent Educational Movement in the South*. Edited by Dan T. Carter and Amy Friedlander. Bureau of Education *Circular of Information*, no. 1. Washington, DC: Government Printing Office, 1892. Reprint, Baton Rouge: Louisiana State University Press, 1978.

Miller, Nora. *The Girl in the Rural Family*. Chapel Hill: University of North Carolina Press, 1935.

Moton, Robert R. "Economic Justice." In *Cooperation in Southern Communities: Suggested Activities for County and City Inter-racial Committees*, ed. T. J. Woofter Jr. and Isaac Fisher, 33–40. Atlanta: Commission on Inter-racial Cooperation, 1921.

Munford, Mary Cooke Branch. "Woman's Part in the Educational Progress of the South." In *The South in the Building of the Nation*, 10:638–645. Richmond, VA: Southern Historical Publication Society, 1909.

Murray, Anna J. "A New Key to the Situation." *Southern Workman* 29 (September 1900): 503–507.

Park, Emily Hendree. "The Educational Work of the Georgia Federation." *Southern Woman*, March 25, 1901.

Parrish, Celeste. "Shall the Higher Education of Women Be the Same as That of Men?" *Educational Review* 22 (November 1901): 383–396.

———. "The Womanly Woman." *Independent* 53 (April 1901): 775–778.

———. "Woman's Problems." *Independent* 53 (October 1901): 2582–2585.

Richie, Andrew J. *The Rabun Industrial School and Mountain School Extension Work among the Mountain Whites*. N.p., ca. 1904. Booklet.

Roosevelt, Theodore. "The Woman and the Home." In *The Works of Theodore Roosevelt*, 18:225–233. New York: Scribner's Sons, 1908.

Shinn, Milicent Washburn. "The Marriage Rate of College Women." *Century* 50 (1895): 946–948.

Sledd, Andrew. "Illiteracy in the South." *Independent* 17 (October 1901): 2471–2474.

Some Interesting Information concerning Child Labor in Georgia. Atlanta: Georgia Federation of Labor, 1902. Pamphlet.

Stewart, J. S. "The Conference for Education in the South." *Southern Educational Journal* 1 (June 1905): 29–31.

Washington, Martha Murray. "The Gain in the Life of Negro Women." *Outlook* 76 (January 1904): 271–274.

White, John E. "Our Southern Highlands." In *The Home Mission Task*, edited by Victor I. Masters, 209–238. Atlanta: Home Mission Board of the Southern Baptist Convention, 1912.

Williams, W. T. B. "The Negro Exodus from the South." In *Negro Migration in 1916–1917*, U.S. Department of Labor, Division of Negro Economics, 93–113. Washington, DC: Government Printing Office, 1919.

Wilson, Samuel Tyndale. *The Southern Mountaineers*. New York: Presbyterian Board of Home Missions, 1906.

Woodward, Mary V. "Woman's Education in the South." *Educational Review* 7 (May 1894): 466–478.

Woofter, T. J., Jr. "Migration of Negroes from Georgia, 1916–1917." In *Negro Migration in 1916–1917*, U.S. Department of Labor, Division of Negro Economics, 75–91. Washington, DC: Government Printing Office, 1919.

Wray, Rev. J. E. *The Herod of the South; or, The Child Labor Iniquity.* Columbus, GA: Central Federation of Labor, n.d. Pamphlet.

Yates, Josephine Silone. "Kindergartens and Mothers' Clubs as Related to the Work of the NACW." *Colored American Magazine* 8 (June 1905): 304–311.

SECONDARY SOURCES

Allen, Ann Taylor. "'Let us Live with Our Children': Kindergarten Movements in Germany and the United States, 1840–1914." *History of Education Quarterly* 28 (Spring 1988): 23–48.

Anderson, Mrs. Clyde F., Jr. *A Walk through History.* N.p.: Georgia Federation of Women's Clubs, 1986.

Anderson, James D. *The Education of Blacks in the South, 1860–1935.* Chapel Hill: University of North Carolina Press, 1988.

———. "Northern Foundations and the Shaping of Southern Black Rural Education, 1902–1935." *History of Education Quarterly* 18 (Winter 1978): 371–396.

Aultman, Ruth Wynn, ed. *Reflections of Georgia Retired Teachers.* Macon: Georgia Retired Teachers Association, 1976.

Ayers, Edward L. *The Promise of the New South: Life after Reconstruction.* New York: Oxford University Press, 1992.

Baker, Gladys L. "Women in the U.S. Department of Agriculture." *Agricultural History* 50 (January 1976): 190–201.

Baker, Paula. "The Domestication of Politics: Women and American Political Society, 1780–1920." *American Historical Review* 89 (June 1984): 620–647.

Bardaglio, Peter. *Reconstructing the Household: Families, Sex, and the Law in the Nineteenth-Century South.* Chapel Hill: University of North Carolina Press, 1995.

Bardaglio, Peter, and Eileen Boris. "The Transformation of Patriarchy: The Historic Role of the State." In *Families, Politics, and Public Policy: A Feminist Dialogue on Women and the State,* edited by Irene Diamond, 70–93. New York: Longman Press, 1983.

Bartley, Numan V. *The Creation of Modern Georgia.* Athens: University of Georgia Press, 1983.

Bartley, Numan V., Kenneth Coleman, William F. Holmes, F. N. Boney, Phinizy Spalding, and Charles E. Wynes. *A History of Georgia.* 2nd ed. General editor Kenneth Coleman. Athens: University of Georgia Press, 1991.

Basch, Norma. "The Emerging Legal History of Women in the United States: Property, Divorce, and the Constitution." *Signs* 12 (Autumn 1986): 97–117.

Beatty, Barbara. *Preschool Education in America: The Culture of Young Children from the Colonial Era to the Present.* New Haven, CT: Yale University Press, 1995.

———. "'A Vocation from on High': Kindergartning as an Occupation for American

Women." In *Changing Education: Women as Radicals and Conservators,* edited by Joyce Antler and Sari Knopp Biklen, 35–50. Albany: State University of New York Press, 1990.

Boatwright, Eleanor Miot. *Status of Women in Georgia, 1783–1860.* New York: Carlson Publishing, 1994.

Bonner, James C., Oscar H. Joiner, H. S. Shearouse, and T. E. Smith. *A History of Public Education in Georgia, 1734–1976.* General editor Oscar H. Joiner, with introduction and epilogue by Claude Purcell. Columbia, SC: Georgia State Board of Education, 1979.

Boydston, Jeanne. *Home and Work: Household, Wages, and the Ideology of Labor in the Early Republic.* New York: Oxford University Press, 1990.

Breen, William J. "Black Women and the Great War: Mobilization and Reform in the South." *Journal of Southern History* 44 (August 1978): 421–440.

Brooks, Robert Preston. "The Agrarian Revolution in Georgia, 1865–1912." Ph.D. diss., University of Wisconsin–Madison, 1914.

Brundage, W. Fitzhugh. *Lynching in the New South: Georgia and Virginia, 1880–1930.* Urbana: University of Illinois Press, 1993.

Butcher, Patricia Smith. *Education for Equality: Women's Rights Periodicals and Women's Higher Education, 1849–1920.* Westport, CT: Greenwood Press, 1989.

Byers, Tracy. *Martha Berry: The Sunday Lady of Possum Trot.* New York: G. P. Putnam's Sons, 1932.

Bynum, Victoria. "Reshaping the Bonds of Womanhood: Divorce in Reconstruction North Carolina." In *Divided Houses: Gender and the Civil War,* edited by Catherine Clinton and Nina Silber, 320–333. New York: Oxford University Press, 1992.

———. *Unruly Women: The Politics of Social and Sexual Control in the Old South.* Chapel Hill: University of North Carolina Press, 1992.

Carson, Mina. *Settlement Folk: Social Thought and the American Settlement Movement, 1885–1930.* Chicago: University of Chicago Press, 1990.

Cashin, Joan. *A Family Venture: Men and Women on the Southern Frontier.* New York: Oxford University Press, 1991.

Cavallo, Dom. "From Perfection to Habit: Moral Training in the American Kindergarten, 1860–1920." *History of Education Quarterly* 16 (Summer 1976): 147–161.

Censer, Jane Turner. "A Changing World of Work: North Carolina Elite Women, 1865–1895." *North Carolina Historical Review* 73 (January 1996): 28–55.

Chapman, Bernadine Sharpe. "Northern Philanthropy and African-American Adult Education in the Rural South: Hegemony and Resistance in the Jeanes Movement." Ed.D. diss., Northern Illinois University, 1990.

Chase, Allan. *The Legacy of Malthus: The Social Costs of the New Scientific Racism.* New York: Alfred A. Knopf, 1977.

Chirhart, Ann Short. "Torches of Light: African American and White Female Teachers in the Georgia Upcountry, 1910–1950." Ph.D. diss., Emory University, 1997.

Church, Robert L., and Michael W. Sedlak. *Education in the United States: An Interpretive History.* New York: Free Press, 1976.

Clinton, Catherine. "Caught in the Web of the Big House: Women and Slavery." In *The Web of Southern Social Relations: Women, Family, and Education,* edited by Walter J. Fraser Jr., R. Frank Saunders Jr., and Jon L. Wakelyn, 19–34. Athens: University of Georgia Press, 1985.

———. *The Plantation Mistress: Woman's World in the Old South.* New York: Pantheon Books, 1982.

———. " 'Southern Dishonor': Flesh, Blood, Race, and Bondage." In *In Joy and in Sorrow: Women, Family, and Marriage in the Victorian South, 1830 –1900,* edited by Carol Bleser, 52–68. New York: Oxford University Press, 1991.

Cott, Nancy F. "Marriage and Women's Citizenship in the United States, 1830–1934." *American Historical Review* 103 (December 1998): 1440–1474.

Cox, Karen Lynne. *Dixie's Daughters: The United Daughters of the Confederacy and the Preservation of Confederate Culture.* Gainesville: University Press of Florida, 2003.

———. "Women, the Lost Cause, and the New South: The United Daughters of the Confederacy and the Transmission of Confederate Culture, 1894–1919." Ph.D. diss., University of Southern Mississippi, 1997.

Cremin, Lawrence A. *The Transformation of the School: Progressivism in American Education, 1876 –1957.* New York: Alfred A. Knopf, 1961.

Cross, Barbara M., ed. *The Educated Woman in America: Selected Writings of Catharine Beecher, Margaret Fuller, and M. Carey Thomas.* New York: Teachers College Press, Columbia University, 1965.

Crowe, Charles. "Racial Violence and Social Reform—Origins of the Atlanta Riot of 1906." *Journal of Negro History* 53 (July 1968): 234–256.

Dabney, Charles William. *Universal Education in the South.* Vols. 1 and 2. Chapel Hill: University of North Carolina Press, 1936.

Dabney, Joseph Earl. *Mountain Spirits: A Chronicle of Corn Whiskey from King James' Ulster Plantation to America's Appalachians and the Moonshine Life.* New York: Charles Scribner's Sons, 1974.

Dale, Lily Farley Ross. "The Jeanes Supervisors in Alabama, 1909–1963." Ph.D. diss., Auburn University, 1998.

Danbom, David. *The Resisted Revolution: Urban America and the Industrialization of Agriculture, 1900 –1930.* Ames: Iowa State University Press, 1979.

Daniel, Pete. *Breaking the Land: The Transformation of Cotton, Tobacco, and Rice Cultures since 1880.* Urbana: University of Illinois Press, 1985.

Davidson, Elizabeth H. *Child Labor Legislation in the Southern Textile States.* Chapel Hill: University of North Carolina Press, 1939.

Degler, Carl N. *At Odds: Women and the Family in America from the Revolution to the Present.* New York: Oxford University Press, 1980.

Dittmer, John. *Black Georgia in the Progressive Era, 1900–1920.* Urbana: University of Illinois Press, 1977.

Downing, Leo, and Ray Rensi. "A Touch of Mountain Dew: Art and History of Whiskey-Making in North Georgia." In *The Many Faces of Appalachia: Exploring a Region's Diversity,* ed. San Gray, 195–204. Boone, NC: Appalachian Consortium Press, 1985.

Dunaway, Wilma A. *The First American Frontier: Transition to Capitalism in Southern Appalachia, 1700–1860.* Chapel Hill: University of North Carolina Press, 1996.

Dyer, Thomas G. *The University of Georgia: A Bicentennial History, 1785–1985.* Athens: University of Georgia Press, 1985.

Dykeman, Wilma. "Appalachia in Context." In *An Appalachian Symposium,* edited by Joel W. Williamson, 28–42. Boone, NC: Appalachian State University Press, 1977.

Edwards, Laura F. *Gendered Strife and Confusion: The Political Culture of Reconstruction.* Urbana: University of Illinois Press, 1997.

Eller, Ronald D. *Miners, Millhands, and Mountaineers: Industrialization of the Appalachian South, 1880–1930.* Knoxville: University of Tennessee Press, 1982.

Epstein, Barbara Leslie. *The Politics of Domesticity: Women, Evangelism, and Temperance in Nineteenth-Century America.* Middletown, CT: Wesleyan University Press, 1981.

Farnham, Christie Anne. *The Education of the Southern Belle: Higher Education and Student Socialization in the Antebellum South.* New York: New York University Press, 1994.

Faust, Drew Gilpin. *A Sacred Circle: The Dilemma of the Intellectual in the Old South, 1840–1860.* Baltimore: Johns Hopkins University Press, 1977.

———. *Southern Stories: Slaveholders in Peace and War.* Columbia: University of Missouri Press, 1992.

Fink, Deborah. *Agrarian Women: Wives and Mothers in Rural Nebraska, 1880–1940.* Chapel Hill, University of North Carolina Press, 1992.

Fink, Gary. *The Fulton Bag and Cotton Mills Strike of 1914–1915.* Ithaca, NY: ILR Press, 1993.

Flanagan, Maureen A. "Gender and Urban Political Reform: The City Club and the Woman's City Club of Chicago in the Progressive Era." *American Historical Review* 95 (October 1990): 1032–1050.

Flexner, Eleanor. *Century of Struggle: The Women's Rights Movement in the United*

States. Cambridge, MA: Harvard University Press, 1959. Reprint, New York: Athenaeum, 1972.

Flynn, Charles L., Jr. *White Land, Black Labor: Caste and Class in Late Nineteenth-Century Georgia.* Baton Rouge: Louisiana State University Press, 1983.

Flynt, Wayne. *Poor but Proud: Alabama's Poor Whites.* Tuscaloosa: University of Alabama Press, 1989.

Foner, Eric. *Reconstruction: America's Unfinished Revolution, 1863–1877.* New York: Harper and Row, 1988.

Foster, Grace Ruth. *Social Change in Relation to Curricular Development in Collegiate Education for Women.* Waterville, ME: Galahad Press, 1934.

Fox-Genovese, Elizabeth. *Within the Plantation Household: Black and White Women of the Old South.* Chapel Hill: University of North Carolina Press, 1988.

Frankfurt, Roberta. *Collegiate Women: Domesticity and Career in Turn-of-the-Century America.* New York: New York University Press, 1977.

Franklin, Barry M. "Progressivism and Curriculum Differentiation: Special Classes in the Atlanta Public Schools, 1898–1923." *History of Education Quarterly* 29 (Winter 1989): 571–593.

Friedlander, Amy. "A More Perfect Christian Womanhood: Higher Learning for a New South." In *Education and the Rise of the New South,* edited by Ronald K. Goodenow and Arthur O. White. Boston: G. K. Hall, 1981.

Friedman, Jean E. *The Enclosed Garden: Women and Community in the Evangelical South, 1830–1900.* Chapel Hill: University of North Carolina Press, 1985.

Genovese, Eugene. *The Political Economy of Slavery: Studies in the Economy and Society of the Slave South.* Middleton, CT: Wesleyan University Press, 1965. Reprint, 1989.

Giddings, Paula. *When and Where I Enter: The Impact of Black Women on Race and Sex in America.* New York: Bantam, 1984.

Gilmore, Glenda Elizabeth. *Gender and Jim Crow: Women and the Politics of White Supremacy in North Carolina, 1896–1920.* Chapel Hill: University of North Carolina Press, 1996.

Ginzberg, Lori. "Pernicious Heresies: Female Citizenship and Sexual Respectability in the Nineteenth Century." In *Women and the Unstable State in Nineteenth-Century America,* edited by Alison M. Parker and Stephanie Cole, 139–161. College Station: Texas A&M University Press, 2000.

Golden Anniversary History, Georgia Congress of Colored Parents and Teachers. Atlanta: The Organization, 1970.

Gordon, Linda. "Family Violence, Feminism, and Social Control." In *Women, the State, and Welfare,* edited by Linda Gordon, 178–198. Madison: University of Wisconsin Press, 1990.

―――. *Heroes of Their Own Lives: The Politics and History of Family Violence, Boston, 1880–1960*. New York: Viking Penguin, 1988.

Gordon, Lynn D. *Gender and Higher Education in the Progressive Era*. New Haven, CT: Yale University Press, 1990.

Grantham, Dewey W. *Southern Progressivism: The Reconciliation of Progress and Tradition*. Knoxville: University of Tennessee Press, 1983.

Green, Elna. "'Ideals of Government, Home, and of Women': The Ideology of Southern White Antisuffragism." In *Hidden Histories of Women in the New South*, edited by Virginia Bernhard, Betty Brandon, Elizabeth Fox-Genovese, Theda Purdue, and Elizabeth Hays Turner, 96–113. Columbia: University of Missouri Press, 1994.

Hagler, D. Harland. "The Ideal Woman in the Antebellum South: Lady or Farmwife?" *Journal of Southern History* 46 (August 1980): 405–418.

Hahn, Steven. *The Roots of Southern Populism: Yeoman Farmers and the Transformation of the Georgia Upcountry, 1850–1890*. New York: Oxford University Press, 1983.

Hall, Jacquelyn Dowd. *Revolt against Chivalry: Jessie Daniel Ames and the Women's Campaign against Lynching*. New York: Columbia University Press, 1974.

Hancock, Carol Stevens. *The Light in the Mountains: A History of Tallulah Falls School*. Toccoa, GA: Tallulah Falls School, 1975.

Harlan, Louis R. *Separate and Unequal: Public School Campaigns and Racism in the Southern Seaboard States, 1901–1915*. Chapel Hill: University of North Carolina Press, 1958.

―――. "The Southern Education Board and the Race Issue in Public Education." *Journal of Southern History* 23 (May 1957): 189–202.

Hartsock, Nancy C. "The Feminist Standpoint: Developing the Ground for a Specifically Feminist Historical Materialism." In *Feminism and Methodology*, edited by Sandra Harding, 157–180. Bloomington: Indiana University Press, 1987.

Hickey, Georgina. *Hope and Danger in the New South City: Working-Class Women and Urban Development in Atlanta, 1890–1940*. Athens: University of Georgia Press, 2003.

Hickson, Shirley Ann. "The Development of Higher Education for Women in the Antebellum South." Ph.D. diss., University of South Carolina, 1985.

Hilton, Kathleen C. "'Both in the Field, Each with a Plow': Race and Gender in USDA Policy, 1907–1929." In *Hidden Histories of Women in the New South*, edited by Virginia Bernhard, Betty Brandon, Elizabeth Fox-Genovese, Theda Purdue, and Elizabeth Hays Turner, 114–133. Columbia: University of Missouri Press, 1994.

History of Home Economics in Georgia. Atlanta: Standards Committee, Georgia Home Economics Association, 1933.

History of the Kindergarten Movement in the Southeastern States, and Delaware, District of Columbia, New Jersey, and Pennsylvania. Washington, DC: Association for Childhood Education, 1939.

Hoffschwelle, Mary S. *Rebuilding the Rural Southern Community: Reformers, Schools, and Homes in Tennessee, 1900–1930.* Knoxville: University of Tennessee Press, 1998.

Horowitz, Helen Lefkowitz. *Alma Mater: Design and Experience in the Women's Colleges from Their Nineteenth-Century Beginnings to the 1930s.* New York: Alfred A. Knopf, 1984.

Hunter, Tera W. "Domination and Resistance: The Politics of Wage Household Labor in New South Atlanta." *Labor History* 34 (Spring–Summer 1993): 205–220.

———. *To 'Joy My Freedom: Southern Black Women's Lives and Labors after the Civil War.* Cambridge, MA: Harvard University Press, 1997.

Hyman, Michael R. *The Anti-Redeemers: Hill-Country Political Dissenters in the Lower South from Redemption to Populism.* Baton Rouge: Louisiana State University Press, 1990.

Janiewski, Dolores. *Sisterhood Denied: Race, Gender, and Class in a New South Community.* Philadelphia: Temple University Press, 1985.

Jellison, Katherine. *Entitled to Power: Farm Women and Technology, 1913–1963.* Chapel Hill: University of North Carolina Press, 1993.

Jensen, Joan. *Loosening the Bonds: Mid-Atlantic Farm Women, 1750–1850.* New Haven, CT: Yale University Press, 1986.

Johnson, Charles S. *Shadow of the Plantation.* Chicago: University of Chicago Press, 1934.

Johnson, Joan Marie. "'This Wonderful Dream Nation!': Black and White South Carolina Women and the Creation of the New South, 1898–1930." Ph.D. diss., University of California–Los Angeles, 1997.

Johnson, Joan Marie, ed. *Southern Women at Vassar: The Poppenheim Family Letters, 1882–1916.* Columbia: University of South Carolina Press, 2002.

Joiner, Oscar H., ed. *A History of Public Education in Georgia, 1734–1976.* Columbia, SC: R. L. Bryan, 1979.

Jones, Alton DuMar. "Progressivism in Georgia, 1898–1918." Ph.D. diss., Emory University, 1963.

Jones, Beverly Washington. "Mary Church Terrell and the National Association of Colored Women, 1896–1901." *Journal of Negro History* 67 (Spring 1982): 20–33.

———. *Quest for Equality: The Life and Writings of Mary Eliza Church Terrell, 1863–1954.* New York: Carlson Publishing, 1990.

Jones, Jacqueline. *Labor of Love, Labor of Sorrow: Black Women, Work, and the Family, from Slavery to the Present.* New York: Vintage Books, 1985.

———. *Soldiers of Light and Love: Northern Teachers and Georgia Blacks, 1865–1873.* Chapel Hill: University of North Carolina Press, 1980. Reprint, Athens: University of Georgia Press, 1992.

Jones, Lu Ann. *Mama Learned Us to Work: Farm Women in the New South.* Chapel Hill: University of North Carolina Press, 2002.

Kane, Harnett T., and Inez Henry. *Miracle in the Mountains.* New York: Doubleday, 1956.

Katz, Michael B. *In the Shadow of the Poorhouse: A Social History of Welfare in America.* New York: Basic Books, 1986.

Keith, Jeanette. *Country People in the New South: Tennessee's Upper Cumberland.* Chapel Hill: University of North Carolina Press, 1995.

Keller, Morton. *Regulating a New Society: Public Policy and Social Change in America, 1900–1933.* Cambridge, MA: Harvard University Press, 1994.

Kerber, Linda K. "A Constitutional Right to Be Treated like American Ladies: Women and the Obligations of Citizenship." In *U.S. History as Women's History: New Feminist Essays,* edited by Linda K. Kerber, Alice Kessler-Harris, and Kathryn Kish Sklar, 17–35. Chapel Hill: University of North Carolina Press, 1995.

———. *Women of the Republic: Intellect and Ideas in Revolutionary America.* Chapel Hill: University of North Carolina Press, 1980.

Kett, Joseph F. "Women and the Progressive Impulse in Southern Education." In *The Web of Southern Social Relations: Women, Family, and Education,* edited by Walter J. Fraser Jr., R. Frank Saunders Jr., and Jon L. Wakelyn, 166–180. Athens: University of Georgia Press, 1985.

Key, V. O. *Southern Politics in State and Nation.* New York: Vintage Books, 1949.

Klotter, James C. "The Black South and White Appalachia." *Journal of American History* 66 (March 1980): 832–849.

Knight, Edgar W. *Public Education in the South.* Boston, Athenaeum Press, 1922.

Knowles, Jane. "Science and Farm Women's Work: The Agrarian Origins of Home Economic Extension." *Agriculture and Human Values* 2 (Winter 1985): 52–55.

Kuhn, Clifford M. *Contesting the New South Order: The 1914–1915 Strike at Atlanta's Fulton Mills.* Chapel Hill: University of North Carolina Press, 2001.

Ladd-Taylor, Molly. *Mother-Work: Women, Child Welfare, and the State, 1890–1930.* Urbana: University of Illinois Press, 1994.

Larson, Edward J. *Sex, Race, and Science: Eugenics in the Deep South.* Baltimore: Johns Hopkins University Press, 1995.

Lebsock, Suzanne D. "Radical Reconstruction and the Property Rights of Southern Women." *Journal of Southern History* 43 (May 1977): 195–216.

Leloudis, James L., II. *Schooling the New South: Pedagogy, Self, and Society in North Carolina, 1880–1920.* Chapel Hill: University of North Carolina Press, 1996.

————. "School Reform in the New South: The Woman's Association for the Betterment of Public School Houses in North Carolina, 1902–1919." *Journal of American History* 69 (March 1983): 886–909.

Lerner, Gerda. "Early Community Work of Black Club Women." *Journal of Negro History* 59 (April 1974): 158–167.

Lewis, Mary Beth Barnett. "A History of Home Economics at Georgia State College for Women from 1891 through 1943." Master's thesis, University of Georgia, 1943.

Link, William A. *A Hard Country and a Lonely Place: Schooling, Society, and Reform in Rural Virginia, 1870–1920.* Chapel Hill: University of North Carolina Press, 1986.

————. *The Paradox of Southern Progressivism, 1880–1930.* Chapel Hill: University of North Carolina Press, 1992.

Litwack, Leon L. *Been in the Storm So Long: The Aftermath of Slavery.* New York: Vintage Books, 1979.

Lumpkin, Katharine Du Pre. *The Making of a Southerner.* New York: Alfred A. Knopf, 1946. Reprint, Athens: University of Georgia Press, 1991.

MacLean, Nancy. *Behind the Mask of Chivalry: The Making of the Second Ku Klux Klan.* New York: Oxford University Press, 1994.

————. "The Leo Frank Case Reconsidered: Gender and Sexual Politics in the Making of Reactionary Populism." *Journal of American History* 78 (December 1991): 917–948.

Matthaei, Julie A. *An Economic History of Women in America: Women's Work, the Sexual Division of Labor, and the Development of Capitalism.* New York: Schocken Books, 1982.

Matthews, John Michael. "Studies in Race Relations in Georgia, 1890–1930." Ph.D. diss., Duke University, 1970.

McArthur, Judith N. *Creating the New Woman: The Rise of Southern Women's Progressive Culture in Texas, 1893–1918.* Urbana: University of Illinois Press, 1998.

McCandless, Amy Thompson. *The Past in the Present: Women's Higher Education in the Twentieth-Century American South.* Tuscaloosa: University of Alabama Press, 1999.

McCluskey, Audrey Thomas. "Mary McLeod Bethune and the Education of Black Girls." *Sex Roles* 21, nos. 1–2 (1989): 113–126.

McCurry, Stephanie. *Masters of Small Worlds: Yeoman Households, Gender Relations, and the Political Culture of the Antebellum South Carolina Low Country.* New York: Oxford University Press, 1995.

McDowell, John P. *Social Gospel in the South: The Woman's Home Mission Movement in the Methodist Episcopal Church, South, 1886–1939.* Baton Rouge: Louisiana State University Press, 1982.

McMath, Robert C., Jr. "Community, Region, and Hegemony in the Nineteenth-Century South." In *Toward a New South? Studies in Post-Civil War Southern Communities,* edited by Orville Vernon Burton and Robert C. McMath Jr., 281–300. Westport, CT: Greenwood Press, 1982.

McMath, Robert C., Jr., James E. Brittain, August W. Giebelhaus, Ronald H. Bayor, Lawrence Foster, and Germaine M. Reed, eds. *Engineering the New South: Georgia Tech, 1885–1985.* Athens: University of Georgia Press, 1985.

Michel, Sonya. "The Limits of Maternalism: Policies toward American Wage-Earning Mothers during the Progressive Era." In *Mothers of a New World: Maternalist Politics and the Origins of Welfare States,* edited by Seth Koven and Sonya Michel, 277–320. New York: Routledge and Kegan Paul, 1993.

Mink, Gwendolyn. *The Wages of Motherhood: Inequality in the Welfare State, 1917–1942.* Ithaca, NY: Cornell University Press, 1995.

Mitchell, Theodore R. *Political Education in the Southern Farmers' Alliance, 1887–1900.* Madison: University of Wisconsin Press, 1987.

Montgomery, Rebecca. "Lost Cause Mythology in New South Reform: Gender, Class, Race, and the Politics of Patriotic Citizenship in Georgia, 1890–1925." In *Negotiating the Boundaries of Southern Womanhood: Dealing with the Powers That Be,* edited by Janet Coryell, Thomas H. Appleton Jr., Anastatia Sims, and Sandra Gioia Treadway, 174–198. Columbia: University of Missouri Press, 2000.

Muncy, Robyn. *Creating a Female Dominion in American Reform, 1890–1935.* New York: Oxford University Press, 1991.

Neth, Mary. *Preserving the Family Farm: Women, Community, and the Foundations of Agribusiness in the Midwest, 1900–1940.* Baltimore: Johns Hopkins University Press, 1995.

Neverdon-Morton, Cynthia. *Afro-American Women of the South and the Advancement of the Race, 1895–1925.* Knoxville: University of Tennessee Press, 1989.

Newby, Idus A. *Plain Folk in the New South: Social Change and Cultural Persistence, 1880–1915.* Baton Rouge: Louisiana University Press, 1989.

Orr, Dorothy. *A History of Education in Georgia.* Chapel Hill: University of North Carolina Press, 1950.

Osterud, Nancy Grey. *Bonds of Community: The Lives of Farm Women in Nineteenth-Century New York.* Ithaca, NY: Cornell University Press, 1991.

Ownby, Ted. *Subduing Satan: Religion, Recreation, and Manhood in the Rural South, 1865–1920.* Chapel Hill: University of North Carolina Press, 1990.

Pascoe, Peggy. *Relations of Rescue: The Search for Female Moral Authority in the American West, 1874–1939.* New York: Oxford University Press, 1990.

Pateman, Carole. *The Sexual Contract.* Stanford, CA: Stanford University Press, 1988.

Perkins, Carol Ortman. "Pragmatic Idealism: Industrial Training, Liberal Education, and Women's Special Needs—Conflict and Continuity in the Experience of Mary McLeod Bethune and Other Black Women Educators, 1900–1930." Ph.D. diss., San Diego State University, 1986.

Pickens, Donald K. *Eugenics and the Progressives*. Nashville, TN: Vanderbilt University Press, 1968.

Plank, David N., and Paul E. Peterson. "Does Urban Reform Imply Class Conflict?: The Case of Atlanta's Schools." *History of Education Quarterly* 23 (Summer 1983): 151–173.

Powers, Jane Bernard. *The "Girl Question" in Education: Vocational Education for Young Women in the Progressive Era*. Washington, DC: Falmer Press, 1992.

Rafter, Nicole Hahn, ed. *White Trash: The Eugenic Family Studies, 1877–1919*. Boston: Northeastern University Press, 1988.

Ragsdale, Annie Laura. "The History of Co-Education at the University of Georgia, 1918–1945." Master's thesis, University of Georgia, 1948.

Range, Willard. *The Rise and Progress of Negro Colleges in Georgia, 1865–1949*. Athens: University of Georgia Press, 1951.

Reidy, Joseph P. *From Slavery to Agrarian Capitalism in the Cotton Plantation South: Central Georgia, 1800–1880*. Chapel Hill: University of North Carolina Press, 1992.

Rosenberg, Rosalind. *Beyond Separate Spheres: Intellectual Roots of Modern Feminism*. New Haven, CT: Yale University Press, 1982.

Ross, Edyth L. "Black Heritage in Social Welfare: A Case Study of Atlanta." *Phylon* 37 (Winter 1976): 297–307.

Ross, Elizabeth Dale. *The Kindergarten Crusade: The Establishment of Preschool Education in the United States*. Athens: Ohio University Press, 1976.

Roth, Darlene Rebecca. *Matronage: Patterns in Women's Organizations, Atlanta, Georgia, 1890–1940*. New York: Carlson Publishing, 1994.

Rouse, Jacqueline A. "The Legacy of Community Organizing: Lugenia Burns Hope and the Neighborhood Union." *Journal of Negro History* 69 (Summer–Autumn 1984): 114–133.

———. *Lugenia Burns Hope: Black Southern Reformer*. Athens: University of Georgia Press, 1989.

Ryan, Mary P. *Cradle of the Middle Class: The Family in Oneida County, New York, 1790–1865*. Cambridge: Cambridge University Press, 1981.

———. *The Empire of the Mother: American Writing about Domesticity, 1830–1860*. New York: Institute for Research in History, 1982.

Salstrom, Paul. *Appalachia's Path to Dependency: Rethinking a Region's Economic History, 1730–1940*. Lexington: University Press of Kentucky, 1994.

Scarborough, Donald Dewey. "An Economic Study of Negro Farmers as Owners, Tenants, and Croppers." Master's thesis, University of Georgia, 1923.

Schoen, Johanna. "'A Great Thing for Poor Folks': Birth Control, Sterilization, and Abortion in Public Health and Welfare in the Twentieth Century." Ph.D. diss., University of North Carolina–Chapel Hill, 1995.

Schwarzweller, Harry K. "Social Change and the Individual in Rural Appalachia." In *Change in Rural Appalachia: Implications for Action Programs,* edited by John D. Photiadis and Harry K. Schwarzweller, 53–57. Philadelphia: University of Pennsylvania Press, 1970.

Scott, Ann Firor. *The Southern Lady: From Pedestal to Politics, 1830–1930.* Chicago: University of Chicago Press, 1970.

Seals, R. Grant. "The Formation of Agricultural and Rural Development Policy with Emphasis on African Americans: II. The Hatch-George and Smith-Lever Acts." *Agricultural History* 65, no. 2 (1991): 12–34.

Sessoms, Josie B., Ella A. Tackwood, Rebecca E. Davis, Maenelle D. Dempsey, Ethel W. Kight, Madie A. Kincy, and Susie W. Wheeler. *Jeanes Supervision in Georgia Schools, A Guiding Light in Education: A History of the Program from 1908–1975.* Athens: Georgia Association of Jeanes Curriculum Directors and Southern Education Foundation, 1975.

Shapiro, Henry D. *Appalachia on Our Mind: The Southern Mountains and Mountaineers in the American Consciousness, 1870–1920.* Chapel Hill: University of North Carolina Press, 1978.

Shapiro, Michael Steven. *Child's Garden: The Kindergarten Movement from Froebel to Dewey.* University Park: Pennsylvania State University Press, 1983.

Sharpless, Rebecca. *Fertile Ground, Narrow Choices: Women on Texas Cotton Farms, 1900–1940.* Chapel Hill: University of North Carolina Press, 1999.

Shaw, Barton C. *The Wool-Hat Boys: Georgia's Populist Party.* Baton Rouge: Louisiana State University Press, 1984.

Shaw, Stephanie. *What a Woman Ought to Be and to Do: Black Professional Women Workers during the Jim Crow Era.* Chicago: University of Chicago Press, 1996.

Sheffer, Marguerite B. *Memorabilia of the Athens Woman's Club.* Athens, GA: Athens Woman's Club, 1982.

Shifflett, Crandall A. *Coal Towns: Life, Work, and Culture in Company Towns of Southern Appalachia, 1880–1960.* Knoxville, University of Tennessee Press, 1991.

Silber, Nina. *The Romance of Reunion: Northerners and the South, 1865–1900.* Chapel Hill: University of North Carolina Press, 1993.

Sims, Anastatia. *The Power of Femininity in the New South: Women's Organizations and Politics in North Carolina, 1880–1930.* Columbia: University of South Carolina Press, 1997.

Sklar, Kathryn Kish. *Florence Kelley and the Nation's Work: The Rise of Women's Political Culture, 1830–1900.* New Haven, CT: Yale University Press, 1995.

————. "The Historical Foundations of Women's Power in the Creation of the American Welfare State, 1830–1930." In *Mothers of a New World: Maternalist Politics and the Origins of Welfare States,* edited by Seth Koven and Sonya Michel, 43–93. New York: Routledge and Kegan Paul, 1993.

Skocpol, Theda. *Protecting Soldiers and Mothers: The Political Origins of Social Policy in the United States.* Cambridge, MA: Harvard University Press, 1992.

Smith, Daniel Blake. *Inside the Big House: Planter Family Life in Eighteenth-Century Chesapeake Society.* Ithaca, NY: Cornell University Press, 1980.

Smith, Dorothy E. "Women's Inequality and the Family." In *Inequality: Essays on the Political Economy of Social Welfare,* edited by Allan Moscovitch and Glenn Drover, 156–195. Toronto: University of Toronto Press, 1981.

Smith, Sandra N., and Earle H. West. "Charlotte Hawkins Brown." *Journal of Negro Education* 51, no. 3 (1982): 199–202.

Solomon, Barbara. *In the Company of Educated Women: A History of Women and Higher Education in America.* New Haven, CT: Yale University Press, 1985.

Stanley, Amy Dru. "Conjugal Bonds and Wage Labor: Rights of Contract in the Age of Emancipation." *Journal of American History* 75 (September 1988): 471–500.

Stetar, Joseph M. "In Search of a Direction: Southern Higher Education after the Civil War." *History of Education Quarterly* 25 (Fall 1985): 341–367.

Strober, Myra H. "Toward a General Theory of Occupational Sex Segregation: The Case of Public School Teaching." In *Sex Segregation in the Workplace: Trends, Explanations, Remedies,* edited by Barbara F. Reskin, 144–156. Washington, DC: National Academy Press, 1984.

Strober, Myra H., and David Tyack. "Why Do Women Teach and Men Manage? A Report on Research on Schools." *Signs* 5 (Spring 1980): 494–503.

Talbot, Marion, and Lois Kimball Mathews Rosenberry. *The History of the American Association of University Women, 1881–1931.* Boston: Houghton Mifflin, 1931.

Taylor, A. Elizabeth. "The Origin of the Woman Suffrage Movement in Georgia." *Georgia Historical Quarterly* 28 (June 1944): 63–79.

Thomas, Leland Clovis. "Some Aspects of Biracial Public Education in Georgia, 1900–1954." Ph.D. diss., George Peabody College for Teachers, 1960.

Thomas, Mary Martha. *The New Woman in Alabama: Social Reforms and Suffrage, 1890–1920.* Tuscaloosa: University of Alabama Press, 1992.

Thompson, Mildred. *Reconstruction in Georgia: Economic, Social, Political, 1865–1872.* New York, 1915. Reprint, Atlanta: Cherokee Publishing, 1971.

Toppin, Edgar A. "Walter White and the Atlanta NAACP's Fight for Equal Schools, 1916–1917." *History of Education Quarterly* 7 (Spring 1967): 3–21.

Townsend, Sara Bertha. "The Admission of Women to the University of Georgia." *Georgia Historical Quarterly* 43 (June 1959): 156–169.

Tucker, William H. *The Science and Politics of Racial Research*. Urbana: University of Illinois Press, 1994.

Turner, Elizabeth Hayes. *Women, Culture, and Community: Religion and Reform in Galveston, 1880–1920*. New York: Oxford University Press, 1997.

Urban, Wayne J. "The Illusion of Educational Reform in Georgia." In *School Reform in the Deep South: A Critical Appraisal*, edited by Joseph L. DeVitis and David J. Vold, 131–141. Tuscaloosa: University of Alabama Press, 1991.

Vold, David J. "Democratic Tension and the Future of the Public School." In *School Reform in the Deep South: A Critical Appraisal*, edited by Joseph L. DeVitis and David J. Vold, 155–167. Tuscaloosa: University of Alabama Press, 1991.

Welter, Rush. *Popular Education and Democratic Thought in America*. New York: Columbia University Press, 1962.

Wheeler, Marjorie Spruill. *New Women of the New South: The Leaders of the Woman Suffrage Movement in the Southern States*. New York: Oxford University Press, 1993.

Whisnant, David E. *All That Is Native and Fine: The Politics of Culture in an American Region*. Chapel Hill: University of North Carolina Press, 1983.

White, Deborah Gray. *Ar'n't I a Woman?: Female Slaves in the Plantation South*. New York: W. W. Norton, 1985.

Whites, LeeAnn. *The Civil War as a Crisis in Gender: Augusta, Georgia, 1860–1890*. Athens: University of Georgia Press, 1995.

———. "The De Graffenried Controversy: Class, Race, and Gender in the New South." *Journal of Southern History* 54 (August 1988): 449–478.

———. "Rebecca Latimer Felton and the Wife's Farm: The Class and Racial Politics of Gender Reform." *Georgia Historical Quarterly* 76 (Summer 1992): 354–372.

Wiebe, Robert. *The Search for Order, 1877–1920*. New York: Hill and Wang, 1967.

Wilhelm, Gene, Jr. "Appalachian Isolation: Fact or Fiction?" In *An Appalachian Symposium: Essays Written in Honor of Cratis D. Williams*, edited by J. W. Williamson, 77–91. Boone, NC: Appalachian State University Press, 1977.

Wilkerson, Doxey A. *Agricultural Extension Services among Negroes in the South*. N.p.: Conference of Presidents of Negro Land Grant Colleges, 1942.

Williamson, Joel. *The Crucible of Race: Black-White Relations in the American South since Emancipation*. New York: Oxford University Press, 1984.

Wilson, Charles Reagan. *Baptized in Blood: The Religion of the Lost Cause, 1865–1920*. Athens: University of Georgia Press, 1980.

Winterer, Caroline. "Avoiding a 'Hothouse System of Education': Nineteenth-Century Early Childhood Education from the Infant Schools to the Kindergartens." *History of Education Quarterly* 32 (Fall 1992): 288–314.

Woodfaulk, Courtney S. "The Jeanes Teachers of South Carolina: The Emergence,

Existence, and Significance of Their Work." Ed.D. diss., University of South Carolina, 1992.

Woodman, Harold D. "Economic Reconstruction and the Rise of the New South, 1865–1900." In *Interpreting Southern History: Historiographical Essays in Honor of Sanford W. Higginbotham,* edited by John B. Boles and Evelyn Thomas Nolen, 254–307. Baton Rouge: Louisiana State University Press, 1987.

———. "Sequel to Slavery: The New History Views the Postbellum South." *Journal of Southern History* 43 (November 1977): 523–554.

Woodson, Carter Godwin. *The Rural Negro.* Washington, DC: Association for the Study of Negro Life and History, 1930.

Woodward, C. Vann. *Origins of the New South, 1877–1913.* Baton Rouge: Louisiana State University Press, 1951.

———. *The Strange Career of Jim Crow.* New York: Oxford University Press, 1955. Reprint, 1974.

———. *Tom Watson: Agrarian Rebel.* New York: Macmillan, 1938.

Woody, Thomas. *A History of Women's Education in the United States.* Vol. 1. New York: Science Press, 1929.

Woofter, Thomas J., Jr. *Negro Migration: Changes in Rural Organization and Population of the Cotton Belt.* New York: W. D. Gray, 1920.

———. *Southern Race Progress: The Wavering Color Line.* Washington, DC: Public Affairs Press, 1957.

Wright, Gavin. *Old South, New South: Revolutions in the Southern Economy since the Civil War.* New York: Basic Books, 1986.

———. *The Political Economy of the Cotton South: Households, Markets, and Wealth in the Nineteenth Century.* New York: W. W. Norton, 1978.

Wrigley, Steven Wayne. "The Triumph of Provincialism: Public Life in Georgia, 1898–1917." Ph.D. diss., Northwestern University, 1986.

Wyatt-Brown, Bertram. *Yankee Saints and Southern Sinners.* Baton Rouge: Louisiana State University Press, 1985.

Young, Elizabeth Barber. *A Study of the Curricula of Seven Selected Women's Colleges of the Southern States.* New York: Teachers College, Columbia University, 1932.

INDEX